Chinese Church in Context

Australian University of Theology Publications

SERIES EDITOR EDWINA MURPHY

Australian University of Theology Publications offers scholars, church leaders, and the wider community uniquely Australian and New Zealand perspectives on matters of significance for research and practice.

Dr Edwina Murphy
Deputy Vice-Chancellor (Research)

Chinese Church in Context

Voices from Downunder
澳洲華人教會本色化之探索

Edited by
Grace Kwan Sik Tsoi
and **Philip P. Chia**

WIPF & STOCK · Eugene, Oregon

CHINESE CHURCH IN CONTEXT
Voices from Downunder

Australian University of Theology Publications

Copyright © 2025 Wipf and Stock Publishers. All rights reserved. Except for brief quotations in critical publications or reviews, no part of this book may be reproduced in any manner without prior written permission from the publisher. Write: Permissions, Wipf and Stock Publishers, 199 W. 8th Ave., Suite 3, Eugene, OR 97401.

Wipf & Stock
An Imprint of Wipf and Stock Publishers
199 W. 8th Ave., Suite 3
Eugene, OR 97401

www.wipfandstock.com

PAPERBACK ISBN: 979-8-3852-4674-8
HARDCOVER ISBN: 979-8-3852-4675-5
EBOOK ISBN: 979-8-3852-4676-2

09/22/25

Contents

Acknowledgments | vii

Contributors | ix

Abbreviations | xiii

Introduction: Contextualization and Appropriation | xv
  GRACE TSOI AND PHILIP CHIA

1. A Brief History of Chinese Churches in Australia | 1
   YUN ZHOU

2. A Study on the Contextualization Process for Chinese Churches in Australia and Its Relevance to the Continuous Influx of Chinese Immigrants | 28
   KA SHING SAMUEL LUI

3. Towards a Contextual Theology for Chinese Australian Conservative Evangelicals | 47
   GRACE LUNG

4. Necromancy: 1 Samuel 28 and Australian Chinese Christians | 71
   GRACE KWAN SIK TSOI

5. Examining Cultural Conflict through the Lens of the Book of Acts | 91
   MING LEUNG

CONTENTS

6. Church Ministry in Light of *Munus Triplex Christi* | 108
   WALLY WANG

7. What Does "Indigenization of a Religion" Mean? An Investigation of Methodological Issues on Sinicization of Christianity in China and Diaspora | 123
   HUNG-EN (TALLIS) TIEN

8. Syncretism and Inculturation: Wang Zheng as an Example | 149
   KAI T. WONG

9. Politics: A Topic That Cannot Be Avoided in Diasporic Chinese Churches | 177
   JASON LAM

Subject Index | 199

Scripture Index | 203

Acknowledgments

THE COMPLETION OF THIS monograph would not have been possible without the assistance and participation of lots of people. A very special thanks to the Australian University of Theology for providing funding to support this project. I would like, in particular, to extend my gratitude to Prof. James Dalziel, Vice-Chancellor of the AUT, for his encouragement in the process. Edwina Murphy and Megan Powell du Toit from the ACT/AUT office are much appreciated for their help in the editing process. I thank all the contributors of this monograph: Yun Zhou, Kai Shing Lui, Grace Lung, Ming Leung, Wally Wang, Tallis Tien, Kai T. Wong, and Jason Lam. Since this monograph is the proceedings of the "Chinese Church in Context: Voices from Downunder" conference held by CTCA in September 2022, the attendees of the conference and their contributed feedbacks enhanced the richness of this monograph.

Soli Deo Gloria

Contributors

Dr. Jason Lam 林子淳 was born and grew up in Hong Kong. After completing his doctorate at the University of Cambridge, he conducted interdisciplinary research in the East Asian context for over a decade before joining Melbourne School of Theology in 2019. He is now Senior Lecturer in Christian Thoughts and Senior Research Fellow of the Australian University of Theology. He has published widely in hermeneutics and modern theology and has been deeply involved in the theological movement called Sino-Christian theology. His recent books include *Moltmann and China: Theological Encounters from Hong Kong to Beijing*, co-edited with Naomi Thurston (Brill, 2023); and *Sino-Christian Theology: A Theological qua Cultural Movement in Contemporary China*, co-edited with Pan-chiu Lai (Peter Lang, 2010).

Rev. Ming Leung 梁明生 is the moderator of Chinese units at the Australian University of Theology. He is a retired Vice Principal (academic) and New Testament Lecturer of CTCA. He is an adjunct faculty member of CTCA, Melbourne School of Theology, Brisbane School of Theology, and Presbyterian Theological College.

Rev. Dr. Ka Shing Lui 呂家聲 is a lecturer and TEE coordinator of the Chinese Theological College Australia, Sydney. He also presently serves at the Praise Evangelical Free Church of Australia as Pastor in Charge. He holds a DMin and ThM from Trinity Evangelical Divinity School, Chicago, USA, and a MDiv from China Graduate School of Theology, Hong Kong. His passion is to develop church leaders as well as to see churches grow healthily. He has written a book, *Truth That Can Be Clearly Explained*, and forty gospel booklets in Chinese. He and his wife, Sophia, have two grown children.

PASTOR GRACE LUNG 歐陽惠 is an independent researcher and pastoral worker in Brisbane, within the Christian and Missionary Alliance of Australia. She is also Director of the Centre for Asian Christianity at the Brisbane School of Theology. Her writing can be found in the SOLA Network, Ethos, Zadok Perspectives, and the journal, *Mission Studies*. She writes and teaches on the topic of Asian Australian Christianity. She completed her theological training through Sydney Missionary and Bible College and Fuller Theological Seminary.

REV. DR HUNG-EN TIEN 田宏恩 is a lecturer of systematic theology and church history at Chinese Theological College Australia. He also serves as the rector (senior minister) at St. Mark's Anglican Church, Granville, with experience in church planting. Rev. Dr. Tallis Tien has been invited by various theological colleges and churches to deliver lectures. He has also written articles on Christian epistemology, church history, and theological education. His main research interests are in ecclesiology, methodology in systemic theology, Christian epistemology, hermeneutics, early Christianity, Reformation, Oxford Movement, Chinese church history, and the development of Chinese indigenous theology.

REV. DR GRACE KWAN SIK TSOI 李君晢 was born in Hong Kong, and migrated to Australia during high school. She lectures in the Old Testament, and her research interest includes narrative criticism, intertextuality, ideological criticism, and contextual criticism. Her thesis, *Who Is to Blame for Judges 19? Interplay between the Text and a Chinese Context*, was published in 2022, and she is currently the Principal and Academic Dean of CTCA.

DR. WALLY WANG 王光正 is a Lecturer and Director of the Chinese Program at Brisbane School of Theology. After obtaining a BSc in Mathematics from Florida State University, he completed a MSc and PhD in Theoretical Physics from Carnegie Mellon University. After serving as a research associate at Argonne National Laboratory and UNSW, he went back to Hong Kong and completed a MDiv at China Graduate School of Theology (CGST). After serving as a pastor in the Chinese Evangelical Free Church in Sydney, he went back to CGST to complete his MTh.

REV. DR. KAI T. WONG 黃啟泰 is currently the Vice Principal and Lecturer of Systematic Theology and Church History at Chinese Theological College Australia. Kai has been involved in theological education in Hong Kong and Australia for more than thirty years. He is also an experienced pastor to Chinese churches in Hong Kong and Australia. Kai's research interest includes inculturation and Christianity in late Ming China.

DR. YUN ZHOU 周韻 is a lecturer at the Australian National University. Her research focuses on the history of Christianity in modern China, gender and mission studies, and women's periodicals in Republican China. She has published articles on the encounter of Christianity, gender, and nation. Recent publications include "Rural Reform in Republican China: Christian Women, Print Media, and a Global Vision of Domesticity," *Modern China* 49, no. 3 (2023) 355–85, and "Singing a New Song: Christian Musical Literature for Chinese Women in the Republican Era," *Studies in World Christianity* 28, no. 1 (2022) 28–48.

Abbreviations

AB	Anchor Bible
ABC RE	*ABC Religion and Ethics*
ABS	*Australian Bureau of Statistics*
ACNT	Augsburg Commentary on the New Testament
AJMS	*Australian Journal of Mission Studies*
AJPS	*Asian Journal of Pentecostal Studies*
AJT	*Asia Journal of Theology*
AOAT	Alter Orient und Altes Testament
AOT	Apollos Old Testament Commentary
ASB	*Austin Seminary Bulletin*
BECNT	Baker Exegetical Commentary on the New Testament
CB	*Christian Bioethics*
CBQ	*Catholic Biblical Quarterly*
CJ	*Concordia Journal*
CLRM	*Chinese Law and Religion Monitor*
CMS VIC	Church Missionary Society of Victoria
CT	*Christianity Today*
EBC	The Expositor's Bible Commentary
EMQ	*Evangelical Missions Quarterly*
ESV	*English Standard Version*
GTJ	*Grace Theological Journal*

ABBREVIATIONS

HBT	*Horizons in Biblical Theology*
HJAS	*Harvard Journal of Asiatic Studies*
IACS	*Inter-Asia Cultural Studies*
IBMR	*International Bulletin of Missionary Research*
ICC	*The International Critical Commentary*
IJPDS	*International Journal of Peace and Development Studies*
IJPT	*International Journal of Public Theology*
JAEAR	*The Journal of American-East Asian Relations*
JBL	*Journal of Biblical Literature*
JBPL	*Journal of Biblical Perspectives in Leadership*
JCCA	*Journal of Current Chinese Affairs*
JCS	*Journal of Church and State*
JEH	*The Journal of Ecclesiastical History*
JQR	*Jewish Quarterly Review*
JSOT	*Journal for the Study of the Old Testament*
JSS	*Journal of Semitic Studies*
LMM	*Lutheran Mission Matters*
NICNT	*New International Commentary on the New Testament*
NRSV	*New Revised Standard Version*
OLP	*Orientalia Lovaniensia Periodica*
PNTC	*The Pillar New Testament Commentary*
R & E	*Review and Expositor*
SJT	*Scottish Journal of Theology*
SWJT	*Southwestern Journal of Theology*
TJ	*Trinity Journal*
TJ	*Taiwan Journal of Democracy*
TNTC	*Tyndale New Testament Commentary*
TT	*Theology Today*
VC	*Vigiliae Christianae*
VHJ	*Victorian Historical Journal*
WLQ	*Wisconsin Lutheran Quarterly*
WTJ	*Wesleyan Theological Journal*
ZAW	*Zeitschrift für die alttestamentliche Wissenschaft*

Introduction: Contextualization and Appropriation

Grace Tsoi and Philip Chia

In 1972, Shoki Coe[1] (August 20, 1914–October 28, 1988) 黃彰輝 臺灣彰化人), a Taiwanese, coined the term "contextualization."[2] He was then the General Director of the Theological Education Fund (TEF), a fund set up to raise the level of theological education in the Third World by the International Mission Council (IMC) founded in 1921, which evolved out of the World Missionary Conference in Edinburgh in 1910, and in 1961

1. Shoki Coe, "was described by Nobel Laureate and Archbishop Emeritus of Cape Town, Desmond Tutu, as 'a man without country' and by the Dean of Southeast Asian Graduate School of Theology, Kosuke Koyama, as 'a homeless guru,'" as presented in Chang, *Shoki Coe*, xi, a translation from the 2004 Taiwan version and also a Japanese version in 2007. Jonah Chang portrayed Shoki Coe as "a 'Thinker Contextual' characterized by a 'life live[d] contextually.'" In the words of the ex-General Secretary of WCC, *Rev. Dr Olav Fykse Tveit*, Shoki Coe was able to "develop and elaborate the analytical tools of 'contextualization' at a global level. His contribution to the universal church was much more than simply presenting a 'term' for defining what must be done for Christianity to be relevant to the world in which it was called to bear witness. He presented the church with both a conceptual and procedural tool for formulating a method of authentic witness that held in creative tension the scriptures (text) and the dynamic changes in the society (context) in which it was read, interpreted and applied." Chang, *Shoki Coe*, viii. See World Council of Churches, "Shoki Coe."

2. According to Shoki Coe, "Contextuality . . . is that critical assessment of what makes the context really significant in the light of the *Missio Dei*. It is the missiological discernment of the signs of the times, seeing where God is at work and calling us to participate in it." Coe, "Contextualized Theology," 19–24; Kinsler, "Mission and Context," 87.

merged into the World Council of Churches (WCC, founded in 1948), to become its Division on World Missions and Evangelism. The TEF has a mission to encourage Third World scholars "to evolve theologies and programs designed specifically for their respective constituencies and culture."[3]

Although the idea of "contextualization" received a somewhat skeptical challenge,[4] it continues to be welcomed generally in biblical, theological, ecclesiastical, and missiological studies, as well as in linguistics studies and science education.[5]

Renowned biblical scholar Walter Brueggemann outlined vividly the process of contextual biblical interpretation in *Revelation and Violence: A Study in Contextualization*:

> The conviction that scripture is revelatory literature is a constant, abiding conviction among the communities of Jews and Christians which gather around the book . . . But that conviction, constant and abiding as it is, is problematic and open to a variety of alternative and often contradictory of ambiguous meanings . . . Clearly that conviction is appropriated differently in various contexts and various cultural settings . . . Current attention to hermeneutics convinces many of us that there is no single, sure meaning for any text. The revelatory power of the text is discerned and given precisely through the action of interpretation which is always concrete, never universal, always contextualized, never "above the fray," always filtered through vested interest, never in disinterested purity.[6]

With reference to Christian missions in Asia, Teresa Chai attempts to delineate the concept of contextualization and concludes that, "Although all these definitions have different nuances, the main point of each one is the description of how to express the message of the Gospel, supreme over all cultures, in new cultural contexts. It is the process that makes the message intelligible in the thought of the receptor people." She agrees with

---

3. Hesselgrave, "Edinburgh Error," 121–49.

4. As reflected in Fluegge, "Dubious History," 49–69.

5. Auer, "Introduction"; Sánchez Tapia, "Introduction," 1, explores how "science learning can be more relevant and interesting for students and teachers by using a contextualized approach to science education . . . the contextualization of science education from multiple angles, such as teacher education, curriculum design, and assessment, and from multiple national perspectives . . . provide and inspire new practical approaches to bring science education closer to the lives of students to accelerate progress toward global scientific literacy."

6. Brueggemann, *Revelation and Violence*, 1.

Hesselgrave and Rommen that "contextualization is a necessity . . . if the Gospel is to be understood, then contextualization must be true to the full message of the Bible and related to the cultural, linguistic and religious background of the listeners." She legitimately raises three concerns of contextualization, which are still very much relevant:

> The first concern is that missionaries tend to introduce their cultural heritage as an integral part of the Gospel. Thus missionaries should decontextualize the message of the Gospel from their own cultural background. The second concern is the necessity of putting the Gospel into the new context so that the Gospel and the resulting church will not seem foreign in its new setting. The third concern is that converts may include elements of their culture, which alters or eliminates aspects of the Gospel, upon which the integrity of the Gospel depends."[7]

Jackson Wu, on the other hand, utters the importance of contextualization in *One Gospel for All Nations* as he remarks that, "contextualization involves multiple cultural and historical contexts as well as a plethora of academic disciplines . . . contextualization concerns more than simply cultural 'relevance.' Contextualization is not merely an important additive to mission theory; it is inevitable. In the same way architectural plans determine the design for a building, so also contextualization is an essential element of mission strategy."[8]

In *Issues in Contextualization*, Charles H. Kraft proclaims that, "In Jesus, God contextualized Himself in a particular society at a particular time in order to reach a particular people in the most appropriate and impactful way. This is an 'insider' approach to communicating and expressing the gospel."[9] He maintains that "'contextualization' refers to the effective communication of the gospel message in a culturally appropriate manner in order that the receptor can respond with understanding and acceptance through the work of the Holy Spirit."[10]

Timothy Keller[11] in *Center Church* wrote that "If there is no single, context-free way to express the gospel, then contextualization is inevitable."

---

7. Chai, "Look at Contextualization," 3–19; Cf. Hesselgrave and Rommen, *Contextualization*, ix, 1.
8. Wu, *One Gospel*, 54.
9. Kraft, "Preface," 10.
10. Kraft, *Christianity in Culture*, xxiii.
11. Keller, *Center Church*, 150.

There is no doubt that the contextualization of the gospel is utterly important for any Christian mission or church planting across the globe, but the translation and transfer of the gospel message into culturally sensitive language is also undeniably crucial for any effective ministry.

With reference to the contextualization of language under Britain's colonized India, Ranjan Kumar Auddy succinctly points out that, "Indians did not throw off their languages; neither did they discontinue using the English language ever since they began to use it. Rather their languages have cast a deep impact upon the English they use, resulting in the 'Indianization' of the English language and subsequently the emergence of a new variant of the English language." He rightly spells out that, "'Indianization' of the English language is itself a process of decolonization, leading to the emergence of a distinct variant of the English language called Indian English. Voices associating the identity with the English language can also be heard."[12] Perhaps this is what "indigenization" means. According to David J. Bosch, "'indigenization' refers to the process that a church, its leadership and relevant theology, through contextualization, develops within and through native peoples, their culture and worldview. The result of indigenization is that a recipient hears, understands, accepts, puts into practice and reproduces the Gospel message within his or her own culture and worldview."[13]

According to Peter Auer on the work of Gumperz's understanding of linguistic contextualization, it implies "a certain conceptualization of 'context' which can be characterized as flexible and as reflexive." A flexible context is one, "that is continually reshaped in time. But the relationship between context and text must also be a reflexive one—i.e. one in which language is not determined by context, but contributes itself in essential ways to the construction of context."[14] He further employs the music of Bach's *St. Matthew Passion*, as a metaphor to express the concept of contextualization, whereby "Bach quite regularly switches into C major to *contextualize* irony," as Auer further elaborates.[15]

> In most general terms, *contextualization therefore comprises all activities by participants which make relevant, maintain, revise, cancel . . . any aspect of context which, in turn, is responsible for the*

12. Auddy, *Indian English*, 1.
13. Bosch, *Transforming Mission*, 389–93.
14. Auer, "Introduction," 3.
15. Auer, "Introduction," 4.

interpretation of an utterance in its particular locus of occurrence. Such an aspect of context may be the larger activity participants are engaged in (the "speech genre"), the small-scale activity (or "speech act"), the mood (or "key") in which this activity is performed, the topic, but also the participants' roles (the participant constellation, comprising "speaker," "recipient," "bystander," etc.), the social relationship between participants, the relationship between a speaker and the information he conveys via language ("modality"), even the status of "focused interaction" itself.

Today, half a century has passed by since the term "contextualization" was coined by Shoki Coe, and the enterprise of constructing contextual theology continues to be a formidable task, though certainly it has been fruitful and multiplied. Contextualization, though a slippery term, demands the awareness of, and sensitivity towards, the subject's locality, adaptation of its environmental consciousness with relevance to its subject, and incorporating it into the subject to make it a part of it. Indigenization denotes the awareness of the subject's identity and essence of existence. Both contextualization and indigenization necessarily implied the presence of the "otherness" incorporating and appropriating into a hybridized subject being. The notion of contextualization involves the exploration of the idea of the context and the text, intertextually and intersubjectively. Inculturation brings about the awareness of the potential danger of indoctrination or forcing down one's culture upon another. Sinicization points to the transformation of the "otherness" into some sort of "self-ness."

With awareness of various relevant sets and subsets on contextualization, and the boldness to explore and engage the subject matter, this volume endeavours to contribute positively towards the global project of contextualization of the gospel from "Down Under"—its locality is Australia, its subject the Chinese Church of Australia, the context is the Chinese Australian community, and the text is the Evangelical Chinese Church, as well as the community of biblical faith. The challenges are manifold; among them the question of how much context is relevant for gospel ministry and how the relationship between context and text should be appropriated.

We first explore the history of the Chinese Australian Church, highlighting key events and happenings for the last two centuries, from the history of its early migration days down to the present *status quo* with reference to its development, struggle, adaptation, and evolution. This is presented in Yun Zhou's "A Brief History of Chinese Churches in Australia," and includes a special interview with the influential Chinese Christian leader in Australia, Rev. Dr Dennis Law, which probes into the future path for the ethnic Chinese Church in Australia.

Tackling the issue of the contextualization process in Australian Chinese churches, Samuel Lui's "A Study on the Contextualization Process for the Chinese Churches in Australia and Its Relevance with Reference to the Continuous Influx of Chinese Immigrants" provides an understanding of the past and present challenges to contextualize the gospel ministry, especially with the continuous influx of migrants; while Grace Lung's "Towards a Contextual Theology for Chinese Australian Conservative Evangelicals" draws examples from Asian American theology and focuses on constructing an urgently needed Chinese Australian contextual theology that is relevant for Chinese Australian evangelicals.

Apart from highlighting key issues of the history of Chinese Australian churches with a path for the present and future strategy for gospel ministry in Australia, this volume also demonstrates the importance of a biblically based contextual theology by providing two essays demonstrating a contextual biblical interpretation. From the Old Testament, Grace Tsoi explores from sociological and theological perspectives the very important issue of "necromancy" with a contextual reading of 1 Samuel 28 in relation to Australian Chinese Christians. Taking on the subject of necromancy is in itself a formidable task culturally and theologically, yet unavoidable, as it continues to be relevant to the present Chinese Christian community worldwide. From the New Testament, Ming Leung's "Examining Cultural Conflict through the Lens of the Book of Acts 6:1–7" reveals the relevance of the biblical text for today's contextual consideration, with a hope for an inclusive community in the making, which consists of various diversified ethnic and dialect-speaking cultures that the Australian Chinese Church vowed to serve and minister to in unity.

Wally Wang, on the other hand, drills into the fundamental of theological essence in Christ's threefold office in "Church Ministry in Light of *Munus Triplex Christi*," expounding the relevance of Christ's "priestly, kingly, and prophetic" office for the formulation of a biblically, theologically, and culturally sound church ministry with the Australian Chinese Church in context. With a similar Chinese Christian context in focus, Tallis Tien's methodological investigation on the concept of "sinicization" addresses the issue of "What Does 'Indigenization of a Religion' Mean?" with a strong interest in Chinese Christianity in the diaspora with China at the core. It proposes a "canonical-linguistic approach" after examining four methodological approaches, recommending such for the construction of an indigenous Chinese theology, with an aim to share with the global churches. Drawing from an example on the contextualization of the gospel ministry from Chinese church history, Kai Wong hammers on the critical issue of "Syncretism and Inculturation" in his essay, with "Wang Zheng as an Example" from the late Ming Christian antique, highlighting "the powerplay between 'church tradition' and 'younger churches,' and the interpenetration of theological traditions and cultures." Finally, equally critical is the issue of "politics" with reference to the construction of a contemporary Chinese theology in the contemporary global political situation, whereby Chinese churches within the Chinese diaspora must undeniably be encountered, in Jason Lam's "Politics: A Topic That Cannot Be Avoided in the Diasporic Chinese Churches." In two parts, Lam explains the importance of taking on the topic proactively rather than passively, lest it may bring about pastoral shortfall. He admits that diverse "political opinions" in a community are unavoidable. Thus, utilizing a positive approach with the "unity" of the church in mind, one should engage in rather than avoid "politics" by allowing everyone to express without fear.

On this note, we go back to the initiator of the concept of "contextualization," to Taiwanese contextual theologian, Shoki Coe, who went into "political" exile without the luxury of returning home until his death; yet introduced and contributed a crucial concept for the gospel message and ministry to be spread effectively and the world evangelized concretely and concisely with the incarnated Christ as the sole exemplified figure to follow. This volume, *Chinese Church in Context: Voices from Downunder*, is an auspicious attempt from colleagues and friends of the Chinese Theological College Australia, from the Chinese evangelical perspective, which marks an attributive effort in contributing to the ongoing discussion on the contextualization of the gospel in Australia for the global Christian community in the advancement of the kingdom ministry of Christ.

Bibliography

Auddy, Ranjan Kumar. *In Search of Indian English: History, Politics and Indigenisation*. London: Routledge, 2020.

Auer, Peter. "Introduction: John Gumperz's Approach to Contextualization." In *The Contextualization of Language*, edited by Peter Auer and Aldo Di Luzio. Amsterdam: John Benjamins, 1992.

Bosch, David J. *Transforming Mission: Paradigm Shifts in Theology of Mission.* Maryknoll: Orbis, 2005.

Brueggemann, Walter. *Revelation and Violence: A Study in Contextualization.* Milwaukee, WI: Marquette University Press, 1986.

Chai, Teresa. "A Look at Contextualization: Historical Background, Definition, Function, Scope and Models." *AJPS: Contextualization in Asia: Theory and Practice* 24, no. 1 (February 2015) 3–19.

Chang, Jonah. *Shoki Coe: An Ecumenical Life in Context.* Geneva: WCC, 2011.

Coe, Shoki. "Contextualized Theology." In *Mission Trends No. 3: Asian, African, and Latin American Contributions to a Radical, Theological Realignment in the Church*, edited by Gerald H. Anderson and Thomas F. Stransky, 19–24. Grand Rapids: Eerdmans, 1976.

Fluegge, Glenn K. "The Dubious History of 'Contextualization' and the Cautious Case for Its Continued Use." *LMM* 25, no. 1 (May 2017) 49–69.

Hesselgrave, David J. "Will We Correct the 'Edinburgh Error'?—Future Mission in Historical Perspective." *SWJT* 49, no. 2 (Spring 2007) 121–49.

Hesselgrave, David, and Edward Rommen. *Contextualization: Meanings, Methods and Models.* Pasadena, CA: William Carey Library, 1989.

Keller, Timothy. *Center Church: Doing Balanced, Gospel-Centered Ministry in Your City.* Grand Rapid: Zondervan, 2012.

Kinsler, F. Ross. "Mission and Context: The Current Debate about Contextualization." *EMQ* 14, no. 1 (1978) 87.

Kraft, Charles H. *Christianity in Culture: A Study in Biblical Theologizing in Cross-Cultural Perspective.* 2nd ed. Maryknoll: Orbis, 2005.

———. "Preface." In *Issues in Contextualization*, 10. Pasadena, CA: William Carey Library, 2016.

Sánchez Tapia, Ingrid. "Introduction: A Broad Look at Contextualization of Science Education across National Contexts." In *International Perspectives on the Contextualization of Science Education*, edited by Ingrid Sánchez Tapia for UNICEF, 1. Switzerland: Springer Nature Switzerland AG, 2020.

World Council of Churches. "Shoki Coe: An Ecumenical Life in Context." https://www.oikoumene.org/resources/publications/shoki-coe-an-ecumenical-life-in-context.

Wu, Jackson. *One Gospel for All Nations: A Practical Approach to Biblical Contextualization.* Pasadena: William Carey Library, 2015.

1.

A Brief History of Chinese Churches in Australia

Yun Zhou

Abstract

This paper explores key events in the development of Chinese Christian churches in Australia over the last two centuries. It shows that evangelical fervor underpinned the development of Chinese Christian churches which then took root and thrived in Australia. Exploring this history illustrates the evangelical commitment by Christians from different denominations, both Western and Chinese, to proselytize Chinese immigrants in different historical periods. In three sections, this paper demonstrates how Chinese churches have taken shape since the nineteenth century and become embedded in Australian society. The first section examines mission work during the first wave of the goldrush in the mid-nineteenth century. Western missionaries of different European denominations targeted a growing population of Chinese migrants, and Chinese missionaries came to play a crucial role in evangelizing local Chinese laborers. The second section explores the emergence of Chinese churches in the late nineteenth century and under the White Australia Policy. It focuses on the development of two Chinese churches by Chinese Christians; one associated with the Wesleyan Church in Melbourne and the other with the Presbyterian Church in

Sydney. The third section looks at the revival of Chinese churches after the Australian Government shifted towards a more open immigration policy in the early 1970s. To conclude, I summarize key issues lingering in ethnic Chinese churches in Australia and discuss future paths based on my interview with the influential Chinese Christian leader Rev. Denis Law conducted in Sydney in September 2022.

The encounter of Chinese immigrants and Christianity in Australia occurred during the British expansion of the nineteenth century. In 1788, Australia became a British colony requiring many laborers to develop agriculture and pastoral industry. Chinese immigrants, primarily from Guangdong, responded to this opportunity and sailed to Australia. The earliest documented Chinese migrant to Australia is Mak Sai Ying 麦世英, who arrived in New South Wales from Guangdong in 1818 as a free settler.[1] The need for cheap labor became more urgent in 1840, when the transportation of British convicts to Australia was abolished. Official Chinese statistics show that ten thousand Chinese people left for Australia between 1801 and 1850.[2] Relocating to Australia meant that these migrants found themselves in a sociocultural context sculpted by Christianity—a religion that was outlawed in China.

Little is known about the early days of evangelical work among the Chinese in Australia, but surviving records show that mission work took place among the Chinese during the mid-nineteenth century. The Chinese population of Australia increased dramatically at that time. Due to the discovery of gold in Victoria in 1851, for instance, the number of Chinese laborers in that state increased from 2,341 in 1854 to 42,000 by 1858/59—12 percent of the state's entire population.[3] In response to the growth of the Chinese demographic, European Protestant churches commenced evangelical work among the Chinese. As noted in the work of Keith Cole, Ian Welch, and Walter Phillips, evangelical work was conducted by different Protestant denominations, individually and collaboratively, to proselytize Chinese workers in the late nineteenth century and early twentieth century.[4]

1. The history of Chinese migrants to Australia can be traced back to 1803 when Ahuto (杜亞許), an experienced carpenter, migrated from Guangdong to New South Wales. See Lung, "Early Arrivals," 39; National Museum Australia, "Early Chinese Migrants."

2. Sheng, "Environmental Experiences," 91.

3. Lung, "Chinese Miners," 51, 59.

4. Welch, "Our Neighbors," 149–83; Cole, *Anglican Mission*; Phillips, "Seeking Souls," 86–104.

By 1920, Chinese migrants could be found attending church services in Methodist, Anglican, Baptist, and Presbyterian churches.[5]

Chinese Christians were active agents in the making of Chinese churches in Australia. A body of scholarship has examined the work of Chinese Christians in establishing churches in Australia. In addition to promoting evangelical work, leading Chinese Christians often found themselves in positions to negotiate surrounding hostility. A prominent study by Ian Welch examines the Chinese Christian leader Cheong Cheok Hong (1851–1928, Zhang Zhuoxiong張卓雄), who was actively involved in building Chinese churches and participated in political lobbying to prevent anti-Chinese discrimination in immigration and employment.[6] The work of Denise A. Austin explores the religious and social contributions of several Chinese Christian merchants in early twentieth-century Australia.[7] As well as struggling with elements of broader society in Australia, Chinese Christians had to internally negotiate how to develop their churches as independent ones. Research on the history of the Chinese Presbyterian church, such as the works of Wendy Lu Mar and Dorothy Low, shows how the ethnic church developed from a foreign mission into a self-supporting church.[8]

This paper aims to provide a history of key events in the development of Chinese Christian churches in Australia over the last two centuries. Evangelical fervor underpinned the development of Chinese Christian churches which then took root and thrived in Australia. Exploring this history illustrates the evangelical commitment by Christians from different denominations, both Western and Chinese, to proselytize Chinese immigrants in different historical periods. The Chinese mission in Australia was initiated by European churches as an expedient means of reaching millions of Chinese people in their home country: European churches assumed that evangelizing Chinese migrants in Australia would extend Christianity's reach into China via the Chinese diaspora. Early evangelistic work among Chinese migrants in Australia took the form of collaboration between Western missionaries and Chinese catechists. Later, Chinese Christians assumed more autonomy in church ministry and endeavored to become self-supporting. Members of Chinese Christian churches in

---

5. Cummines and Leung, "Chinese Australian Timeline History Scroll," 24.
6. Welch, "Alien Son."
7. Austin, *Kingdom-Minded*, 185–212.
8. Mar Lu, *So Great a Cloud*; Low, *History*.

Australia demonstrated an ongoing evangelical fervor, reaching out to different waves of ethnic Chinese immigrants who emigrated to Australia in the second half of the twentieth century.

In three sections, this paper shows how Chinese churches have taken shape since the nineteenth century and become embedded in Australian society. The first section examines mission work during the first wave of the goldrush in the mid-nineteenth century. Western missionaries of different European denominations targeted a growing population of Chinese migrants, and Chinese missionaries came to play a crucial role in evangelizing local Chinese laborers. The second section explores the emergence of Chinese churches in the late nineteenth century and under the White Australia Policy. It focuses on the development of two Chinese churches by Chinese Christians; one associated with the Wesleyan Church in Melbourne and the other with the Presbyterian Church in Sydney. The third section looks at the revival of Chinese churches after the Australian Government shifted towards a more open immigration policy in the early 1970s. To conclude, I summarize key issues lingering in ethnic Chinese churches in Australia and discuss future paths drawing from my personal communications with the influential Chinese Christian leader Rev. Denis Law conducted in Sydney in September 2022.

Chinese Mission Work during the Gold Rush Period of the Mid-Nineteenth Century

The Chinese mission work of Australian Protestant churches started with diaspora Chinese in the mid-nineteenth century.[9] By the early nineteenth century, Euro-American missionaries had travelled to China, but it was not until the rapid increase of Chinese migrants to the goldfields during the goldrush of the mid-nineteenth century that Chinese mission work emerged in Australia. Anti-Chinese sentiments were common among European settlers who believed their livelihood was threatened by the cheap labor of Chinese miners. However, a small group of European Christians viewed the growth in the Chinese population as an opportunity to evangelize foreigners locally. The Wesleyan clergyman Rev. James Bickford raised the issue of mission work among the Chinese in Victoria in a letter dated 1857. With no missionaries employed to evangelize Chinese laborers,

---

9. Ian Welch identifies Mary Reed of the China Inland Mission as the first "Australasian" missionary who sailed for China in 1888. See Welch, "Mary Reed."

Bickford suggested that Wesleyan missionaries in China who needed to recover from health conditions could come to Victoria while they recuperated.[10] Although local missions received limited support from the wider Australian Christian community,[11] several denominations including the Anglican Church, Presbyterian Church, and Wesleyan Church responded to the call and engaged in the Chinese mission.

The mission work with Chinese migrants in the nineteenth century centered on goldfields such as Ballarat, Bendigo, Castlemaine, and Beechworth in Victoria, and later in Bathurst in NSW. The first mission directed at Chinese migrants was the interdenominational Victoria Chinese Mission established in 1855. It was financially supported by the Anglican Bishop of Melbourne and the Wesleyan Methodist Missionary Society.[12] Rev. John Legg Poore, a Congregational minister and founder of the Christian mission to the Chinese in Victoria, explained in 1855 the origin and purpose of the mission:

> China with its 300 million heathens is not far off. But China is sending a portion of her population to this land, and thousands of the inhabitants of that vast empire are now learning the English language on our goldfields and will return to explain the Christian religion to their countrymen.[13]

At the time Australian churches perceived Chinese migrants as their neighbors but not as their countrymen.[14] Echoing Poore's words, the report of the Wesleyan Methodist Missionary Society in 1859 stated that it valued the mission work among "the vast masses of population in China" and considered that "the temporary sojourn of the Chinese of this colony (Victoria) affords an opportunity of attempting their evangelization, and of thus preparing an agency for influencing their fellow countrymen to receive" the gospel.[15] Therefore, the work to proselytize the Chinese workers was considered a foreign mission.

The Victoria Chinese Mission was based in Castlemaine. The mission team was initially composed of Eurasian missionary Rev. William Young[16]

10. Bickford, *Christian Work*, 109–10.
11. Welch, "Our Neighbors," 159.
12. Welch, "Our Neighbors," 158.
13. Welch, "Alien Son," 47.
14. Welch, "Our Neighbors," 150.
15. Danks, *Mission Fields*, 11.
16. William Young was the son of a Chinese Malay mother and a Scottish father.

and two Chinese evangelists who arrived in Australia in mid-1855, Ho A. Low and Chu A. Luk.[17] Rev. Young often conducted itineration accompanied by a Chinese catechist. The agents of the mission would distribute tracts and copies of the New Testament in Bendigo, Castlemaine, and Ballarat and ask a series of questions related to the gospel and explain biblical verses to Chinese people in the region. As the superintending missionary, Rev. Young led discussions while the Chinese catechist worked as translator and helped answer questions about Christianity. On October 2, 1855, for example, Rev. Young went into a Chinese store with Ho A. Low. Noting a New Testament lying open on the counter, Rev. Young asked the storekeeper whether he understood the portion he had read. With a negative response, Rev. Young asked Ho A. Low to explain the chapter that was open before him. When the man was asked whether he worshipped idols, he replied with a no, as they were not useful in a foreign land. Rev. Young and Ho responded that idols were useless in China as well and recommended the men to abandon idols and worship the true God. They further said that "Europeans and Chinese, all form one great family, to live in love, and worship one God."[18] The notion of the unity of Chinese and Europeans in Christ was a novel concept to Chinese migrants, who lived separately from European settlers. The collaboration of Young and his Chinese counterparts was a visual example of the possibility of coexistence and cooperation.

According to another account on May 13, 1856, Rev. Young visited a Chinese store in Little Bendigo with Chu A. Luk. The storekeeper intended to become a Christian but was ridiculed by his Chinese fellows. Rev. Young and Chu encouraged him to feel honored instead of ashamed. They wished that all the Chinese would become Christians. When a man overheard them, he asked them whether Jesus was a sage like Confucius. Chu replied that "Jesus is greater than all earthly sages; he is even the son of God." Hearing this the man left the store. Rev. Young then asked Chu to read the twenty-first chapter of Revelation and explained further about the "character of those who should be admitted into the kingdom of heaven" to the storekeeper.[19] The evangelistic work of the agents of the Victoria Chinese Mission was fruitful in terms of church service attendance. In October

---

After his missionary service in Java and China with the London Missionary Society, Young went to Australia in 1854. See Cole, *Anglican Mission*, 17.

17. "Castlemaine," 6.
18. Young, "Fourth Report," 6.
19. "Chinese Mission," *MAR*, 3.

1855, a total of six hundred Chinese people attended four Sabbaths held in different places (including one in Forrest Creek and another in Campbell's Flat). The number increased to 675 in June the following year.[20] The Victorian Chinese Mission, nevertheless, ceased in 1858 due to economic recession.[21]

The second interdenominational mission was the Ballarat Chinese Evangelization Society formed in 1858. It was closely related to the Victoria Chinese Mission and managed by a local Ballarat interdenominational committee. The purpose of the society was to enlighten and instruct the Chinese "in the sacred and soul-saving truths of the redemptive work of the Lord Jesus Christ."[22] The Chinese Anglican catechist Lo Sam-yuen, sent by the Anglican Bishop of Hong Kong, James Legge, to help with the Victoria Chinese Mission in 1856, played a crucial role in the Ballarat Chinese Mission. In 1857, Lo was moved from Castlemaine to Ballarat and raised funding to build a Chinese Christian chapel at Red Hill in Ballarat East.[23] Lo's work included addressing "his countrymen every Lord's Day" and "visiting and conversing with them on week days." During the year of 1858, Lo "had visited the camps at Red Hill, Magpie, Eureka, Canadian, Little Bendigo, and Golden Point no less than 436 times, visited 1061 tents, conversed with 9165 persons, distributed 669 books, and employed 1253 hours in the active duties of his mission."[24] Despite the progress made in its first year, as Welch notes, the Ballarat Chinese Mission ended in 1860 with no reasons provided. In the following years, different denominations took up the evangelization of Chinese migrants.[25]

The Presbyterian Church conducted mission work among the Chinese in Ballarat and established its Chinese mission in NSW in the 1860s. For a

---

20. Young, "Fourth Report," 6; "Chinese Mission," *MAR*, 3.
21. Welch, "Alien Son," 104.
22. "Chinese Mission," *Star*, 2.
23. Welch, "Alien Son," 105–106.
24. "Chinese Mission," *Star*, 2.
25. According to Welch, the Wesleyan Methodists took over the work at Castlemaine. The Presbyterians focused on the Ballarat area and the Anglicans briefly commenced work at Yackandandah in the northeast. See Welch, "Our Neighbors," 159. There are some cases when different denominations worked together to promote Chinese missions following the Ballarat Chinese Mission. One example is the Western District Chinese Mission in Bathurst established in 1889. This mission was supported by all evangelical denominations and in 1892 a missionary called David Shing conducted services on behalf of the mission for Chinese people in Bathurst. See "Western District," 72.

period, the Presbyterian Chinese Mission at Ballarat had two missionaries: Superintendent William Young, and Cheong Peng-nam, a lay missionary. Cheong arrived in Australia from Canton in the 1850s and converted to Christianity in 1860, the same year that he was employed. The evangelical work of Cheong, according to his journals, included visiting shops to spread the word of the gospel and pointing out the evil of opium smoking to Chinese workers. Cheong believed the opium would endanger the body and soul and urged his country fellows to quit it and find peace in Christ.[26]

In NSW, the Presbyterian minister J. B. Laughton of Bathurst commenced a mission in 1864 to "2000 Chinese goldminers camped at Sofala, on the Turon River, just south of Mudgee."[27] The lack of suitable Chinese evangelists, however, hindered the development of the Bathurst Chinese mission. A centralized effort in Chinese mission work took place after the Presbyterian Church of New South Wales formed in 1865, uniting the scattered Presbyterianism in the colony. In the same year, the General Assembly passed a resolution to fund foreign missions to the Chinese in NSW, "the natives of the New Hebrides," and the Aborigines of Australia.[28] In the following years, the Foreign Missions Committee of NSW made efforts to find missionaries who could work among the Chinese in the colony. Initially, the thought was to employ a European minister who could speak the Cantonese language. From 1867 to 1880, the Presbyterian Foreign Missions Committee corresponded with missionaries in Hong Kong and Amoy but found no qualified minister. The China mission progressed when evangelists were found among the Chinese converts in Australia.

In the Braidwood area, a Chinese Christian called Philip Lee Hyung engaged in Presbyterian mission work with the Chinese from 1869. Hyung had been trained by the minister Mr. Matthew of Pleasant Creek in Victoria, who had learnt the Chinese language (most likely Cantonese). However, Hyung was unable to communicate with the superintendent Rev. Henry Macready, who found it impossible to guide the mission and understand how it was progressing. This led to Hyung being discharged in 1871 and the Chinese mission work there ceasing. In Sydney, George Ah Lin engaged in the Presbyterian Chinese mission in 1872 and continued his work there for eight years. The progress "was not great" and the meetings were held in different places "where the Chinese were at work, or in the Ragged School

---

26. Welch, "Alien Son," 47–48.
27. Mar Lu, *So Great a Cloud*, 2.
28. Lamont, *Foreign Mission Work*, 3.

at Harrington-street."²⁹ It was in the 1880s that the Chinese mission in Sydney flourished: the Chinese catechist John Young Wai (Zhou Rongwei) commenced his labors in 1882 and advanced the establishment of Chinese churches in Sydney.

The Church Missionary Society of Victoria (CMS VIC), independent from the Church Missionary Society in London, formed the Anglican Mission to the Chinese in Victoria in 1859. With evangelism at its core, CMS VIC conducted mission work among the Australian Aboriginal, Chinese, and Jewish populations. According to Keith Cole, the mission to the Chinese was the main activity of CMS VIC, which established five missions in Central Victoria from 1864 to 1875. Like the mission work to Chinese by other European churches at the time, Chinese missionaries were crucial to the development of such a mission yet received limited recognition and power. In the case of CMS VIC, the mission benefited from the labor of Chinese Christians such as William Ching Wah of Golden Square in Sandhurst and James Lee Wah from St. Arnaud (also called New Bendigo), who were enthusiastic and dedicated in helping to commence the mission work in Central Victoria. Despite the invaluable contributions of Chinese Christians, there was reluctance to appoint Chinese Christians to positions of authority. While each Anglican mission center had its own Chinese catechist, the Chinese catechist was always supervised by a local European parish incumbent, regardless of the supervisor's ability to speak Chinese. At the annual meeting of the Anglican Mission to the Chinese in 1883, James Moorhouse, the Bishop of Melbourne, appealed for a European superintending missionary who could speak Chinese.³⁰ CMS VIC did not consider appointing Chinese Christians as superintendents until the mid-1880s.

In the 1880s, at the same time as the Central Victorian mission was struggling to find a suitable European mission superintendent, a growing number of Chinese people were moving to Melbourne seeking work. This urbanization led to new evangelical efforts in the Victorian capital. In 1885, the Anglican CMS VIC appointed Chinese Christian Cheong Cheok Hong as the superintendent tasked with overseeing the five country mission districts and developing the Chinese ministry in Melbourne. A son of the Presbyterian missionary Cheong Peng-nam, Cheong Cheok Hong was initially affiliated with the Presbyterian Church but left when he was

---

29. Lamont, *Foreign Mission Work*, 5. Lin used the school on Sunday afternoons to address Chinese workers. See "Sydney Ragged School," 2.

30. Cole, *Anglican Mission*, 21–27, 34.

not appointed superintendent by the Presbyterian Mission Board. During his role as the Anglican superintendent, Cheong persuaded CMS VIC to establish a mission site at 110 Little Bourke Street (currently located at 123 Little Bourke Street), which opened in May 1894.[31] Chinese church buildings became convergence points for the Chinese Christian community, and Chinese mission work started to take root more firmly in Australian society accompanied by the growing autonomy of Chinese Christians.

Constructing Chinese Churches from the 1870s to the 1960s

The new phase of the Chinese mission work conducted by different denominations during the early years of the goldrush took place in two main forms: constructing Chinese church buildings and forming Chinese Christian communities. In the early days missionaries walked around the goldfields, visited Chinese stores and camps, held open-air meetings, and used local chapels for sermons and worship. Constructing church buildings specifically for these purposes embedded the Chinese mission in local communities. As a physical place for Chinese Christians, the Chinese church buildings became physical embodiments of a "spiritual home" where Chinese Christians could gather and form their own religious community. These church buildings represent a crucial point in Australian history when Chinese Christians, previously seen as temporary residents, were increasingly integrated into local society.

The first Chinese Christian church building in Melbourne and the earliest evangelical Chinese church in Australia[32] is the Wesleyan Chinese Mission Church, currently the Uniting Church Gospel Hall. It was established in the 1870s as Chinese miners drifted to urban areas for employment opportunities. The Chinese mission was an integral part of the global evangelical vision of the Australasian Wesleyan Church, which took "the world for Christ" as its motto at its conference in January 1872. The Wesleyan Church perceived the evangelization of Chinese people in Australia as a divine call and enthusiastically promoted the establishment of a Chinese

---

31. Cole, *Anglican Mission*, 37–44.

32. Keith Cole notes that the first Chinese Christian Church in Australia was built in Castlemaine in 1859 by the Wesleyans. See Cole, *Anglican Mission*, 17. For a brief history of the Chinese church in Castlemaine see Australia's Christian Heritage, "Chinese Christian."

church building. Although it had no mission station in China at the time, the Wesleyan Church believed that purchasing a site for a Chinese church in Australia would be an efficient and practical way to evangelize this demographic. In 1872, the Chinese population living in areas where the Australasian Wesleyan Methodist Missionary Society ministered was forty thousand, half of whom were residents in Victoria. The mission work of the Wesleyan Church in Victoria at the time was confined to Castlemaine, where twelve Chinese people attended, and Melbourne, where twenty-four Chinese Methodists gathered initially in their own hall in Little Bourke Street. In Melbourne, opposition to Christianity from Chinese Christians' countrymen and later the demolition of another place Chinese Methodists used in Russell Street led to the need for a permanent place for Chinese Christians to use in the city. Funds were raised to purchase land and pay building costs.[33]

On Sunday July 14, 1872, the Chinese Wesleyan Mission Church was opened on Little Bourke Street in Melbourne (now 196 Little Bourke Street). The two-story building of red and white brick was situated in the center of the Chinese quarter of the city. The Wesleyan minister Rev. J. Watsford conducted services on the opening day which were interpreted by the Chinese catechist Rev. James Moy Ling (1832–1911, also known as James Ah Ling and Lee Moy Ling). The services in the following weeks were conducted in Chinese language (Cantonese) by Rev. Ling on Sunday and Thursday evenings. An illustration published in a local newspaper in August 1872 depicted a Thursday evening sermon as follows:

> The church interior has four windows shaded with venetian blinds. The building is lit by a couple of gas lights. The Chinese preacher wearing an orthodox white tie is preaching to a group of Chinese. One man with a white beard is gazing at the lips of the preacher, and one is perusing a prayer book printed in Chinese characters.[34]

An annual report of the Chinese Wesleyan Church in August 1876 shows that Rev. Ling had two assistants, Jacob Wah Fat and Joseph Le Tak. The size of the congregation varied from twenty to sixty-five people. The report estimated that at least a quarter of the congregation at each sermon was different. Many were new arrivals making their way to the diggings, sailors, or visitors to Melbourne from other parts of Australia. Regular

33. "Wesleyan Mission," 2.
34. "Chinese Mission Church," 170.

services included two sermons on Sunday, "prayer meetings on Saturday and Monday evenings, class meeting on Thursday evening, and Scripture class on Tuesday evening, in addition to regular house-to-house visitation and services at the house of Jacob." In 1876, the Chinese Wesleyan Church had thirteen people convert to Christianity.[35] In 1899, over three hundred Chinese people attended the twenty-seventh anniversary of the Wesleyan Chinese church, indicating ongoing growth of the church in the local community.[36]

Rev. James Moy Ling played an important role in establishing the Chinese Mission Church in Melbourne. Ling arrived in Daylesford in Victoria in 1856 and converted at the local Methodist Chapel in 1865. He worked as a Methodist catechist in Castlemaine and later in Bendigo.[37] In around 1870, Ling was employed as a Chinese missionary for mission work in Melbourne. A report from December 1870 shows that Ling worked as an interpreter for the baptism of two Chinese people at the Lonsdale Street Wesley Church. These conversions were the fruits of the mission work by "missionaries in connection with the Little Lonsdale-street Sunday services for Chinese, conducted principally by James Ah Ling, catechist."[38] In 1871, three Chinese people were baptized in the Lonsdale Street Wesley Church, the conversion of whom was "chiefly due to the labors of the Rev. James Ah Ling, who was employed in the mission."[39] In 1872, Ling worked towards the opening of the Chinese Mission Church on Little Bourke Street.

Ling's efforts to establish the Chinese Mission Church were evident in a letter from the congregation in 1873 when he was about to return to China to marry. A partial translation to provide the general gist of the letter is: "We, the undersigned Christian Chinese residents of Melbourne, Victoria" express to you "our warm feeling and attachment" and "deeply thank you for teaching us the true doctrine of God, and that He sent His only beloved Son as a Redeemer for us all." We hope that you and your partner "may enjoy good health and happiness" and return "to your flock as soon as possible."[40] From 1879 to 1885, the Melbourne Chinese Mission Church

---

35. "Chinese Wesleyan Church," 6.
36. "Chinese Church Anniversary," 6.
37. For a brief introduction of Rev. James Moy Ling, see Chinese-Australian Historical Images in Australia. https://www.chia.chinesemuseum.com.au/biogs/CH00046b.htm.
38. "Wesleyan Chinese Mission," 5.
39. "Chinese Christians," 11.
40. "Victoria," 3.

was supervised by another Chinese missionary, Rev. Leong On Tong. When Tong returned to China in 1885, Ling took his place.[41] Records show that Ling worked as the superintendent of the Chinese Mission in Victoria in 1888 and was active in advancing the Chinese Mission work within and outside of Victoria.[42]

From 1880, due to the slowing of the goldrush and the downturn of the mining industry, many Chinese migrants moved from rural and mining areas to cities. Most chose to live in Sydney and Melbourne. Statistics show that Chinese communities in cities doubled or tripled between 1880 and 1901.[43] After 1881, the number of Chinese people in NSW overtook Victoria, making NSW the state with the largest Chinese population. By 1891, there were approximately 3,500 Chinese living in Sydney.[44] The increased Chinese population in Sydney led to the Presbyterian Chinese mission work undertaken by Rev. John Young Wai, whose efforts contributed to the establishment of the Chinese Presbyterian Church Sydney in 1893: the first Chinese church building in NSW.

John Young Wai was born in Canton in 1847 and arrived in Australia in 1867. He worked as a goldminer in Victoria and converted to Christianity. In 1872, together with five other Chinese people, he undertook training for ministry with the Foreign Missions Committee of the Presbyterian Church of Victoria. John Young Wai engaged in mission work in Ballarat, Beechworth, and other towns. After serving the church in Victoria for eight years, in 1882 he was invited by the NSW Foreign Missions Committee to conduct mission work among Chinese people in NSW. In 1886, he asked for leave and returned to China. In the first month of the lunar new year in 1887, John Young Wai married a woman in Hong Kong whose surname was Dai 戴. The couple returned to Sydney in May that year and engaged in Chinese mission work.[45]

As Chinese mission work developed rapidly in the early 1890s, the meeting place for Chinese Christians on Goulburn Street was no longer able to accommodate the congregation, which averaged between seventy

---

41. Phillips, "Seeking Souls," 97.

42. "Wesleyan Methodist Church," 503. For Ling's work of establishing a Chinese mission in Perth, see "Chinese Mission: Inaugural," 3.

43. David Lung, "After the Gold Rush," 149.

44. Mar Lu, *So Great a Cloud*, 2.

45. "Obituary," 10; 〈周牧師容威事略〉, 5.

and eighty people.[46] On one occasion, John Young Wai had to stand in the doorway between two rooms to deliver a sermon, with thirty men in each room. Young Wai urged the Foreign Missions Committee to secure larger facilities.[47] The committee agreed to build a Chinese Presbyterian Church in Foster Street in 1892, and with permission from the convener of the committee, Young Wai actively solicited "donations to purchase a site and erect a church in Sydney."[48] Young Wai's hard work led to a sum of £372 being contributed by both Christian and non-Christian Chinese people as part of the total cost of £1,000. On March 14, 1893, the foundation stone was laid by Lady Darley, wife of the Chief Justice of New South Wales, Sir Frederick Matthew Darley. On behalf of the Chinese, Young Wai presented Lady Darley "with a valuable screen."[49] Two months later, the newly constructed church building was opened in Foster Street. On September 24 that year, Young Wai was ordained as a Presbyterian minister "by the Presbytery of Sydney by the laying on of hands" in the Chinese Presbyterian Church.[50] As an ordained minister, Young Wai "now possessed the authority to baptize the Chinese he converted himself, without needing to utilize an Australian minister." Young Wai was expected by the Presbyterian Church to "serve as 'a Missionary among the Chinese in this Colony,'" which was deeply encouraging for the Chinese congregation.[51]

A report published in November 1893 in *The Presbyterian Messenger* detailed the usual weekly duties of John Young Wai. On the Sabbath morning from nine thirty to ten thirty, a Bible class numbering ten people would meet in the Chinese Presbyterian Church. The afternoon service was given from one thirty to two forty-five to a congregation of sixty to eighty people. The service was followed by the Sabbath School at three o'clock, attended by twenty children and ten young Chinese for Bible reading. On the evening of the Sabbath, an open-air service would start at six thirty in Wexford Street and the Sunday school teachers would come to help with the singing. A church service would then be held at seven o'clock, usually attended by 120 to 200 people. On Mondays, Young Wai would visit a few Chinese patients at the Sydney Hospital and the Prince Alfred Hospital. On

46. "Presbyterian Chinese Church," 3.
47. "New Chinese Presbyterian," 8.
48. "Sydney Chinese Church," 71.
49. "New Chinese Church," 214.
50. "Chinese Church, Sydney," 87.
51. Mar Lu, *So Great a Cloud*, 4–5.

Tuesday, he would visit Chinese gardeners at Rushcutters Bay and Double Bay. About twenty Chinese would attend the evening service at Double Bay. On Wednesdays, he would visit Chinese stores, workshops, and houses in the city. A weeknight service would be held at seven thirty with an attendance of thirty to forty people. On Thursdays and Fridays, Young Wai would visit suburbs and places such as Waterloo, St. Peters, Alexandria, Newtown, Botany, and the North Shore.[52] Noting the development of the Foster Street Mission, "the Foreign Missions Committee requested the Presbytery of Sydney to raise the Foster Street Mission to the status of a sanctioned charge," which means to become a self-supporting church.[53] In 1897, the Chinese Presbyterian Church was given the status of a sanctioned charge, and in the following year Young Wai was inducted as the minister in charge of the church and had ministerial status in the General Assembly.[54]

Chinese churches demonstrated resilience after the White Australia Policy was implemented in 1901. Under this law, the immigration officers had "the power to make any non-European migrant sit a 50-word dictation test," which was "initially given in any European language and after 1905 in any prescribed language." The number of non-European immigrants drastically declined. Only fifty-two non-white migrants were granted entry to Australia before 1909 and no non-white migrant passed the test after 1909. Small numbers of non-white migrants were granted exemption.[55] This testing system led to the decline of the Chinese population in Australia: by 1921 it was 20,800, nearly half of the number in 1881. In 1947, the Chinese population had nearly halved again, down to 12,100 people. Sydney was the main center of the Chinese community: about 3,400 Chinese resided there between 1891 and 1947. By 1966, following waves of post-war migration, the Chinese population in Australia had risen back up to 26,700 people.[56]

Chinese Christians in Australia under the Immigration Restriction Act of 1901 remained a small but faithful community. Research shows that the Chinese Presbyterian Church was without a minister from 1935 to 1943 after the deaths of Rev. John Young Wai in 1930 and his successor Rev. Lan San Leung in 1935. During this period laymen played a crucial role in church life. From 1943 to 1959, the church only supplied temporary

52. "Chinese Church, Sydney," 87.
53. Mar Lu, *So Great a Cloud*, 5.
54. "Personal," 9.
55. National Museum Australia, "White Australia."
56. Mar Lu, *So Great a Cloud*, 11–12, 21.

ministers to the pulpit due to the war in the Pacific. The year 1959 marked a critical node in the history of the Chinese Presbyterian Church as it had its own inducted minister for the first time since Rev. Young Wai and became totally self-supporting. Its long relationship with the Board of Foreign Missions thus ended.[57] This change demonstrates the growing agency of Chinese Christians in managing their churches.

Against a backdrop of racism and segregation, Chinese Christians in Australia had to unite to make sure their voices were heard. At the turn of the twentieth century, the social network of the Chinese community, which was previously based on blood and place of origin (mostly from the districts of Siyi, Taishan, and Zhongshan in Guangdong Province), gradually transformed into a new network shaped by bilingual people such as missionaries, reporters, and merchants.[58] Research has shown that Chinese Christian businesspeople in early twentieth-century Australia played a key role in bridging the Chinese community and their adopted society. They demonstrated their Christian identity through fundraising for local charities and Chinese missions, including projects such as building Chinese churches and training Chinese missionaries. They also expressed their opposition to the anti-Chinese sentiments that were common in Australia at the time.[59]

Chinese Christian merchant and missionary Cheong Cheok Hong was a pioneer figure in promoting "greater unity within the broader Chinese community." Educated in Victoria and supported by his Christian father Cheong Peng-nam, Cheong's bilingualism enabled him to "develop a deep understanding of his religious identity and trained him to strive for the extension of Chinese Christianity in Australia."[60] Cheong was engaged in the Victorian Chinese merchant community and joined the Melbourne Chinese Merchants' Association in 1875–76. Cheong co-authored a pamphlet titled *The Chinese Question in Australia 1878–1879* in response to "anti-Chinese polemics following a decision by the Australian Steam Navigation Company to replace Europeans with lower paid Chinese crew on its Australian routes."[61] This public comment submitted to the Victorian Government aimed to protect Chinese laborers under the "Beijing Treaty"

57. Mar Lu, *So Great a Cloud*, 16–25.
58. Lung, "After the Gold Rush," 149.
59. Austin, *Kingdom-Minded*, 185–212.
60. Austin, *Kingdom-Minded*, 195, 197.
61. Welch, "Alien Son," 71.

signed between Britain and China that allowed the Chinese to enter British colonies freely.[62]

Cheong also endeavored to promote unity among Chinese Christians in Australia. In the early 1900s, Cheong co-founded the Victorian Chinese Christian Union that was composed of the Chinese members of the Anglican, Presbyterian, Methodist, and Church of Christ communions to spread the gospel among Chinese people in Australia and in China. In addition to supporting evangelistic work, the union was active in matters that were seen as being of concern to Chinese Christians. In 1906, the union participated in a Victorian protest against "the anti-Chinese amendments to the Victorian Factories Act" that aimed to end "the employment opportunities of Chinese in the furniture and laundry trades."[63] The union joined the wider cooperation of Chinese Christians in Australia to support the 1911 revolution, led by Rev. John Young Wai, who played a significant role "in bringing members of the Chinese Christian districts from New Zealand, Victoria, and New South Wales together."[64]

The century-long period discussed in this section captures a slow but profound development of Chinese Christian churches in Australia. This period saw the ethnic religious community become more visible and integrate into local society. The emergence of Chinese Christian leaders and Chinese church buildings in Australia facilitated the formation of religious and ethnic community in the Chinese diaspora, and the leading role of Chinese Christians in evangelistic work and church ministry demonstrates their growing agency. Following the abolishment of the White Australia Policy in 1973, Chinese Christian churches in Australia were reinvigorated and began to evangelize new tides of Chinese immigrants in the following decades.

The Expansion of Chinese Churches in Australia from the 1970s Onward

Chinese Christian churches in Australia developed rapidly after the end of the White Australia Policy. As Australian society embraced a multicultural policy that valued equality, waves of immigrants arrived in Australia from different countries and regions in the Asia-Pacific. There was an influx of

62. Lung, "Chinese Fighting for Equality," 79.
63. Welch, "Alien Son," 563–64.
64. "Chinese Christians Favor Revolution," 9.

Asian migrants in the 1970s as nationalism and conflicts surged in postwar Southeast Asia. Many people from the Chinese diaspora living in Malaysia, Singapore, Indonesia, Vietnam, and East Timor migrated to Australia, and immigration from Hong Kong increased prior to the handover of Hong Kong to the People's Republic of China in 1997. When China implemented its economic reforms in the 1980s, a growing number of mainland Chinese went overseas, and Mandarin speakers became a prominent group in the Chinese diaspora in Australia. Table 1 shows the Chinese population in Australia based on birthplace in 1976, 1981, and 1991.

Table 1. Census of Population and Housing

Birthplace	1976	1981	1991
China	19,542	25,883	78,866
Hong Kong	8,818	15,717	58,984

Source: Australian Bureau of Statistics

Chinese churches in Australia experienced rapid development with the increase in immigration. In the 1980s, there were thirty-two Chinese churches in Australia according to the report of Chinese Coordination Centre of World Evangelism.[65] However, Chinese churches in Australia increased rapidly in the following decades. By 2019, the website of the Chinese Christian Mission Australia showed a total number of 239 Chinese churches in Australia, concentrated in NSW (see Table 2).

Australian-Chinese Christians and new immigrants were two major influences in the development of Chinese churches. The expansion of the Chinese Christian Church at Milson's Point (CCC) is an example of the local development of an ethnic church and its responses to the immigration wave.[66] The CCC is an interdenominational Chinese church at which over 1,300 people have been baptized during its fifty-year history. Some of the churches it planted became independent and baptized many more. In 2015, there were over 2,500 people attending the CCC or one of its daughter churches.

Table 2. Ethnic Chinese Churches in Australia

---

65. 世界華福中心,《海外華人教會名錄》, 322–23.

66. The section on the history of CCC is based on the following publication if not noted otherwise: *Chinese Christian Church*, 13–42.

NSW	103
VIC	82
Queensland	24
South Australia	13
West Australia	11
ACT	3
Tasmania	2
Northern Territory	1
Total	239

Source: Chinese Christian Mission Australia Website ©2019[67]

The founders of the CCC were four elders of the Chinese Presbyterian Church (CPC). When the CPC became an independent church under the Presbyterian Church in 1959, the CPC was no longer required to report to the Foreign Missions Committee (FMC) but was accountable to the Australian Presbytery which was not as sensitive to cultural differences as the FMC. The four CPC elders were concerned about "the spiritual welfare of the rising number of Chinese migrants" and an unwillingness among Chinese Christians "to be a part of the Presbyterian Church due to differences in denominational beliefs."[68] Coupled with the involvement of the Australian Presbytery in the re-election of the minister for the CPC, the four elders decided it was time to establish an interdenominational church where the congregation had the right to select their own Chinese minister and run the church by and for the Chinese.

In 1964, the four elders left the CPC and formed the Chinese Christian Fellowship. In August that year, the fellowship adopted a constitution that aimed to "establish an independent, self-governing and self-supporting Chinese Christian Church by uniting Christians of like faith" and to "surge forward in spreading the Gospel."[69] They found a place for worship one month later at the AMP Auditorium in Circular Quay and held a bilingual worship service in English and Cantonese. In May 1965, the fellowship formed the Chinese Church Formation Committee. In the following month, the committee registered the Chinese Christian Church Limited

67. "澳洲教會索引."
68. *Chinese Christian Church*, 15.
69. *Chinese Christian Church*, 19.

as a company and the fellowship dissolved. In 1967, the CCC purchased a property at Milson's Point from North Sydney Congregational Church.

The CCC expanded its ministry works as immigration increased. In 1975, in response to the influx of refugees after the civil war in East Timor, it established the East Timorese Bible Study Group. Noting the needs of the Timorese refugees, a CCC church member called Timothy Tjoe committed to serve them. Each Sunday Mrs. Tjoe drove the old and feeble to the CCC and Mr. Tjoe and his daughter led "the other several dozens in total" to travel from Coogee to Milsons Point "by foot, by bus and by train."[70] Many of the Timorese refugees converted to Christianity and became part of the CCC.

The CCC ministry also reached out to refugees from Vietnam, Laos, and Cambodia. With new migrants joining, the CCC grew rapidly and increased from 150 in 1975 to 240 in 1977. To cope with the growing congregation numbers, the CCC started a 9 a.m. English service in addition to the bilingual congregational worship at 11 a.m. In 1978, the CCC established a branch church in the Burwood/Strathfield area in response to the growing Chinese population who lived in remote suburbs. With the encouragement of the CCC, the branch became independent and was renamed the West Sydney Chinese Christian Church in 1982.

In the 1980s, the CCC established three branch churches and two monolingual services. The East Sydney Asian Christian Church was integrated into the CCC in 1986 as a branch church. It focused on evangelizing Chinese students studying at UNSW. In 1987, the Timorese Bible study class was reorganized into the Chung Chen Chinese Christian Church. A Chinese fellowship group was established following the rise of immigrants from Hong Kong in 1983. This Cantonese language Bible study divided into two groups in 1986. The second group later became a branch church of the CCC in 1989 and was renamed the Northern District Chinese Christian Church. In 1988, the CCC commenced a Mandarin Service at 2 p.m. attended by thirty people, including Mandarin-speaking residents and mainland Chinese students. The following years saw an increase in Chinese migrants from both Hong Kong and mainland China.

In addition to established Australian Chinese churches, new immigrants who were Christians prior to coming to Australia were another group advancing ministry work among diaspora Chinese. The history of the Chinese Methodist Church in Australia (CMCA) demonstrates the

---

70. *Chinese Christian Church*, 36.

important role of new immigrants in expanding Chinese churches.[71] Unlike any other Methodist Church, which dispatches a missionary from a sponsoring Methodist Conference, the CMCA was formed independently.[72] It was established by Pastor James Ha who received a divine call to evangelize the Chinese diaspora in Australia. He left Malaysia for Melbourne in May 1986. Ha started the Kew Chinese Christian Fellowship in the following month. In June 1987, the fellowship was formally registered as the Kew Chinese Christian Church. In 1988, Rev. Ha was commissioned to be a missionary in the Sarawak Chinese Annual Conference under the Methodist Church in Malaysia to establish a church in Brisbane.[73] In 1990, the fellowship was renamed the Chinese Methodist Church of Melbourne (CMCM, 謝恩堂). In 1992, Rev. Ha flew to Malaysia, Singapore, and Taiwan to share with local Methodists about the ministry and financial needs of the CMCA.

By 1994, there were seven Chinese Methodist churches and one preaching point.[74] Chinese Methodist churches in Australia shared the vision of establishing a connected system and consequently formed the Mission Conference in 1994 under the guidance of the Bishop of the Methodist Church in Malaysia. The conference became a Provisional Annual Conference in 2000 and one year later a full member of the World Methodist Conference within which the CMCM played a leading role.

As of 2020, the CMCA has twenty-one churches, three preaching points, and one preaching center in Australia, providing Mandarin and English services, as well as two mission districts that provide Mandarin services outside of Australia. In Papua New Guinea (PNG) there is currently one church, four preaching centers, and one preaching point. Its history can be traced back to 1999 when a Mandarin Bible study group was formed by Mandarin-speaking migrants for laborers from Malaysia and mainland

71. The section on the history of Chinese Methodist Church in Australia is based on the following publications if not noted otherwise: 《滿有恩典之路》；《紀念特刊》.

72. Chinese Methodist Church in Australia, "Annual Conference."

73. The term "annual conference" in the framework of the United Methodist refers to a regional body, an organization unit, and a yearly meeting. See United Methodist Church, "Annual Conferences."

74. The Chinese Methodist Church in Australia uses three terms to refer to the progress of their evangelical work: church 教會, preaching center 佈道站, and preaching point 佈道所. A preaching point is to be established at places where the gospel was preached. Along with its growth, a preaching point will then develop into a preaching center and eventually a Methodist church. See Eight Mile Plains, "Our Faith." https://emp.cmca.org.au/faith/.

China. When the CMCA learned about the need of a minister for the Mandarin ministry in PNG, it established a preaching point at Port Moresby in 2005, which is now a Methodist Church.[75] In the Solomon Islands, there is one Chinese Methodist church, which was initially established in 2010 as a preaching point. Eight years later, the preaching point became an affiliated church of the CMCA.[76]

Amidst these church expansions, to cope with the fast-growing Mandarin-speaking ministry, Chinese theology training became a shared vision of Chinese church leaders. Compared with the last two centuries, when Australian-Chinese Christians were predominantly Cantonese speakers, a growing number of Mandarin speakers gave rise to the need to train pastoral workers who could understand Chinese culture and preach in Mandarin. A vision to train pastoral workers locally was shared among delegates who attended the Australia and New Zealand Chinese Congress on World Evangelization in 1991. The delegates from Sydney worked to establish an interdenominational Chinese theological college. In 2000, the Chinese Theological College Australia Inc. (CTCA, 澳洲華人教牧神學院) was formed and registered as a non-profit theological education organization. Initially supervised by and a teaching agent of Christ College, from January 1, 2020, the CTCA became the first independent Chinese theological college affiliated with the Australian University of Theology, a national self-accrediting provider of courses in theology and ministry established in 1891. The CTCA is tasked with equipping pastors and church leaders with the skills and knowledge to serve the Chinese Christian communities in Australia and provide lay theological education to Chinese Christians in Australia.[77]

The 1991 world evangelization meeting inspired delegates from Melbourne to develop theological education, and as of 2022 there are three institutions in Australia that provide theological training in Mandarin. The Melbourne Chinese Christian Churches Association (墨爾本華人基督教聯會) formed a Chinese theology education committee and collaborated with the Melbourne School of Theology (MST, previously known as the Melbourne Bible Institute and then Bible College Victoria) to establish a Chinese department (墨爾本神學院中文部). From 1993 to 2003, twenty-three lecturers from different denominations worked to promote Chinese

---

75. Chinese Methodist Church in Australia, "Mission Districts."
76. See Chinese Methodist Church in Solomon Islands.
77. CTCA, "Birth of the Vision"; Law, "Dream Come True," 1.

theology education at the MST Chinese department.[78] To form an in-depth understanding of Christianity in an era of postmodernism and multiculturalism, the MST Chinese department established the Centre for the Study of Chinese Christianity (華人神學研究中心) in February 2012. The center is tasked with promoting Chinese contextual theology and enhancing academic communication with local and overseas scholars.[79]

In addition to the independent and affiliated models, the Brisbane School of Theology has a Chinese program and has offered courses taught in Mandarin since 1997. The small yet vibrant Chinese program at this interdenominational college currently has two lecturers and one sessional lecturer, and a diverse community of students.[80] The Mandarin-taught theology at these institutions represents an endeavor to develop Chinese churches by blending Chinese culture and the Australian context.

The late twentieth century and early twenty-first century witnessed a revival of Chinese churches in terms of church numbers. The growing ethnic religious community is also becoming increasingly diverse, with ethnic Chinese people coming from different regions and countries. The large number of immigrants from mainland China prompted the establishment of Mandarin-speaking theology education, filling the need for modern theological training in Australia that is of, by, and for Chinese Christians. The Chinese churches in Australia thus entered a new phase marked by the establishment of institutions that conduct research on Chinese theology and locally train Chinese church ministers.

Advancing Chinese Churches in Australia's Diverse Society

From the Chinese mission during the goldrush period to the expansion of Chinese churches in an era of multiculturalism, evangelism has underpinned the development of Chinese churches in Australia. In the latter half of the nineteenth century, Chinese migrants converted to Christianity due to the joint efforts of Euro-Sino missionaries. Some converts later became church leaders and engaged in ministry and establishing Chinese church buildings in urban areas. Under the White Australia Policy, Chinese Christian leaders responded to public anti-Chinese sentiment by attempting to bridge the gap between mainstream society and the broader Chinese

78. 陳廷忠, 《墨爾本神學院中文部廿週年數主恩》, 3–20.
79. "華人神學研究中心."
80. "學院簡介."

community. Many Chinese Christian leaders united to protest racism and simultaneously worked to promote evangelical ministry among Chinese people in Australia and China. Chinese churches currently uphold this evangelical vision and develop missionary strategies to cater to the spiritual needs of an increasing ethnic Chinese population. The leading role of Chinese Christians as well as the establishment of Chinese church buildings and theology institutions in Australia demonstrates the growing agency of Chinese Christians in ministry and theological training. The development of Chinese churches in Australia has illustrated a process of gradual integration into the host country.

With the rapid expansion of churches and the growing complexity of ethnic Chinese groups, Chinese churches are struggling to find senior pastors. Rev. Denis Law,[81] an influential senior church leader who served as Principal of CTCA from 2013 to 2022, notes that there is a shortage of senior pastors who have the language skills (English and Chinese, including Cantonese and Mandarin) and cultural knowledge to minister to the broader Chinese community. Due to the restrictions on overseas applicants, who can only obtain temporary visas to enter Australia for pastoral work, a long-term solution is to train pastors locally. Law therefore highlights the important role of Chinese theological training in securing church leaders.

In addition to cultivating senior pastors, Law points out the importance of youth ministry. Chinese Christians, especially second-generation Chinese immigrants, experience tension between their Chinese background and Australian society. New immigrants often want their children to learn Chinese, but as they grow up, second-generation Chinese Australians often want to integrate into mainstream culture by using only English. According to Law, it is common to see the children of Chinese Christians leaving Chinese Christian churches for Western churches. However, Western churches do not provide them with the same sense of comfort: second-generation Chinese Christians are sandwiched between two cultures. The issue of identity and the challenge of integrating the younger generation requires ethnic Chinese churches to invest in youth ministry to foster the personal and spiritual growth of young people.

Embedded in an increasingly diverse Australian society, the Chinese Christian community is also diverse. Developing a unified ethnic church for people of Chinese heritage with different languages and birthplaces is, according to Law, a challenge in an era divided by competing political

---

81. For a detailed biography of Rev. Denis Law, see 《曠野牧聲》.

agendas and ideologies. Law points to the Great Commission as a shared mission of ethnic Chinese churches to spread the gospel to people of all nations. The evangelical zeal that has permeated the history of Chinese churches in Australia over the last two centuries continues to be of great relevance to their future paths.

Bibliography

Austin, Denise A. *"Kingdom-Minded" People: Christian Identity and the Contribution of Chinese Business Christians.* Leiden: Brill, 2011.
Australia's Christian Heritage."Chinese Christian Church—Former." https://www.churchesaustralia.org/list-of-churches/denominations/methodist-wesleyan-and-other/directory/4381-chinese-christian-church-former.
Bickford, James. *Christian Work in Australasia.* London: Wesleyan Conference Office, 1878.
"Biographical Sketch of Rev. John Young Wai." *The Chinese Republic News*, July 4, 1930, 5.
Brisbane School of Theology. "A Brief Introduction of the Chinese Program." https://bst.qld.edu.au/chinese-program/.
"Castlemaine: Christian Mission to the Chinese." *Age*, July 14, 1855, 6.
Chinese Christian Church Milson's Point: 50 Anniversary. Milson's Point: Chinese Christian Church, 2015.
"Chinese Christians." *Leader*, May 13, 1871, 11.
"Chinese Christians Favor Revolution." *The Daily Telegraph*, November 1, 1911, 9.
"A Chinese Church Anniversary." *Age*, July 27, 1899, 6.
"Chinese Church, Sydney." *The Presbyterian Messenger*, November 4, 1893, 87.
Chinese Methodist Church in Australia. "Chinese Methodist Church in Australia Annual Conference—About Us." https://cmca.org.au/index.php/aboutus/.
———. "Chinese Methodist Church in Australia Annual Conference—Mission District." https://cmca.org.au/index.php/districts/mission-district/.
Chinese Methodist Church in Solomon Islands. https://www.facebook.com/cmcsolomonislands.
"Chinese Mission." *Mount Alexander Mail*, July 11, 1856, 3.
"Chinese Mission." *Star*, January 28, 1859, 2.
"Chinese Mission: The Inaugural Meeting." *Daily News*, July 14, 1896, 3.
"The Chinese Mission Church Illustrated." *Australian News for Home Readers*, August 13, 1872, 170.
"Chinese Wesleyan Church." *Argus*, August 15, 1876, 6.
CTCA. "Birth of the Vision." https://www.ctca.edu.au/the-birth-of-the-vision/?lang=en.
Cummines, Cheryl, and Michael Leung, eds. "Chinese Australian Timeline History Scroll." In *A Comprehensive Chinese Australian History 1818-2018, Vol. 1.* Chatswood, NSW: New Century, 2018.
Cole, Keith. *The Anglican Mission to the Chinese in Bendigo and Central Victoria, 1857-1918.* Bendigo, Vic: Keith Cole, 1994.
Danks, B. *Our Mission Fields: The Chinese in Australia, the Indians in Fiji, Samoa, Fiji, Rotuma, New Britain, Papua, Solomon Islands, India.* Sydney: Epworth, nd.
Eight Mile Plains Methodist Church. "Our Faith." https://emp.cmca.org.au/faith/.

Lamont, James. *The Foreign Mission Work of Our Church: Historical Summary*. Sydney: s.n., 1899.
Law, Denis. "A Dream Come True." *Chinese Theological College Australia Inc. Newsletter* 50 (February 2020) 1.
Low, Dorothy. *The History of the Chinese Presbyterian Church, Melbourne, Victoria 1860–1995*. Bendigo, Vic: Doug Morey, 1997.
Lung, David. "Early Arrivals Apart from the Aborigines." In *A Comprehensive Chinese Australian History 1818–2018, Vol. 1*, edited by Cheryl Cummines and Michael Leung, 38–40. Chatswood, NSW: New Century, 2018.
———. "The Chinese After the Gold Rush." In *A Comprehensive Chinese Australian History 1818–2018, Vol. 1*, edited by Cheryl Cummines and Michael Leung, 149. Chatswood, NSW: New Century, 2018.
———. "The Chinese Fighting for Equality." In *A Comprehensive Chinese Australian History 1818–2018, Vol. 1*, edited by Cheryl Cummines and Michael Leung, 79–82. Chatswood, NSW: New Century, 2018.
———. "The Chinese Miners in the Gold Rush." In *A Comprehensive Chinese Australian History 1818–2018, Vol. 1*, edited by Cheryl Cummines and Michael Leung, 47–63. Chatswood, NSW: New Century, 2018.
Mar Lu, Wendy. *So Great a Cloud of Witnesses: A History of the Chinese Presbyterian Church Sydney, 1893–1993*. Sydney: The Centenary of the Chinese Presbyterian Church, 1993.
Melbourne School of Theology. "Centre for the Study of Chinese Christianity." http://chinese.mst.edu.au/?page_id=1987.
National Museum Australia. "Early Chinese Migrants." https://www.nma.gov.au/explore/features/harvest-of-endurance/scroll/early-chinese-migrants#:~:text=Records%20show%20that%20about%202018,and%20purchased%20land%20at%20Parramatta.
———. "White Australia Policy." https://www.nma.gov.au/defining-moments/resources/white-australia-policy.
"New Chinese Church." *The Woollahra Messenger*, April 1893, 214.
"The New Chinese Presbyterian Church." *The Sydney Morning Herald*, May 31, 1893, 8.
"Obituary." *The Sydney Morning Herald*, June 23, 1930, 10.
"Personal: Induction of the Rev. J. Young Wai." *The Daily Telegraph*, October 29, 1898, 9.
Phillips, Walter. "Seeking Souls in the Diggings: Christian Missions to the Chinese on the Victorian Goldfields." *Victorian Historical Journal* 72 (2001) 86–104.
"Presbyterian Chinese Church." *The Sydney Morning Herald*, May 29, 1893, 3.
Sheng, Fei. "Environmental Experiences of the Chinese Miners." In *A Comprehensive Chinese Australian History 1818–2018, Vol. 1*, edited by Cheryl Cummines and Michael Leung, 85–105, Chatswood, NSW: New Century, 2018.
"Sydney Chinese Church." *The Woollahra Messenger*, July 1892, 71.
"Sydney Ragged School." *The Sydney Morning Herald*, August 31, 1875, 2.
United Methodist Church. "Annual Conferences." https://www.umc.org/en/content/annual-conferences.
"Victoria." *Launceston Examiner*, March 8, 1873, 3.
Welch, Ian. "Alien Son: A Life of Cheok Hong Cheong, (Zhang Zhuoxing) 1851–1928." PhD diss., Australian National University, 2001.
———. "Mary Reed of Australia and the China Inland Mission," 2014. https://openresearch-repository.anu.edu.au/bitstream/1885/13040/1/Welch%20Mary%20Reed%202014.pdf.

———. "'Our Neighbors but Not Our Countrymen': Christianity and the Chinese in Nineteenth-Century Victoria (Australia) and California." *The Journal of American-East Asian Relations* 3 (2004-2006) 149-183.

"Wesleyan Chinese Mission in Victoria." *Cornwall Advertiser*, December 6, 1870, 5.

"Wesleyan Methodist Church of Australasia." In *The Yearbook of Australia*, 503-4. London: Trübner &Co., 1888.

"Wesleyan Mission to the Chinese." *Herald*, January 24, 1872, 2.

"Western District Chinese Mission." *The Woollahra Messenger*, July 1892, 72.

Young, W. M. "Fourth Report of the Chinese Mission." *The Argus Melbourne*, December 11, 1855, 6.

陳廷忠.《墨爾本神學院中文部廿週年數主恩1996-2016：神學耕耘錄》.Melbourne: MST Chinese Department, Melbourne School of Theology, 2016.

楊錦華等編,《基督教華人衛理公會墨爾本謝恩堂十五週年紀念特刊》.Melbourne: 澳洲基督教華人衛理公會謝恩堂, 2001.

陳鐘桂蘭等編,《曠野牧聲: 羅德麟院長七秩榮壽紀念集》.Sydney: 澳洲華人教牧神學院, 2017.

《滿有恩典之路: 基督教華人衛理公會二十週年紀念特刊》.Melbourne: 澳洲基督教華人衛理公會, 2006.

〈周牧師容威事略〉.《民國報》(1930年7月4日) 5.

世界華福中心編,《海外華人教會名錄（當代華人教會第七冊）》.Hong Kong: Logos Book House Ltd., 1986.

"學院簡介." https://bst.qld.edu.au/chinese-program/.

"華人神學研究中心." http://chinese.mst.edu.au/?page_id=1987.

"澳洲教會索引." https://ccma.org.au/%E6%BE%B3%E6%B4%B2%E6%95%99%E6%9C%83%E7%B4%A2%E5%BC%95/.

2.

A Study on the Contextualization Process for Chinese Churches in Australia and Its Relevance to the Continuous Influx of Chinese Immigrants

Ka Shing Samuel Lui

Abstract

It is right to understand that one should be more creative, critical, and understand the real situation of a particular circumstance as well as sensitive to the environment when sharing the gospel in a meaningful way.

When the apostle Paul taught us that we are all in one church in union with our Lord Jesus Christ (Gal 3:28), he didn't mean that we need to speak in the same language or we need to forsake our own cultures before we can integrate into the body of Christ, but rather he only said that when we are in Christ, there is no difference between Jew and gentile, slave and free, male or female.

In this article, we examine how the gospel was proclaimed in the past and in the present, and we would agree that the circumstances are very different; in the past when missionaries had to go overseas to share the gospel with non-believers, they needed to consider how they could "contextualize" the gospel so that people with different cultures could understand in their own cultural contexts. However, because people movements nowadays are so common, when applying "gospel contextualization" in the modern era one can notice that the contextualization process isn't the same.

When looking into the Chinese churches in Australia, we need to find out the actual situation in our society regarding Chinese immigrants. When analyzing the demographic of Chinese communities, the statistical research data show that there has been a continuous influx of Chinese immigrants for the past fifty years, and for Chinese immigrants from mainland China, we see an overall strong increase in percentage for the last decade even though there was a slowdown in the last three years due to the COVID-19 pandemic.

Therefore, every Chinese church in Australia should construct a practical approach of contextualization in their own contexts so as to make the outreaching and the nurturing effort effective. In short, Chinese churches will need to adapt the environment and be sensitive to the development of different congregations with different backgrounds.

Introduction

In his paper "Contextualization and Methodology: The Praxis of Gospel Communication," John Farquhar Plake rightly pointed out that "Globalization, urbanization, and migration have transformed contextualization from a missionary issue into a *missio Dei* issue for the global church."[1] He argued by mentioning the concept of critical contextualization introduced by Paul Hiebert "respects both biblical revelation and cultural diversity, bringing them together through the mediatorial work of missionaries, guided by a critical realist epistemology."[2] So for sharing the gospel in a more meaningful and effective way, one should be more creative, critical, and understanding of the real situation of a particular circumstance as well as sensitive to the environment.

---

1. Plake, "Contextualization," ii.
2. Steps in understanding how we interpret the process of contextualization: (1) exegete the culture through phenomenological analysis, (2) exegete relevant Scripture in cooperation with the hermeneutical community, (3) engage in a community-wide (primarily ethnic) critical evaluation of cultural practice in light of Scripture and decide how to respond, and (4) arrange any new practices into a contextualized ritual that expresses the Christian meaning of the event. This was mentioned in Plake, "Contextualization," 21.

Looking at "Gospel Contextualization" Differently

In the past when using the term "gospel contextualization," one would interpret culture through the lens of the Bible, that is, how we can effectively bring the gospel message to unreached people with sensitivity to their cultures without compromising the core of the Christian faith. So, missionaries went to foreign countries and tried to "contextualize" the gospel message (Christian faith), with the hope it would be relevant to different cultures, and people could understand it in their cultural contexts without any barriers such as cultural differences, ways of thoughts, and languages. It is therefore essential to understand that gospel contextualization is both a process and a product,[3] that is, a way towards the propagation of faith in new sociocultural settings, as well as being central to the life of believers in a particular society or people group.

As we know, Christianity began to spread widely into China in the early nineteenth century, and it went through a process of trying to contextualize Christian faith. In the 1920s, Chinese theologian Tzu-Chen Chao hoped to construct a set of Chinese Christian beliefs that were different from the Western way of understanding Christianity. He worked hard to integrate the gospel with Chinese culture and find common points, hoping that the Chinese at that time could comprehend and accept the gospel.[4]

Having said that, we can look at "gospel contextualization" from a different angle in the modern era. Nowadays a multicultural society sees different cultures of people living together in one nation, such as Australia (the country in our discussion). According to the Britannica Australia website, Australia has more than 270 ethnic groups living in the country now, a rapid increase in non-English speaking immigrants for the past half century was recorded.[5] We may use the term "missions by the doorsteps" to describe the change of concept about missions in modern multicultural societies. Before, when we thought about missions, we associated

---

3. See the abstract of Plake, "Contextualization," n1.

4. 賈嘉文 (Jia),《趙紫宸1917至1937年之著作和聖詩中的本色化神學思想》.

5. When describing the ethnic groups in Australia, the Britannia Australia mentions that there are more than 270 people groups now living in Australia. Until the mid-twentieth century, however, Australian society was, with some accuracy, regarded in the wider world as essentially British or at any rate Anglo-Celtic. The ties to Britain and Ireland were scarcely affected by immigration from other sources until then. The complex demographic textures in Australia at the beginning of the twenty-first century contrasted quite sharply with the homogeneity of the country during the first half of the twentieth century.

missionaries with those who went overseas (mission fields) in order to share the gospel message with foreigners. They had to adapt to the environment, learn the cultures, languages/dialects, and try to understand their way of thought, for example, so that the gospel message could be conveyed in a meaningful way that people could understand. Today, we may say that this is not the only way to do missions—that is, missionaries would need to go to other foreign countries physically to reach out to unreached groups of people—but those people groups are now actually living in countries like Australia by immigration. How ethnic churches seize opportunities to reach out to immigrants with similar backgrounds can be through a focus on local missions, and how ethnic churches minister to their people in different stages, including new immigrants, older generation immigrants, and second and third generations of immigrants would be crucial to their overall church growth.

Biblical and Theological Perspectives on Gospel Contextualization

As God's people, Christians all over the world need to constantly reflect on how to spread the gospel of our Lord Jesus more effectively, and how we can edify believers in ways that are most appropriate in their environment and circumstances. Without doubt the gospel is for all nations, different people groups, and cultures; on the other hand, we also know from the incidence of the Tower of Babel in Genesis, people were scattered to different parts of the world, and they have used different languages or dialects since then. And in terms of evangelistic priorities, in order not to make language a barrier for people to hear the gospel of Jesus, we also agree that using the same language of non-believers will be the best way for them to understand the gospel message. So, it stands to reason, "few would argue that culturally homogeneous churches are intrinsically superior to multicultural ones."[6]

From the perspective of faith, the gospel of Jesus is cross-cultural and transforms culture. The message of one Lord, one God, one faith, and one baptism is what believers must pass on in every age. Cultural differences should not affect our respect for each other. That is to say, the importance

---

6. Quoted from Howell, "Multiculturalism," 1. Howell mentioned other church growth advocates have suggested that while there is no argument necessary for multiculturalism, such a focus is unhelpful insofar as it undermines what they believe is the most important function of the church, i.e., bringing more people into the church.

of having a common belief must be emphasized, and it must also be clearly distinguished which are core beliefs (the truths of the Bible, missions of the church) and which are just cultural differences (for example, ways of worship, how messages are delivered, rituals and liturgies, the collection of offerings, the way the church operates, differences in attire and appearance). Therefore, since there are constantly new immigrants and the next generations (in this study, Chinese immigrants) are growing up, we must pass on the mission of proclaiming the gospel with sensitivity to our audience: "To the weak I became weak, to win the weak. I have become all things to all people so that by all possible means I might save some" (1 Cor 9:22).

From a pastoral perspective, the Bible says, "Be shepherds of God's flock that is under your care, watching over them—not because you must, but because you are willing, as God wants you to be; not pursuing dishonest gain, but eager to serve" (1 Pet 5:2). Biblical teaching is always true and unchanged, but how to reconcile cultural differences within the church, especially in multilingual churches, really requires mutual respect, appreciation, acceptance, and making every effort to keep the unity of the Spirit through the bond of peace (Eph 4:3).

As a matter of fact, most of the overseas Chinese churches that have a longer history are bilingual or trilingual. And of course, for those churches that have a shorter history, say, for those established less than twenty years, they do not necessarily have bilingual services or multilingual congregations.

Although Chinese churches have to adapt to different languages and cultures in shepherding different congregations, the mission is the same—that is, we must equip believers to be "mature in Christ and be fishers of men." It is also affirmative and understandable that Chinese churches are moving toward multicultural congregations.

Contextualization and Homogeneous Unit

Donald McGavran, the advocate of modern missiology and church growth, suggested that the Homogeneous Unit (HU) is the most effective mode of evangelism and shepherding. Therefore, it would be the best for people to listen to the gospel without crossing the language barrier, and this can also apply to those who are believers—they can learn, grow, and serve in the church using their most confident languages.

McGavran suggested the "Homogeneous Unit as a basic ecclesiastical building block . . . The anthropologist recognizes it as a wider and more elastic term than culture. The missionary uses it constantly as he evangelizes out beyond the Church. The minister and shepherd discover that he serves his flock better when he sees Christians in their particular societies. The theologian finds the homogeneous unit firmly imbedded in the Bible."[7] Each homogeneous unit has therefore a right to be different and to maintain that difference as it comes into the body of Christ.[8]

"The concept of the homogeneous unit is extremely useful to the missionary movement because of the particularity of church growth. The Church never grows in a vacuum it always grows among men. It never grows among mankind in general—it always grows in homogeneous units."[9] What is not so generally recognized is that each homogeneous unit has its own culture language and ethnic stream, and that the church must become indigenous to it. Till it does, the church grows slowly if at all.[10]

McGavran's observations regarding the homogeneous unit principle helps us realize the importance of contextualization when doing ministries. Missionaries as well as church growth advocates can gain practical insights of seeing how the gospel can be effectively proclaimed, and how a church can grow healthier and faster when applying the principle.

As a matter of fact, when Christians see the needs and opportunities to start a new Christian community in a particular area, most of the church planting effort or the initiation of a new church starts small. And it comes to make sense that the small bunch of people would probably have a similar background, essentially speaking the same language and banding together for the sake of spreading the gospel and building a Christian community among unreached people with a similar culture. And it works well when they can communicate and understand each other without crossing any cultural and language barriers.

Cultural sensitivity is essential if we want to win people for Christ; it would be ineffective if we asked someone to become a Christian but they needed to learn a new language, a new culture, and the worst scenario, if they were asked to give up their cultural inheritance. Let us not forget that

---

7. McGavran, "Homogeneous Unit," 403.
8. McGavran, "Homogeneous Unit," 410.
9. McGavran, "Homogeneous Unit," 405.
10. McGavran, "Homogeneous Unit," 409.

we are to have one Lord, one Savior, one baptism, one faith—but we won't say we need to become one culture or one language.

We are all in one church in union with our Lord Jesus Christ (Gal 3:28), and when the apostle Paul said both Jews and gentiles are united as one people, he didn't mean that we need to speak the same language or forsake our own cultures, but rather that when we are in Christ, there is no difference between Jew and gentile, slave and free, male or female. McGarvan described it in this way: "Oneness in Christ does not mean being run through a blending machine which turns peas, carrots and cucumbers into a bland vegetable soup."[11] The Bible does not say something against people from different cultural backgrounds but rather we need to embrace our differences and maintain cultural diversities such that no matter what languages we speak, we are still one in Christ and were all made to drink of one Spirit.

Is the Homogeneous Unit Principle Unbiblical?

Yet there are some who don't think it is biblical to build a homogeneous church, and one of these critics is Aubrey Sequeira. She wrote an article "Re-Thinking Homogeneity: The Biblical Case for Multi-Ethnic Churches"[12] and argued that in the early church, the apostles faced different issues within the church as there were differences among the believers. The famous passage of Acts 6:1–6 describes the tensions that arose between those from different cultural-linguistic groups, but the apostles never "partitioned the church into homogeneous units." Instead, they resolved the issues through appointing men from the minority groups for the work of service, for example. She further suggested, wherever possible, establishing multiethnic churches is not only more faithful to Scripture but that multiethnic churches more fully display the glorious gospel of Jesus Christ.[13]

However, when carefully examining how Donald McGavran used the term "homogeneous unit," he had no intention to segregate ethnic groups so that churches should only be run according to their ethnicities. When he mentioned that "The homogeneous unit principle of church growth

---

11. McGavran, "Homogeneous Unit," 414.

12. Sequeira, "Re-Thinking," 1. In the article Aubrey Sequeira strongly argued against the homogeneous unit principle.

13. Sequeira tried to argue from the biblical point of view to support the establishment of multiethnic churches.

maintains that such homogenous churches grow faster because they are more accommodating to outsiders who might feel uncomfortable crossing cultural, ethnic, or other boundaries,"[14] McGavran didn't suggest this as the only way of building God's church. It was merely suggested to his audience that from his observations over the years with many churches in different countries, this was what he found out, and never suggested that all churches in the world should be built as homogeneous churches. If we carefully read his book *Understanding Church Growth*, he argues that church leadership should consider more effective ways of reaching to the unreached. He doesn't say that all churches should be built according to the homogenous unit principle, but rather urges to his readers that we should be sensitive to the cultural-linguistic factors when we want to reach out to non-believers as well as shepherding believers. So then, in a multicultural society with different languages or dialects being used, we can further develop the concept by embracing churches in such an environment to consider having different language/dialect congregations under one roof. And if that is the case, then Sequeira misunderstood what McGavran suggested, and her statements against the homogeneous unit principle would be overstated. Referring to the passage in Acts 6, the main problem wasn't related to the language barrier but that some of the widows were being overlooked in the daily distribution of food. Possibly most of the people at that time could understand Greek, no matter whether they were of Jewish or Hellenistic background. If this is the case, this passage shouldn't be used to criticize McGavran's suggestion.

Early History of the Chinese Immigrants in Australia

By recognizing that whilst multiculturalism refers to the sociological notions or social policies of countries, contextualization, in the context of church, would mean the process of considering something in its context (the situation within which it exists or happens), which can help in understanding it.[15] Let us learn more about the history of the Chinese population in Australia before we formulate how we can reach out to the Chinese community as well as minister to Chinese Christians in the country.

---

14. Sequeira quoted McGavran's saying in her article. See "Re-Thinking," 1.

15. See *Cambridge Dictionary*, s.v. "contextualization," https://dictionary.cambridge.org/dictionary/english/contextualization.

According to the historical records of *A Comprehensive Chinese Australian History (Vol. 2)*, the long history of Chinese migration to Australia dates from the early nineteenth century. In the 1850s tens of thousands of Chinese people arrived to provide a source of cheap labor as workers in the goldfields. After the gold rushes, many Chinese miners returned home to their families in China, but others stayed to establish businesses or work on the land. Though there were some setbacks for Chinese immigrants because of legislation applied in the 1920s known as the "White Australia" policy, after the abolishment of this legislation in 1973 migrants of Chinese origin have arrived in increasing numbers.[16]

While the Australian Government embraces multiculturalism in the country, immigrants are encouraged not only just to stay in the country but also to integrate into mainstream society. Nevertheless, it is inevitable that immigrants continue to use their own mother tongues for communication and even to live close by to each other.

Current Trend of Chinese Immigrants in Australia

The situation at present for the past decade is quite unique. When examining the statistics published by the Australian Bureau of Statistics (ABS), we can notice that despite the not-so-good relationship between Australia and China, coupled with the adverse effect of COVID19 on new immigrants to Australia, new Chinese migrants are in second place behind India! And the rate of increase for the past ten years is stunning at an increase of over 50 percent for this period.[17]

At present, 27.6 percent of Australia's population are born overseas. Two of the top five languages used at home, other than English, are Mandarin (2.7%) and Cantonese (1.2%).[18]

It is understandable that use of culture and language would remain even after immigrants have been settled in the country for a long period of time. In Australia, the number of new immigrants is constantly increasing, and has no sign of decreasing. According to statistics, in 2020 Australia

---

16 The information can be found in *Comprehensive History (Vol. 2)*, an important piece of literature regarding Chinese immigrants in Australian history which was written in Chinese and published in two volumes in September 2021.

17 The information can be found in the newly released report by the ABS. See ABS, "Australia's Population."

18 These figures were released by the ABS on June 28, 2022. See ABS, "Snapshot."

became the ninth most immigrant country in the world. Therefore, there is an understanding that Australia is a country of immigrants, and people of different nationalities and cultures coexist together. And as a multicultural society, the important thing is to respect and appreciate different cultures, though we would also like to see immigrants one day integrate with the mainstream.

According to the Australian Bureau of Statistics in 2016, about 6.9 million people in the country were born overseas. The Chinese population was about 650,000. Besides British immigrants (1 million), Chinese immigrants (including people from China and Hong Kong) ranked second, followed by New Zealand immigrants (about 570,000), and Indian immigrants (490,000).[19]

For the 2021 census, overseas-born immigrants together accounted for 29.1 percent of the Australian population, about 7.5 million people, so it is clear that the trend of immigrants keeps growing.[20]

Table 3

Year	2016	2021
Overseas-born population	6.9 million	7.5 million (29.1%)
Overseas-born Chinese population (China and Hong Kong)	Approx. 660,000	Approx. 700,000

Source: Australian Bureau of Statistics

Overseas-born immigrants in 2021 included:

- UK: 967,000
- India: 710,000
- China: 595,630 (not including immigrants from Hong Kong).

So, it shows that Chinese overseas-born immigrants ranked third overall. In the past ten years from 2011 to 2021, according to the Australian Bureau of Statistics, the Chinese immigrant population increased by 208,000, an increase of 53.74 percent (2011: 387,420), only next to India. This data has not included immigrants from Hong Kong.

By looking at the ABS statistics released in 2021, statistically we continue seeing the influx of Chinese, especially from China, for the last ten

---

19. The statistical data are from ABS, "Population."
20. The statistical data are from ABS, "Statistics."

years. Though the number of Chinese immigrants slowed down over the past two years due to the effect of the pandemic, the tension in Sino-Australian relations between the two countries, and the strict immigration policy from the Australian Government; as time goes by, the pandemic will be a matter in the past, and the relationship will be getting on its feet again as the Australian Government tries to mend the situation. Gestures like softening comments on the Chinese issues, high profile government officials visiting China from time to time, and relaxation of the immigration policies for the last two years (such as allowing overseas students to stay in Australia after their graduation by issuing bridging visas for five years) show that the present Australian Government is more ready to accept immigrants. So the overall trend leads us to see a further growth of the Chinese population and immigrants in Australia in the next five to ten years, and of course, we can also imagine that the number of second- and third-generation Chinese immigrants will continue to rise as well.

Brief History of the Chinese Church in Australia

From the earliest Chinese church to the present, Australian Chinese churches have a history of about 150 years. The Gospel Church at 196 Little Bourke Street in Melbourne was established by the Chinese Methodist Church in 1872;[21] and the Chinese Presbyterian Church in Sydney will celebrate its 130th anniversary next year.[22]

Over the past four decades, Chinese immigrants from mainland China and Hong Kong have sprung up like mushrooms in Australia, and we have also seen Chinese churches increase in number rapidly. Just to give an example, by memory, there were only five Chinese churches in Sydney before 1980, namely, Chinese Presbyterian Church, Central Baptist Church, Chinese Christian Church at Milson's Point, West Sydney Chinese Christian Church, and Grace Chinese Christian Church at Kogarah.

Then around the beginning of the 1980s, the Australian Government somehow changed their foreign policies and allowed more migrants and overseas students to the country; and the number of Chinese immigrants especially from Hong Kong peaked around the year 2000 amid the issue of the British returning Hong Kong to China in 1997. The number of Chinese churches increased as well, reflecting that the Chinese Christian immigrants

21. See *Comprehensive History (Vol. 2)*, 29.
22. Sourced from the website of the Chinese Presbyterian Church, Sydney.

from Hong Kong were eager to plant more churches in different suburbs. At the time of writing, the total number of Chinese churches in Sydney exceeds one hundred. This trend is also seen in Melbourne, especially for the last twenty years.

Until the turn of the century, the rise of modern China saw more Chinese get richer and have more freedom going overseas for migrations and studies. Australia became one of the most popular migration options for the Chinese from mainland China, and as a result, a strong influx of both categories (immigrants and overseas students) could be seen for the last two decades in all states of Australia. Because of the continuous increase in Chinese immigrants, Chinese churches in Australia overall seize opportunities to reach out to the Chinese community, and the number of congregations are in a steady increasing rate correspondingly.

If the above context is a true and fair view for the future trend regarding Chinese immigrants, Chinese churches should try to prepare their outreach strategies and at the same time Chinese languages (Mandarin and Cantonese) will still be the main languages ministering to the Chinese congregations. Having said that, as more and more second and third generations of Chinese immigrants grow in number, Chinese churches also need to carefully put appropriate resources to develop the English ministry within their churches.

Contextualization Process for the Chinese Churches in Australia

Obviously, contextualization is a process where we need to consider the "context" in different circumstances. For a country like Australia, it is a vibrant, dynamic, and robust country where there is a continuous influx of immigrants from different parts of the world. As such the ethnic churches in Australia need to evaluate from time to time how they can be faithful in "doing" church ministries, as 1 Chronicles 12:32 says, "For Issachar, men who understood the times and knew what Israel should do . . ." If we see it from the biblical and theological point of view, surely the missions of churches throughout the centuries are to evangelize to all nations (people groups), however, without having the lens of "cultural relevance," we may not be able to reach different people groups effectively.

Pragmatically, for example, ethnic churches such as Chinese churches in a Western society like Australia can attract and draw a similar group of people together, primarily immigrants from the same backgrounds with the same languages (immigrants coming from China, Taiwan, Hong Kong, Macau, Vietnam, Singapore, and Malaysia, for example, have similar cultures, and most of them can speak and understand either Mandarin and/or Cantonese, the two most commonly used languages among Chinese people).

How the gospel can be effectively shared would be without crossing cultural and language barriers. Surely the best way to communicate with a Cantonese-speaking person will be to use the language that he or she can understand the best.

As such, if we try to construct a practical approach to the contextualization process for Chinese churches in Australia, we must wear a different lens to understand what "contextualization" means in its context. It doesn't necessarily mean Chinese churches will need to conform or evolve themselves to the Australian culture and become the same as other Australian English-speaking churches so as to reach out to Australians. Rather the Chinese churches can still have their own uniqueness and identity in being ethnically Chinese, yet being ethnic churches in Australia they may need to adapt the environment, so then their mandates are still reaching mainly Chinese (and beyond) for the sake of the gospel in a multicultural society.

However, this is not referring to how Australian Chinese churches keep their own historical and cultural originality but rather how they should adapt the surrounding environment and make necessary adjustments so as to fulfill the Great Commission which was given by our Lord Jesus before he ascended to heaven (Matt 28:19–20). How they can effectively convey the gospel message to Chinese immigrants (including the second and third generation) will depend on how they interpret the "context" in Australian society.

In his article, "Multiculturalism, Immigration and the North American Church: Rethinking Contextualization," published in *Missiology: An International Review*, Brian M. Howell rightly pointed out that "The question facing the North American Church [in our case, Australian Chinese churches] today is not principally one of the theological imperatives, but of missiological strategy. In the present, does it make sense, in terms of evangelistic priorities, to pursue culturally specific congregations, or should we pursue multicultural congregations? The answer to this is somewhat more complex and depends in part on our understanding of the culture concept."[23]

Somehow, it's not so pragmatic and simple as to whether an ethnic church should develop as a multicultural congregation church or not. For a newly developed ethnic church, it makes sense that it will probably start up with one language (in fact, we know that people who come from different places, especially from Asia, may have the same mother tongue, such as Cantonese, as people from Canton China, Hong Kong, Macau, Vietnam, Singapore, and Malaysia, for example) rather than holding bilingual services, as this would only prolong the service and people would probably feel quite bored hearing a language that they can't understand much. In this sense, the contextualization process will depend on a number of facts about a particular church, for example, age distribution, demographic, development of the youth ministry, and backgrounds of newcomers, and if the church leadership finds an opportunity to reach out to another language group (provided that there are people who can communicate with this group), this would probably be a good indication as to whether the church will be able to develop multicultural congregations in the long run.

In the following discussion, it is unique to argue from the perspective of Chinese churches in Australian society. As Chinese churches in Australia (an English-speaking country), the missiological sense of looking at what "contextualization" means will be quite different. We are not talking about how Australian churches (English-speaking) are to reach out to new immigrant groups by missiological approaches, but how Chinese churches will reach out to Chinese immigrants. Thus, when we talk about contextualization, it depends on which angle we are looking at the matter.

If we are looking from the perspective of Chinese churches in Australia serving Chinese immigrants and younger generations, then there are at least six to seven different categories of Chinese in Australia:

1. Chinese immigrants who came to Australia and settled in the early twentieth century, before the 1950s.

2. Fourth-generation Chinese immigrants whose great grandparents' mother tongue was probably Mandarin or Cantonese but they integrated fully into Australian society and possibly had mixed marriages.

3. Chinese immigrants who came to Australia and settled in the mid-twentieth century, between 1960 and the 1980s.

23. Howell, "Multiculturalism," 1.

4. Third-generation Chinese immigrants whose grandparents' mother tongue was probably Mandarin or Cantonese but they integrated fully into Australian society and may not understand any Chinese, and possibly have mixed marriages.

5. Chinese immigrants who came to Australia and settled in the late twentieth century and early twenty-first century, between 1990 and 2010.

6. Second-generation Chinese immigrants whose parents' mother tongue was probably Mandarin or Cantonese but they integrated pretty well into Australian society and may not understand any Chinese, and possibly have mixed marriages.

7. New Chinese immigrants who came to Australia and settled after 2010.

The question will be how the gospel message can be effectively shared and ministered to the whole spectrum of Chinese immigrants and not so much as to how the Chinese churches in Australia should integrate to mainstream society.

Should we try our best to fit into the mainstream culture or should we examine what we can do to evangelize Chinese immigrants from Asian countries, namely, China, Hong Kong, Macau, Taiwan, Malaysia, Singapore, and Vietnam, more effectively when compared to local Australian churches. In order to reach out to immigrants effectively, surely we need to use their languages and understand their cultures.

In a culturally pluralistic context such as Australia, it might seem logical to adapt globally successful missiological principles among the same peoples now living next door. So, the Chinese churches should look at the present trend of immigrants and the evolution of the Chinese population as a whole in Australia.

We need to examine the context of Chinese churches in Australia, that is, we are not seeing the Chinese community as an unreached group in terms of the gospel, but how we can continually be effective in evangelizing Chinese communities in Australia. Chinese churches need to work out the most effective way to reach out to the Chinese population (including second or third generations).

In the meantime, how Chinese churches should practically address the culture of the newest immigrant groups from China, Taiwan, and Hong Kong, without neglecting older Chinese immigrants and their second and third generation, will be the key for their effectiveness in witnessing to the Christian faith in this present age. As "one size doesn't fit all" for Chinese churches, they will need to measure how they can do ministries effectively in their own "contextualized" circumstances, that is, being sensitive, flexible, and understanding, so that they can respond well to the recent trends of Chinese immigration as well as the large population present in the country.

It is true that ultimately there should be some kind of paradigm shift from a single-language group to multicultural congregations, and in the later stage, the second, third and even fourth generation of Chinese immigrants will somehow merge with the mainstream culture, and we may see more and more international churches established. Having said that, we will only see such a paradigm shift after more than fifty years after the establishment of an ethnic church, as evident in North America and in Australia.

It would depend on how long a particular Chinese church has been established and what the density of the Chinese population is in the vicinity. So, using a "dynamic contextualization" concept would be appropriate for any Chinese church to apply in their own circumstances. For example, from time to time a Chinese church may consider how they can serve the Chinese community in context with a lens of understanding the migration trend in their area, as well as the demographic within the church. There will be no fixed formula for an ethnic church as to how the church should be developed over time.

Without a doubt, if we look at opportunities to share the gospel with these new Chinese immigrants and the Chinese community in Australia, using Cantonese and Mandarin would still be the most effective way to convey the gospel message. And for the second and third generation of Chinese immigrants, setting up an English ministry is a must for an effective multigenerational ethnic Chinese church.

Today, Australia is a multicultural society with immigrants from all over the world. Overseas Chinese churches (Chinese churches outside China, Taiwan, and Hong Kong), including Australia, have their own unique characteristics but we also need to seek ways to gradually integrate into mainstream society, so that Chinese immigrants from overseas, second- and third-generation Australian Chinese, and Australians of different races can also be cared for and reached and their cultural differences addressed, so that the ultimate objective of making the gospel known to different groups of people can be achieved. As such, Chinese churches in

Australia should have the mandate to "contextualize" themselves and be transformed gradually into either multi-congregational churches or multi-cultural churches! And it would not be surprising to see emerging Chinese churches with three or four homogenous unit churches under one roof.

Precautions in Relation to the Contextualization Process in Chinese Churches

Because of the special characteristics of overseas Chinese churches, the role of pastors is particularly important. Pastors who serve in different languages under one roof must have good communication with each other, respecting different cultures, and being sensitive to similarities and differences in different language congregations so as to serve together with humility.

Church pastors and leadership can deliberately create opportunities for different congregations to have joint meetings or ministries, so as to create oneness among themselves, for example, festival worship, joint retreat camps, church anniversary celebrations, church sports days, and short-term missionary work. These are great opportunities to bring the whole church together for one purpose, or for one ministry. In addition, through music, such as praise and worship events and thanksgiving gatherings, congregations of different languages can be encouraged to participate together. In this way, the sense of belonging and unity in the church can be seen, and the name of God will be glorified.

The leadership of the church (e.g., pastors, elders, and deacons) must also be aware of the similarities and differences between different language congregations, so they do not impose on a congregation some of the practices of other language congregations. From the Bible, we can derive and appreciate the concept of "unity in diversity, diversity in unity." As a multicultural or multi-congregational church, we have to mandate ourselves to embrace unity in diversity and allow differences in unity.

Due to cultural differences, it is quite common to have conflicts, disagreements, or misunderstandings with each other's practices and so on. Therefore, for overseas Chinese churches, it is necessary to give sufficient room and autonomy to congregations of different languages (Cantonese, Mandarin, and English), allowing them to develop their own characteristics and use different strategies to reach out to different groups of people. Yes, we need to make sure that everyone has the same understanding and confession in terms of our beliefs, yet there is no need to deliberately create conformity or uniformity among congregations in other aspects.

Conclusion

To sum up, Australia is a country of immigrants, and there is still a steady influx of new immigrants coming from overseas every year. How can the gospel most effectively reach these groups of new immigrants? We must use the languages they are familiar with and be sensitive to the cultures they come from. At the same time, we would welcome the second and third generation, and even the fourth generation of Chinese immigrants to integrate into mainstream society, and there is no need for any Chinese church to maintain a uniform "Chinese" traditional style of doing ministries. In short, Chinese churches will need to adapt the environment and be sensitive to the development of different congregations with different backgrounds. Ultimately the mandate of Chinese churches in Australia is to develop their own characteristics to effectively bring the gospel to the wide spectrum of backgrounds of Chinese communities and beyond.

Bibliography

Australian Bureau of Statistics. "Australia's Population by Country of Birth." https://www.abs.gov.au/statistics/people/population/australias-population-country-birth/latest-release.
———. "Population." www.abs.gov.au/statistics/people/population/.
———. "Snapshot of Australia. https://www.abs.gov.au/statistics/people/people-and-communities/snapshot-australia/latest-release.
———. "Statistics." www.abs.gov.au/statistics/people/population/.
Chinese Presbyterian Church. "Welcome to the Chinese Presbyterian Church." https://www.cpc.org.au/.
A Comprehensive Chinese Australian History (Vol. 2). New Century Publications Fund Inc. (September 2021).
Engle, Richard W. "Contextualization in Missions: A Biblical and Theological Appraisal." Grace Theological Journal 4, no. 1 (1983), 85–107.
Howell, Brian M. "Multiculturalism, Immigration and the North American Churches—Rethinking Contextualization." Missiology: An International Review, Vol. XXXIX, no. 1 (January 2011). http://mis.sagepub.com/.
賈嘉文 (Jia, Jiawen). 《趙紫宸1917至1937年之著作和 聖詩中的本色化神學思想》. 道學碩士論文.台灣神學院神學研究所，2021.
McGavran, Donald. "The Homogeneous Unit in Mission Theory." First Fruits, Asbury Theological Seminary 11th Biennial Meeting 1972.

Plake, John Farquhar. "Contextualization and Methodology: The Praxis of Gospel Communication." Paper presented to the Hiebert Track at the *North Central Regional Conference of the Evangelical Missiological Society* (April 2015).

Sequeira, Aubrey. "Re-Thinking Homogeneity: The Biblical Case for Multi-Ethnic Churches." *9Marks Journal* (Summer/Fall, 2015). https://www.9marks.org/article/re-thinking-homogeneity-the-biblical-case-for-multi-ethnic-churches/.

Sheffield, Dan. "Making the Transition to a Multicultural Church." *Multicultural Church Leaders Dialogue, St. Louis* (2008).

Wu, Jackson. "The Gospel With Chinese Characteristics: A Concrete Example of Cultural Contextualization." *Global Missiology* 1, no. 11 (October 2013). www.GlobalMissiology.org.

3.

Towards a Contextual Theology for Chinese Australian Conservative Evangelicals

GRACE LUNG

Abstract

WHILE CHINESE AUSTRALIAN CHRISTIANS have come of age, their theology is overwhelmingly Anglocentric, hampering their ability to minister in a nuanced and appropriately contextual way within their community and also to non-Christian Chinese Australians. To continue this path will see Chinese Australians follow the slowing and decline of Western Christianity, instead of the evangelistic fervor of the Global South.

Drawing on theoretical analyses, this paper firstly explores the current situation of contextualization in Chinese Australians and demonstrates two reasons for under-contextualization: spiritual formation in Western contexts, and elevation of Anglocentric Christianity as normative. A brief literature review shows a small body of work which has attempted to address the issue. Second, a potential way forward for contextualization is proposed through outlining three developments in the Asian American space: (1) Daniel D. Lee's Asian American Quadrilateral, (2) Sang Hyun Lee's Theology of Liminality, and (3) Neo-Calvinist Theology as proposed by Andrew Ong.

The development of a Chinese Australian contextual theology is urgently needed, as the opportunities for edification and evangelism amongst and outside this community only increase. As Asian American theology demonstrates, in a contextualized theology, salient themes of identity, and intergenerational and intercultural relations are addressed, impacting migrant, multicultural, or independent Asian Australian churches.

Introduction

Chinese Australians self-identify as being in-between cultures, neither fully Chinese nor fully Australian. Because of this, they have carved out a distinct culture and consider themselves, and are regarded as, their own people group. They gather for community, whether it be online with Subtle Asian Traits, physically at the bubble tea shop, or spiritually, in their own ministries and their own churches. But how well has theology and the gospel been contextualized within the Chinese Australian context? And what opportunities are lost while this contextualization is lacking? While Chinese Australian Christians have come of age, their theology is overwhelmingly Anglocentric, hampering their ability to minister in a nuanced and appropriately contextual way within their community and also to non-Christian Chinese Australians. Ultimately, this Anglocentrism can imply a gospel of whiteness, that the acceptable way to be Christian is not to be Chinese Australian. However, this obstacle does not need to remain, and there are promising developments in Asian American theology that can inform and guide the Chinese Australian context if Chinese Australians are willing to engage with it.

The first half of this paper will explore the current situation of contextualization for Chinese Australians, by considering their sociohistorical background and a literature review. It is clear there is a deep lack of contextualization among Chinese Australian Christians and indeed an impetus against contextualizing the gospel for this community. The second half of the paper supplies a proposed direction for contextualization for Chinese in Australia by outlining three developments in the Asian American space as a potential way forward for Chinese Australian contextual theology.

For this paper, *Chinese Australians* are defined primarily as those who are second generation, that is, children of the first generation/migrants to Australia. This is a broad category that includes people with ancestries in Hong Kong, Taiwan, Malaysia, and mainland China.[1] They are in-between both their ancestral context and their host context. Chinese Australians may also refer to the first generation, insofar as they resonate with the inbetweenness experience, which may be determined by their degree of integration and the duration of settlement in Australia.

Chinese Australian Christians are mostly *conservative* and *evangelical*. Recounting the migration history of Chinese Christians, historian Tim Tseng argues that the volatile political situation in China was more conducive to a "generic evangelical identity . . . that allowed Chinese Christians in the Diaspora to bond . . ."[2] Hence, not only is the first generation largely conservative and evangelical,[3] they and their offspring, the second generation, continue this theological tradition, particularly in its Scottish Reformed stream as they settle into conservative and evangelical Anglo-Australian Christian spaces.

While in a missiological context there is a recognition by evangelicals that a subjectivist epistemology and postcolonial criticism ought to be adopted, recognizing the hegemony of Western Christianity in global theological discourse thus far.[4] There needs to be further recognition that contextualization is not just a task for the Global South, and unreached people groups in mission contexts. Established diasporic Christian communities also require self-theologizing, including the Chinese Australian church. Venn's three-selves for churches are well known: "self-governing, self-supporting, self-propagating." But Hiebert identified a fourth self that is required as an indicator of growth and health in the indigenous church: "*self-theologizing*,"[5] that is, the development of *contextual theology*. Hiebert grounds his theory of critical contextualization in a critical realist epistemology and within the field of missiology,[6] a field that recognizes the distinct needs of distinct cultural groups. As a distinct group, Chinese Australian Christians are as much in need of this task of developing a contextual theology as people groups in the Global South. This need not be a task that

---

1. While Hong Kong is part of mainland China, I have made a distinction here based on the differing cultural context of people with ancestries in these regions.

2. Ong, "Chinese American," 51.

3. Though there is also a sizeable Renewalist group amongst Chinese Australians, this paper will seek to propose a theological direction that serves the Evangelical and Conservative theological position. See Lam et al., "Chinese Church Attenders."

4. Green, "Challenge."

5. Cathcart and Nichols, "Self Theology," 211.

6. Cathcart and Nichols, "Self Theology," 211–12.

is outside a conservative and evangelical orientation but can be undertaken with a high view of Scripture and aligned with Reformed theology. It is only through this process that Chinese Australians can clearly critique and embrace aspects of both Asian and Anglocentric theologies, contributing and shaping evangelicalism for the future, just as Anglocentric Christianity has shaped global Christianity already.

The State of Chinese Australian Christianity

Chinese Australian Christians are largely Anglocentric in theology and, hence, Chinese Australian theology is in its infancy. Underdeveloped localized theologies can also be observed in the wider Asian diaspora. Yung laments this "banana Christianity" within Asian contexts: "'yellow' outside, but 'white' inside."[7] At the same time, leaders have acknowledged Anglo Christianity in Australia does not address specific issues faced by the Chinese churches, so some steps have been taken to address this.

Reasons for Under-Contextualization

There are two key reasons for under-contextualization in the Chinese Australian context.

1. Spiritual Formation in Western Contexts

Because second-generation Chinese Australian Christians self-identify as being between identities, many feel disengaged from their migrant church but do not want to give up the faith. Campus ministries often become a significant site where many second-generation Chinese Christians gather, for education and for spiritual growth. They can function as refuges from collectivist and hierarchical first-generation familial and church communities, where the second generation experience generational and cultural disconnection. Here, they are welcomed into an Anglocentric space where they can grow in their faith with others in the Chinese Australian community. The Anglo-Australian pathway continues onto ministry apprenticeships and theological training, usually disconnected from their migrant church,

---

7. Yung, *Mangoes*, 190–91.

and can function as a reprieve from "unintentional marginalisation"[8] and wounds endured as leaders ministering in the Chinese migrant church.

However, these spaces have failed to adequately equip Chinese Australians in their migrant church context. There are three factors. First, reflecting on the Australian University of Theology, Philip Scheepers writes that those curricula are "fairly narrowly focussed on equipping students to minister in a broadly Western context," and second, "cross-cultural training tends to be relegated to units specifically aimed at those preparing for overseas missionary service."[9] That is, contextual understanding is aimed at the Other's culture, not for the self. Hence those ministering in local Chinese churches tend to miss out on cross-cultural reflection unless they intentionally seek it outside of core unit offerings. Additionally, Anglo-Australians themselves leave their own context—histories, and Western culture (i.e., whiteness)—unexamined.

A third factor is evangelicalism's emphasis on an individual's spiritual identity in Christ. This emphasis is attractive for second-generation Chinese Australians experiencing a confusion of ethnic identity.[10] But, this is often adopted to the exclusion of collective identities. Not only does this stunt ethnic formation, faith and ethnic identity remain unintegrated. This manifests in two ways. First, Chinese Australian Christians value community of their own but struggle to articulate why their Asian heritage is relevant to faith other than a hindrance. Specifically, this refers to how the gospel "fixes" Chinese problems, for example, the rejection experienced from family for failing to meet high standards in faith and life.

The second way is that Chinese Australians struggle to biblically justify why they gather in so-called "segregated" and ethnocentric churches.[11] This accusation is not uncommon[12], arising from Anglo-Australian leaders who fail to see the national (e.g., Mainland Chinese, Malaysian, Hong Kong, Australian), linguistic (e.g., Mandarin, Cantonese, Vietnamese, English), and cultural diversity within migrant churches, subconsciously adopting only a racial lens. All the while, they fail to see the Anglocentric nature of

---

8. Chan and Chan, "Mission," 104–7.

9. Scheepers, "Theological Education," 221.

10. Alumkal, *Asian American*, 84.

11. This common accusation and appropriate response is articulated by Rev. Ken Fong, see DeYoung et al., "Separate but Equal," 113–27.

12. Eng, "Your Church." This author has also been challenged with this accusation on some occasions.

their own multicultural endeavors, or the normativity and proliferation of Anglo-majority, English-only churches. For those whose identity is solely "in Christ," like the Anglo-Australian community, Chinese Australians lack the language to articulate their racial and ethnocultural context. Hence, Chinese Australians function as honorary Anglo-Australian Christians in the local context.

2. Elevation of Anglocentric Christianity as Normative

Another reason for under-contextualization is the elevation of Anglocentric theology at the expense of Chinese culture. Conservative evangelicalism can be overly cautious about contextualization that results in "relativism and shifting pluralism" even for those with ". . . a high view of scripture."[13] Yet Anglo theology itself is derived through Enlightenment and Cartesian thought,[14] tending to be individualistic, and is "shaped by empiricist, linear-thinking white Western males."[15] Also, N. T. Wright describes an obsession with individualistic emphases on one's relationship with God and dualistic attitudes that neglect the physical body and material world in favor of knowledge such as the mechanics of personal salvation which occupies systematic theology texts.[16] Further, the modernist epistemology that Anglocentric evangelicalism often adopts means that theology tends to be taught as universal and normative without examination of its social location and captivity to an ancient Greek and Enlightenment worldview. This assumes an objective, rational, and pure theology "out there" which Anglo Christianity has formulated, and so contextualization is treated as merely the translation of this objective knowledge for different people groups, which can function as infallible as Scripture itself.[17] The implication is then, that anything that looks different can be viewed with suspicion, that is, the Chinese church could be seen as, unbiblical, liberal, or inherently captive to a Confucian worldview, as opposed to the "correct" Western Enlightenment worldview.

Soong Chan Rah writes in *The Next Evangelicalism*, "Because of the imbalance of power, the receptor culture is oftentimes unable to discern

13. Green, "Challenge," 52–53.
14. Chan, *Grassroots*, 10.
15. Shaw and Dharamraj, *Challenging Tradition*, 143.
16. Wright, *Surprised by Hope*, 209–13.
17. Ong, "Chinese American," 140.

or distinguish between the gospel message and the Western, white cultural captivity of the church."[18] Consequently, there can be a superior and uncritical view of the Anglo-Christian world, and an inferior and cynical perspective on the local Chinese church. This phenomenon is internalized oppression,[19] and has brought disastrous outcomes within the Chinese migrant church. Adding to the cultural marginalization they already feel, numerous second-generation Chinese Australian Christians follow the "Silent Exodus."[20] Graduands are ill-equipped to engage with the Chinese church, preferring their Anglocentric contexts which do not provide adequate tools for local cultural reflection and praxis. As "honorary" Anglo-Christians, there is little interest in the task of theologizing for the Chinese Australian context.

Nonetheless, there is nothing inherently wrong with learning the theology of another culture, for all cultures are created inherently valuable in God's sight. However, when Anglo theology is elevated as universal and normative it is at the expense of other theologies, which must be inherently viewed as wrong. There can only be an examination from curiosity, not openness. Hiebert also reminds us that theology is not infallible but a human understanding of Scripture, and that ultimately all theologies need to be measured against the Bible, not a human interpretation of the Bible. This requires a global hermeneutic[21] as guided by the Holy Spirit. This does not mean Anglo theology should be discarded. However, there ought to be a recognition of the historic developments arising out of a Western social location, permeating its systematic theologies, its hermeneutical tools, and what doctrines are considered core and which are not.

In summary, while there is an identifiable Chinese Australian Christian culture, there is not a robust, contextualized Chinese Australian Christian theology because the spiritual formation of most second-generation Chinese Australian Christians involves adopting the spaces and practices of Anglocentric Christianity, becoming honorary Anglo-Christians, and in these spaces, Anglocentric theology is elevated to a superior position, discouraging the development of a contextualized non-Western theology for the Chinese Australian church.

---

18. Rah, *Next Evangelicalism*, 129.
19. Lung, "Internalized Oppression," 415.
20. Lee, "Silent Exodus."
21. Cathcart and Nichols, "Self Theology," 212.

Chinese Australian Literature

While second-generation Chinese Australians generally emulate Anglo-Australian theologies and praxis, there has been some acknowledgment that these have been insufficient for the Chinese church context. Whilst Chinese Australian leaders and pastors' networks and events have focused on providing community, training, and raising up the next generation,[22] only small steps have been taken to develop Chinese Australian contextual issues through scholarship.

Historically, there is evidence that during the 1990s, Chinese Australian leaders accessed resources[23] addressing the differences from what was termed ABCs (American Born Chinese) from OBCs (Overseas Born Chinese), most likely through newsletters from *The Fellowship of American Chinese Evangelicals* (FACE) written between 1979 and 2003.[24] In this period, Asian Americans continued to produce works addressing the two key themes of second-generation identity and intergenerational relations.[25] A noteworthy mention is Helen Lee's *Christianity Today* article coining the phrase, "Silent Exodus" to describe the large scale departure of second-generation Asian Americans from migrant churches. Notable books include *Growing Healthy Asian American Churches* produced by Catalyst Leadership Centre, IVP's *Following Jesus without Dishonoring Your Parents*, D. J. Chuang and L2 Foundation's *Asian American Youth Ministry*, and *Honoring the Generations*, which was compiled from a conference held at Trinity Evangelical Divinity School. Sadly, Asian Australian practitioners have barely accessed, much less interacted with this work. The exception is those in academic contexts.

In Australia, former minister, and PhD candidate Andrew Hong, ran a popular blog,[26] writing short articles on such topics, especially from a

---

22. Second-generation Chinese Australian networking and events have come from organizations such as RICE Movement, Sydney Chinese Christian Churches Association (https://www.sccca.org.au/), ACROSS Youth Training Hub (https://www.acrosshub.org/), and TGC Australia Asian Network (thegospelcoalition.org.au/Asia). A notable mention must go to Rev. Ying Yee, a pioneer and recognized thought leader in this space; see also yingyee.wordpress.com that was active between 2015–18.

23. See *Moving Forward*, 43–44.

24. The collated newsletters from this period appear in Eng et al., *Completing the Face*.

25. Busto, "Gospel," 64–65.

26. Andrewhong.net is now closed.

Confucian perspective. Dissertations at this time also focused on these two themes: Scott Litchfield (1995) and Mei Chung (2006), both on identity issues, and Michael Chu (2017) on the opportunities of cultural intelligence models for first- and second-generation relationships in the church. Regarding published works, Samuel and Kim Chan produced book and journal articles on first- and second-generation relations (2015)[27] and second-generation identity (2016)[28] respectively, while both Chung and Chu's dissertations were published in 2012[29] and 2019 respectively. Most of the works in this period tend to use missiological frameworks of the second generation as third culture, or cross-cultural models to bridge the first and second generation or frame identity crises.

But recently, Asian America has entered a new age, and this has been reflected within evangelical spaces.[30] Even though Asian American theologies are very developed with a long history in America,[31] the activity came from "liberal" and mainline Christians.[32] But recently, a wave of work has been produced in the evangelical space, centered around Intervarsity Press[33] and two seminaries—Fuller Theological Seminary and Talbot School of Theology—both of whom have faculty catering for Asian American concentrations and Doctor of Ministry programs. Their theological reflection arises from a subjectivist and postcolonial paradigm as well as out of the Dutch Reformers' emphasis on "cultural engagement, and the lordship of Jesus over all aspects of life" rather than the Scottish Reformed stream's emphasis on doctrines of salvation,[34] which Anglo-Australian conservative evangelicals have adopted. In the US, this has resulted in a large and growing body of work at all levels, academic, websites, podcasts, and conferences catered specifically to Asian Americans covering theology-proper, race, social justice, preaching, youth, psychology, and more,

27. Chan and Chan, "Mission."
28. Chan and Chan. "Finding an Identity."
29. Chung, "Missional Church."
30. Chow, "Asian American."
31. Asian Americans joined Blacks in the Civil Rights movement, establishing Asian American studies as a discipline, later spreading to other universities. See Umemoto, "On Strike," 54–55.
32. Busto, "Gospel," 69–71.
33. See their commitment to, and list of Asian American authors: IVP, "Meet Our Authors."
34. Holcomb, "Two Major Streams."

significantly deepening the discipline. This increase of activity has not yet been matched in Australia.

Facilitated by the increased online interconnectivity, popular-level Chinese Australian engagement with these developments in the US has grown. Chinese Australians Heidi Tai[35] and Grace Lung[36] have gained some traction, writing in both evangelical Asian Australian and Asian American online spaces with pieces relating to their personal stories, ethnicity, gender, and church contexts. In terms of scholarship, Cyrus Kung writes about spiritual formation in displaced and postcolonial contexts (2021).[37] Also, Graham Joseph Hill published research on the topic of Asian Australian women's experiences in ministry and mission (2022).[38] Works here deal with subjectivist themes such as decolonisation, racism, and sexism.

Despite this, the Chinese Australian context remains under-contextualized, due to Chinese Australians' spiritual formation in Western contexts, as well as the elevation of Anglocentric Christianity as normative and superior over local theologies. The small amount of contextualization work centered around second-generation identity issues, and first- and second-generation relations has generally been unused or unpublished. Consequently, Chinese Australian leaders and pastors' networks are not primarily informed by contextualized scholarship. Also, the large body of work from Asian Americans is relatively untapped. The result of this is that as a people group, Chinese Australian Christians have yet to develop to adulthood since their own needs, questions, and pains have not yet undergone "faith seeking understanding" self-theologizing. They are informed, rather, by the priorities and concerns of Anglocentric Christianity. Hence, there is a great opportunity to significantly enhance ministry and missions to Chinese Australians, through contextual theology. This paper will begin this task by exploring Asian American scholarship to determine its suitability for the Chinese Australian context.

---

35. See Tai, "Heidi Tai."
36. See Lung, "Welcome."
37. Kung, "Why Do I?"
38. Hill, *Sunburnt Country*.

Towards a Contextual Theology for the Australian Context

As previously mentioned, lessons from more developed Asian American theology may provide a way forward in contextualizing theology to the Chinese Australian context. The history of contextual theology amongst Asian Americans has come primarily with its mainline and progressive streams, but even for the more conservative and Reformed Chinese-Australian context, there are three perspectives from the recent wave worth considering. These are Daniel D. Lee's Asian American Quadrilateral, Sang Hyun Lee's theology of liminality, and Andrew Ong's neo-Calvinist approach. These developments can be utilized by the conservative and Reformed community with a high view of Scripture.

Asian American Quadrilateral

Firstly, the Asian American Quadrilateral (AAQ) is a promising hermeneutical tool for Chinese Australians to make sense of their context. The AAQ helps individuals and groups analyze their ethnoracial and spiritual identities. It was developed by Korean American, Daniel Lee, who teaches the material as a core subject of Fuller Theological Seminary's Asian American program. Lee particularly wanted to challenge essentialist and stereotypical Eastern and Western categorizations that cast Asians "as the other, and not part of our hybridic West."[39]

His tool is simple enough to adopt as a methodology but also retains a flexibility and depth. The AAQ can be used for analyzing collective ethnospecific (e.g., Chinese, Korean, Indian) and individual reflection. Each of the four AAQ categories ("Asian Heritage and Cultural Archetypes," "Migration and Loss," "Western Culture and Representation,"[40] and "Racialization"[41]) will be outlined, with a brief analysis made for the Chinese Australian context.

---

39. Lee, "Cultural Archetypes," 39–40.

40. Lee's original, "American Culture and Representation" has been modified here to "Western Culture and Representation" in recognition of the influences of Australian, American, and British contributions in the Chinese Australian context.

41. Lee's original, "Racialization and Navigating the Binary" has been modified here to only address "Racialization." The Black/White binary he refers to is a less common phenomenon in Australia and out of scope for this paper.

Asian Heritage and Cultural Archetypes

This category is most similar to what has been addressed within Chinese Australian literature. It employs a cultural anthropological approach examining a culture's worldview, values, and practices. Chinese Australians engage with their Asian heritage through their family and migrant community, including church. Key learnings from this category are the influence of a Confucian worldview, honor/shame, Hofstede's cultural dimensions, and third culture paradigms. But to avoid stereotypes and static categories that have thus far been employed, Lee argues for the concept of cultural archetypes, analyzing each archetype as theologically neutral,[42] then discerning how it functions, in good or sinful ways.[43] For example, he draws on the archetype of filial piety as good—in alignment with the fifth commandment, while still corrupted when applied oppressively from parents to children.[44] An understanding of Asian heritage through cultural archetypes can illuminate the relationship between the first and second generations. However, this lens alone is insufficient since the Chinese Australian experience needs to be examined through the categories below as well.

Migration and Loss

Migration studies explain why the second-generation experience cannot be generalized and solutions simply transferred across ethnicities. Though Chinese Australians may have shared Asian heritage—cultural revolution, Confucianism, and language—each wave of migration has experienced differing social conditions. This may be migration due to the gold rush, economic reasons, war and or political reasons. The gospel therefore must address each group differently. For example, middle to upper class skilled migrants from Hong Kong have different idols and needs compared with economic migrants from Hong Kong struggling with poverty. Chinese Cambodian migrants with little education and multigenerational war trauma cannot be lumped in with Chinese Malaysian international students even if they are both from South-East Asia. Chinese Pacific Islanders migrated during similar periods as earlier HK migrant waves but have different national histories and cultural practices. Migration in the AAQ

---

42. Lee, *Asian American Theology*, 93.
43. Lee, *Asian American Theology*, 95.
44. Lee, *Asian American Theology*, 94–96.

is an opportunity to clearly articulate why Chinese Australians who share a Confucian worldview and history can have distinct needs, multigenerational wounds,[45] and resources[46] that inform faith. Chinese Australian Christians who dominate the Asian Australian Christian space ought to use this category to listen carefully before attempting to generalize their experiences to other ethnic groups.

Western Culture and Representation

Examining this aspect requires examining the Western worldview that Chinese Australians are exposed to. Exposure to this worldview occurs in two ways: firstly, through transmission of the colonial and Christian legacies of ancestral countries and secondly, through participation in Australia's multicultural society.

First, the Western worldview (as described earlier under "Elevation of Anglocentric Christianity as Normative") is deeply embedded within the Chinese Australian context. Utilizing this aspect of the AAQ illuminates why there is a diversity of theological views amongst Chinese Australians. While conservative evangelicalism is common, there are differences in theology which arise from the differing spiritual traditions brought by British missionary engagement. In the Chinese Australian church, for example, Arminianism is prevalent amongst the large group of Chinese Malaysian Methodists, and female preachers are commonplace amongst Hong Kong churches through the legacy of Chinese Bible women in Southern China. This religious heritage clashes with the dominant Scottish Reformed and Calvinist streams adopted amongst the second generation whose spiritual formation is influenced by White American and Sydney Evangelical theology. This demonstrates that theological clashes within Chinese Australian Christians simply mirror the competing tribes of Anglo-Christianity.

Historically, Chinese were excluded as a part of "White Australia." Although multiculturalism has now been officially adopted, multiculturalism here is often expressed through tokenistic representation or multicultural attendance, and "contained artefacts of difference" such as Lunar New Year and Harmony Day, while maintaining Anglocentrism and white privilege. This extends to the Christian community, where similar paradigms of "happy hybridity" and contained expressions of multiculturalism are

---

45. Lee, *Asian American Theology*, 114–16.
46. Lee, *Asian American Theology*, 121–22.

performed,[47] while Anglocentric paradigms and theological concerns are centered and considered universal, superior, and worse, "more biblical." Internalized oppression explains why Chinese Australians themselves engage in self-orientalist representation[48] and/or subordinate themselves to this status quo as perpetual foreigners.[49]

Racialization

Examining the Chinese Australian context through this category elucidates the impact of race; at its most basic level, how one's appearance has impacted individuals and groups. Asian Australians struggle to articulate their ethnoracial identities, often labelling themselves in exclusively "cultural" terms or adopting color-blind language. This is likely because Anglo-Australian society and faith does the same while functionally denying that systemic racism exists. Racism is largely spoken of as overt acts, mostly occurring in the past.

But racism is ongoing. Recent reports by the Lowy Institute[50] and the Human Rights Commission[51] demonstrate this. Racism exists both overtly and especially, in systemic and/or vicarious experiences of racism through microaggressions, stereotypes, lack of visibility, and the bamboo ceiling. To accept racial categories means conceding to the existence of racism, which wider Australian society considers a threat to its pursuit of unity and "happy hybridity," and hence, is discouraged.[52]

As mentioned previously, this results in marginalization with internalized oppression and self-orientalism as coping mechanisms. This is clearly at odds with God's design and purposes. God's design is that all people are created in his image, not some more in that image than others. Rather than color-blindness, there are no generic Christians, but different people groups and languages are retained in the new creation. Chinese Australians can be affirmed in their embodied and ethnic selves and need not assimilate to Anglocentric Christianity or adopt a multicultural stance

---

47. I refer to practices in churches where ethnic (non-white) food and clothing are adopted on special occasions.
48. Liu, "White Gaze," 781–804.
49. Lung, "Internalized Oppression," 428.
50. Hsu and Kassam, "Being Chinese."
51. Soutphommasane, "Anti-Racism."
52. Lung, "Internalized Oppression," 420.

which is ultimately Anglocentric, while the realities of racial oppression still marginalize them in these spaces.

Lee theologizes out of a Barthian "double particularity" approach. Lest Barth be dismissed as outside Reformed and conservative evangelicalism, consider that prominent evangelicals and evangelical missiologists[53] have called for exegesis of both the Scripture and context. This includes Chinese Australians that are considered reached and established. All four categories are significant when it comes to exegeting context. Hence, the AAQ significantly expands the exegesis of the Chinese Australian context and is a sophisticated tool worthy of consideration for use in the formulation of a contextualized theology.

Theology of Liminality

The late Sang Hyun Lee was a Professor at Princeton Theological Seminary specializing in Asian American studies and Jonathan Edwards. His theology of liminality is a promising framework for Chinese Australians who are caught between two majority worldviews or contexts, both the Chinese and Western. His framework moves beyond simplistic framing of the two in missiological and cross-cultural terms.

The theology of marginality that has been developed previously by mainline theologians[54] recognizes that the two centers of identity are not merely culturally different but employ power, constantly applying pressure to conform so that Chinese Australians can receive love, belonging, social or monetary reward. Hence, non-conformity means relegation to the margins of both Chinese and Western contexts, a double marginality. To avoid this, Chinese Australians negotiate this tension using multiple strategies: (1) elevate Western worldview, suppress Chinese worldview, (2) elevate Chinese worldview, suppress Western worldview, (3) become proficient in bicultural code switching,[55] and (4) hide in ABC spaces but remain exclusive as a protective layer ("refuge model"). The strategy used can differ depending on context, whether it is food, education, or parenting style. These are all maladaptive coping mechanisms to marginality and produce unhealthy psychological and ethnospiritual developmental outcomes.[56]

---

53. See Hiebert, "Critical Contextualization," 109–10.
54. Phan and Lee, *Journeys*.
55. Lee, "God's Shalom," 57–58.
56. Lee, "God's Shalom," 59–61.

For many Chinese Australians who have experienced upward mobility, the concepts of marginalization and its associated image of victimhood does not resonate, nor would they want to see themselves in those terms. There are three reasons for this. The first is that there is shame in association with weakness. The second is a belief that racism is only active, overt, and individual.[57] And thirdly, they have yet to experience marginalization as emerging adults who grow closer to centers of power.[58] Marginalization is felt most acutely when marginalized peoples draw closer to centers of power, whether this is an interaction with Chinese elders and pastors, or the majority white senior leadership at the workplace. Often only the English pastor and some key English leaders feel the marginalization as they attempt to bridge and advocate for the second generation in the church. In the workplace, Chinese Australians are younger in comparison to Chinese Americans and so are only encountering the bamboo ceiling in more recent times.

Often a denial of marginalization is employed as a survival mechanism, for accepting the reality of racism may erect a barrier to success and acceptance. This position is also at odds with the Anglo-Australian majority and, hence, can be unexpressed for fear of rejection and failure in the majority culture.

However, Sang Hyun Lee offers a hopeful perspective on marginality:

> Marginality is dehumanizing and oppressive. And the space of marginality as the space into which a minority is marginalized is a space of dehumanization, and there is nothing good in it. The liminal space that results from marginalization, however, has the potential of being used as a creative space of resistance and solidarity.[59]

Rather than simply describing a sociocultural phenomenon, he argues for the Trinitarian and incarnational nature of liminality. The "entrance into a liminal space in Jesus Christ is rooted in a liminality within God's internal life and being."[60] Also, he argues, about Jesus:

> Jesus' life and ministry were not devoted to the fulfilment of some anthropologically conceived creation of liminality but, rather, to

---

57. Morsi, "Framing Racism."
58. Lee, *Asian American Theology*, 111.
59. Lee, *Liminal Place*, 5.
60. Lee, *Liminal Place*, 43.

the utilization of liminality's creativity for God's own purposes for created existence.⁶¹

This deepens the solution of being "in-between" or "third culture" beyond missiological approaches and offers an alternative to the primary posture of victimhood which mainline Christians tend to employ. Instead, it lays down a hopeful and convincing response through a theology of liminality: the creative space in the margins as God ordained and intrinsic to his being and purpose.

Accepting a marginal status is incredibly at odds with the Chinese migrant's core values of status, comfort, and worldly successes for their children. But it is marginal people (e.g., Israel, Moses, Joseph, Daniel, and women) whom God uses to initiate his purposes rather than people in the powerful center.

> So God chose to approach first the liminal and marginalized people of the world. It is not that God loves them any more than the people at the centers . . . Healing and freeing up a marginalized people's suppressed liminal creativity is the first step God takes in God's grand project . . .⁶²

Liminality is a promising category to help Chinese Australians, spiritually and socioculturally, make sense of and glorify God in their "in-betweenness." Liminality encourages Chinese Australians to view marginalized persons (including themselves) truthfully and yet does not end there, as mainline and/or progressive scholars tend to.⁶³ Chinese Australians are simultaneously marginalized and privileged. The concept of liminality is appealing and still accurately describes their lived experience while offering a challenge to consider how privileged people can deploy the creative opportunities and responsibilities they have as honorary whites.

Adopting this theology radically changes Chinese Australian's view of themselves. Rather than pursuing honorary Anglo status in the secular and Christian spaces, it challenges Chinese Australians to accept the truth and shame of marginalization and other marginalized peoples. Adopting a liminal stance allows for the transformation of margins to a spiritually ordained, prophetic, and creative space. Being on the margins of both

---

61. Lee, *Liminal Place*, 50.
62. Lee, *Liminal Place*, 36.
63. Derived from Black scholarship, mainline Asian American scholarship tends to emphasize the marginalized position. See Tan, "Asian American," 131.

contexts frees one to be able to embrace and critique both without being held captive by the centers' precarious monetary and/or social reward.

Neo-Calvinist Theology

Thirdly, Chinese American pastor and scholar, Andrew Ong, proposed in his dissertation that neo-Calvinism, as developed through Kuyper, Bavinck, Vos, and Van Til, is a promising direction for the development of Chinese Americans. He demonstrates three areas where neo-Calvinism is relevant: ethnic particularity, individualism, and dualism in creation.

Ethnic particularity is affirmed in neo-Calvinism, unlike conservative and Scottish Reformed streams of evangelicalism. Using Genesis 11, Ong argues that the Tower of Babel narrative is ultimately an affirmation of God's purposes and plans for diverse people groups from the Table of Nations (Gen 10), not just a curse.[64] Further, Revelation 21 brings this into its ultimate fulfillment where diverse peoples retain their distinctiveness and contribute in their own ways in the new creation.[65] From this, neo-Calvinism offers an antidote to the color-blindness, multicultural attendance, and/or Anglocentricity that can characterize Chinese Australian evangelicalism. It is also a convincing response to charges that Chinese Australian churches are homogenous and therefore exclusive by nature.[66] It lends credence to the contextualization of work for Chinese Australians.

Western evangelical *individualism* is critiqued within Neo-Calvinist thought, recognizing the "pervasive individualism" that shaped the "public life of Western nations," including its non-Anglo citizens. His analysis offers a balanced perspective of both individualism and collectivism. He says that this nuance:

> ... contains much promise to Chinese American Christians who often fall prey to an individualistic approach to mission, disharmonious multi-generational church dynamics, a "me and my Bible" theological methodology, and the problem of shame.[67]

Here, he is highlighting the holistic nature of mission, the "collective, social and structural solutions" that can be neglected in the pursuit of

---

64. Ong, "Chinese American," 253.
65. Ong, "Chinese American," 254.
66. Ong, "Chinese American," 259.
67. Ong, "Chinese American," 265.

individual conversions.⁶⁸ Not only that, he demonstrates Bavinck's theology of family that holds together the "collective unity of family [which] does not ignore individuality and diversity within" again, a corrective to the multigenerational church that can pursue conformity as family, but true family as diverse.⁶⁹ Also, in response to the "me and my Bible" theological methodology, he quotes Vanhoozer saying, "*sola scriptura* functions properly only in the context of the whole church," not just the Anglocentric version currently adopted and widespread within Chinese Australians and non-Anglos across the world. Lastly, he reflects on shame, demonstrating neo-Calvinists teaching on the union of Christ and its benefits of belonging into Christ's family, as an antidote to the antisocial and marginal experience of Chinese Australians as minorities in both Chinese migrant communities and/or majority Western society.⁷⁰

Like the rest of Western evangelicalism, Chinese Australians can be captive to Western *dualism* in relation to the sacred/secular and soul/body. Neo-Calvinism identifies inherent worth and value in creation, countering Chinese migrant attitudes which can elevate academic pursuit of knowledge and success at the expense of the body, both mental and physical. Further, it gives proper acknowledgment to non-word ministries, by challenging Chinese Australians to engage in the brokenness of humanity and address immediate mental and physical needs, traditionally seen as inferior.⁷¹

While Ong acknowledges that this approach holds a marginal position amongst Chinese in the diaspora, it is a very promising direction for the Chinese Australian context. First, he highlights its reception by various Reformed Chinese theologians, more specifically, Stephen Tong in Indonesia and Asia, as well as Samuel Ling and Jonathan Chao in Chinese American churches.⁷² Second, its Reformed heritage makes his arguments more palatable for Chinese Australian Reformed Evangelicals compared with other works in contextual theology so far. Having said this, it is relatively underdeveloped compared with the work of Korean American theologians, Daniel D. Lee and Sang Hyun Lee. Yet, it can act as a gateway for conservative and Reformed Chinese Australian evangelicals to consider its critiques

---

68. Ong, "Chinese American," 265.
69. Ong, "Chinese American," 266.
70. Ong, "Chinese American," 274.
71. Ong, "Chinese American," 277–78.
72. Ong, "Chinese American," 246–47.

of mainstream Western theology, and therefore, consider the task of a Chinese Australian contextual theology seriously.

Conclusion

Some have highlighted the potential of culturally hybrid persons to act as mediators who assist globalized society in bridging together the Global South and Global North[73] and to reach new migrants in Australia. Indeed, Chinese Australian Christians have the potential to lead the way, locally and globally. Not only are they the most established and resourced minority group in Australia, anecdotally, Australians are widely liked on the mission field for their cultural adaptability and non-colonial history.[74] But can Chinese Australians rise to this opportunity?

Ironically, Chinese diasporic Christians can only be effective bridges between the Global North and Global South by focusing on themselves, and their own theology. It is only by accepting their doubly marginalized vantage point that Chinese Australians can both embrace but soberly critique both. Yet, at their worst, undergirded by a modernist epistemology, Chinese Australians are captive to an Anglocentric Christianity, still being colonized in the mind and functionally convinced that when it comes to theology, "West is best, East is least."[75] At their best, Chinese Australian Christians have been open to missiological paradigms operating out of a critical realist epistemology which recognizes that contextualization is important so that the gospel can address culturally specific needs. But to take this further, a subjectivist epistemology is urgently required which accepts the power that majority and dominant cultures hold, and which has silenced or punished self-theologizing. This is a collective sin of omission which has resulted in generations of Banana Christians, and ought to be acknowledged. To continue this path will see Chinese Australians follow

---

73. See Weerakoon, "Intercultural Identity," 45–61. However, I caution against an idealistic approach that does not account for the tendency of the elevation of Anglocentric Christianity in diasporic hybrid Christians on the world stage.

74. Online communications with ministry worker Armen Gakavian, and current and former missionaries in the Sydney and Missionary Bible College alumni group, November 2022.

75. Tseng, "Foreword," iii.

the slowing and decline of Western Christianity, instead of the evangelistic fervor of the Global South.[76]

Currently, Chinese culture, particularly in the migrant church and family, has often been framed either as a problem to be fixed by Anglo theology, or as cultural products to be consumed (pop, dramas, food, and travel). While Anglocentric Christianity has certainly provided a much-needed refuge and corrective to dysfunctional and works-based orientations within Chinese migrant churches, Chinese Australian theology also has much to offer. A utilization of recent Asian American theological developments yields much potential in growing and strengthening Chinese Australian self-theologizing. Three perspectives have been examined: a theology of liminality, the AAQ as a contextual exegetical tool, and justification from neo-Calvinism for the task of contextual theology. Employing these perspectives does not discount *sola scriptura* but can be done with a high view of Scripture, indeed, each tool examines and dialogues with Scripture. This self-theologizing endeavor is not a descent into relativism but a move to encourage and hear the contributions of historically marginalized groups. When this theologizing is absent, it sends a message that Jesus is also absent, or worse, favors only Anglocentric forms of faith. It creates a Christianity where conversion and faithfulness must require a change of ethnic identity, which the New Testament writers speak fiercely against.

The development of a Chinese Australian contextual theology is urgently needed, as the opportunities for edification and evangelism amongst and outside of this community only increase. In a contextualized theology, salient themes of identity, and intergenerational and intercultural relations are addressed, whether they are part of the migrant, multicultural, or independent Asian Australian church. Once contextual theology is undertaken, the opportunity to bridge the Global North and South becomes a welcoming and exciting prospect. As opportunities grow for non-Anglo representation, Chinese Australians, with a sober view of both worlds can critique and embrace contributions from multiple contexts. Through the Holy Spirit, Chinese Australians can feel confident in the way God has gifted them to contribute and bless the national and global church.

---

76. Lung, "Internalized Oppression," 427.

Bibliography

Alumkal, Antony William. *Asian American Evangelical Churches: Race, Ethnicity, and Assimilation in the Second Generation.* New York: LFB Scholarly, 2003.

Busto, Rudy V. "The Gospel According to Rice: The Next Asian American Christianity." *Amerasia Journal* 40, no. 1 (2014) 57–79.

Cathcart, Rochelle, and Mike Nichols. "Self Theology, Global Theology, and Missional Theology in the Writings of Paul G. Hiebert." *Trinity Journal* 30, no. 2 (2009) 209.

Chan, Samuel, and Kim Chan. "Finding an Identity in a Multicultural World." *Australian Journal of Mission Studies* (June 2016) 32–41.

——— "A Mission of the Second Generation (Australian Born Chinese) in South Australian Migrant Churches: Dealing with Unintentional Marginalization Due to Confucian Values." In *We Are Pilgrims: Mission from, in and with the Margins of Our Diverse World,* edited by Darren Cronshaw and Rosemary Dewerse, 97–110. Dandenong, Victoria: UNOH, 2015.

Chan, Simon. *Grassroots Asian Theology: Thinking the Faith from the Ground Up.* Downers Grove, IL: IVP Academic, 2014.

Chinese Christian Church Milson's Point 50 Anniversary: Moving Forward. Rockstar Memoirs.com, 2015.

Chow, Alexander. "An Asian American in the Diaspora in an Age of Crazy Rich Asians." August 21, 2018. https://alexanderchow.wordpress.com/2018/08/21/asian-american-diaspora-in-an-age-of-cra/.

Chung, Mei. "A Missional Church in Relation to the Tri-Cultural Generation." *Australian Journal of Mission Studies* 6, no. 2 (2012) 2–8.

DeYoung, Curtiss Paul, et al. "Separate but Equal." In *United by Faith: The Multiracial Congregation as an Answer to the Problem of Race,* 113–27. New York: Oxford University Press, 2003.

Eng, Daniel K. "Your Church Is Not Biblical." https://aapastor.wordpress.com/2008/06/20/your-church-is-not-biblical-why-ethnic-specific-ministries-exist-in-america-part-2/.

Eng, William L., et al. *Completing the Face of the Chinese Church in America.* Oakland, CA: Fellowship of American Chinese Evangelicals (FACE), 2009.

Green, Gene L. "The Challenge of Global Hermeneutics." In *Global Theology in Evangelical Perspective: Exploring the Contextual Nature of Theology and Mission,* edited by Jeffrey P. Greenman and Gene L. Green, 50–64. Wheaton Theology Conference Series. Downers Grove, IL: InterVarsity, 2012.

Hiebert, Paul G. "Critical Contextualization." *International Bulletin of Missionary Research* 11, no. 3 (1987) 104–11.

Hill, Graham Joseph. *Sunburnt Country, Sweeping Pains: The Experiences of Asian Australian Women in Ministry and Mission.* Eugene, OR: Wipf and Stock, 2022.

Holcomb, Justin. "Two Major Streams of Reformed Theology." September 24, 2012. https://www.thegospelcoalition.org/article/two-major-streams-of-reformed-theology/.

Hsu, Jennifer, and Natasha Kassam. "2021 Being Chinese in Australia: Public Opinion in Chinese Communities." Lowy Institute, 2022.

IVP. "Meet Our Asian and Asian American Authors." https://www.ivpress.com/pages/meet-our-asian-and-asian-american-authors.

Kung, Cyrus. "Why Do I Remain a Christian?" *Australian Journal of Mission Studies* 15, no. 2 (2021) 43–47.

Lam, Hoi, and Miriam Pepper. "Chinese Church Attender—A Demographic Profile." NCLS Research Fact Sheet 17012. Sydney: NCLS Research, 2017.

Lee, Daniel. "Cultural Archetypes for a Theology of Culture in a Global Age." *Cultural Encounters* 12, no. 1 (2016) 37–53.

Lee, Daniel D. *Doing Asian American Theology: A Contextual Framework for Faith and Practice.* Kindle ed. Westmont, IL: IVP Academic, 2022.

———. "God's Shalom to All of Ourselves: Integrating the Asian American Double Self." *ChristianityNext* (Winter 2021) 53–77.

Lee, Helen. "Silent Exodus: Can the East Asian Church in America Reverse the Flight of Its Next Generation?" *Christianity Today* (August 1996). https://www.christianitytoday.com/ct/1996/august12/6t9o5o.html.

Lee, Sang Hyun. *From a Liminal Place: An Asian American Theology.* Minneapolis: Fortress, 2010.

Liu, Helena. "Beneath the White Gaze: Strategic Self-Orientalism among Chinese Australians." *Human Relations: The Tavistock Institute* 70, no. 7 (2017) 781–804.

Lung, Grace. "Internalized Oppression in Chinese Australian Christians and Its Mission Impact." *Mission Studies* 39 (2022) 415–40.

———. "Welcome! I'm Grace Lung." https://gracelung.com.

Morsi, Yassir. "Framing Racism: Why Sbs's #Fu2racism Doesn't Get Race Right." *ABC Religion and Ethics*, 2017. https://www.abc.net.au/religion/framing-racism-why-sbss-fu2racism-doesnt-get-race-right/10096010.

Ong, Andrew. "Toward a Chinese American Evangelical Theology: The Promise of Neo-Calvinism." Unpublished thesis, University of Edinburgh, 2019.

Phan, Peter C., and Jung Young Lee., eds. *Journeys at the Margin: Toward an Autobiographical Theology in American-Asian Perspective.* Collegeville, MN: Liturgical, 1999.

Rah, Soong Chan. *The Next Evangelicalism: Releasing the Church from Western Cultural Captivity.* Downers Grove, IL: IVP, 2009.

Scheepers, Philip. "Theological Education for Cross-Cultural Ministry." In *Theological Education: Foundations, Practices, and Future Directions*, edited by Andrew Bain and Ian Hussey, 215–27. Australian College of Theology Monograph Series. Eugene, Oregon: Wipf and Stock, 2018.

Shaw, Perry, and Havilah Dharamraj. *Challenging Tradition: Innovation in Advanced Theological Education.* Icete Series. Carlisle, Cumbria: Langham Global Library, 2018.

Soutphommasane, Tim. "Anti-Racism in 2018 and Beyond: A Report on the Activities of the National Anti-Racism Strategy (2015–18)." Australian Human Rights Commission, 2018.

Tai, Heidi. "Heidi Tai Writes." heiditai.com.

Tan, Sharon M. "Asian American Liberative Ethics." In *Ethics: A Liberative Approach*, 127–42. Minneapolis, MN: Augsburg Fortress, 2013.

Tseng, Timothy. "Foreword." In *Conversations: Asian American Evangelical Theologies in Formation*, edited by Timothy Tseng and D. J. Chuang, i–iv. Washington, DC: L2 Foundation, 2006.

Umemoto, Karen. "'On Strike!' San Francisco State College Strike, 1968–1969: The Role of Asian American Students." In *Contemporary Asian America (Third Edition): A Multidisciplinary Reader*, edited by Min Zhou and Anthony Christian Ocampo, 25–59. New York: NYU, 2016.

Weerakoon, Kamal. "Evangelical Intercultural Identity: A New Resource for Twenty-First Century Mission?" *Colloquium* 47, no. 1 (2015) 45–61.

Wright, N. T. *Surprised by Hope: Rethinking Heaven, the Resurrection, and the Mission of the Church*. New York: HarperCollins, 2009.

Yung, Hwa. *Mangoes or Bananas?: The Quest for an Authentic Asian Christian Theology*. Regnum Studies in Mission. 2nd ed. Minneapolis, Minnesota: Fortress, 2014.

4.

Necromancy: 1 Samuel 28 and Australian Chinese Christians

GRACE KWAN SIK TSOI

Abstract

THE INTERPRETATION OF 1 Sam 28 has been a topic of interest for biblical scholars since the early church, with the focus of the debate anchored on whether the ghost of Samuel actually came to speak to Saul. In the past the controversy was mainly investigated from a theological perspective, and seldom was the sociological understanding of necromancy considered. This article begins with the perspective of Australian Chinese Christians and their understanding of necromancy in the Chinese culture. Combined with the use of historical studies on ancient Hebrew culture, it demonstrates a potential reading within a context that is familiar with communicating with the dead. Through narrative studies on the characters and rhetoric of the discourse, it contends for the authenticity of Samuel and the implicit criticism on necromancy in the text and provides a fresh interpretation for Chinese churches in Australia.

While Asian contextual hermeneutics have flourished in North America in the past decades,[1] similar dialogue is still pending in the Australian biblical studies landscape. One would imagine, with the geographical

---

1. E.g., Liew, "Bible"; *Biblical Hermeneutics*.

proximity to Asia, and the ethnic diversity in churches here in Australia,[2] Australian Chinese Christians are equally,[3] if not more, situated at the intersection of Western and Eastern cultures.[4] The amalgamation of cultures and languages render this community unique characteristics among Australian churches,[5] and considerations on this particular reading context is therefore significant to the interpretation of the Bible in this community.

Following the lead of Athalya Brenner-Idan,[6] I have proposed in *Who Is to Blame for Judges 19* that a contextual interpretation that is meaningful to Chinese Christians is a "back-and-forth" exercise that involves both the reading context and the ancient biblical context.[7] "Beginning with a reading that is sensitive to the Chinese context, it unveils the potential meaning of the text for readers within our culture. It is then necessary to examine how this "Chinese" reading relates to the ancient contexts of the biblical text. Using tools of biblical criticism, one may be able to recover the

---

2. According to 2021 Census data provided by the Australian Bureau of Statistics (www.abs.gov.au), among those who reported their religion as Christian, 5.11 percent had at least one ancestor from Southeast Asia, 3.82 percent from Northeast Asia, and 2.34 percent from South or Central Asia. In terms of languages used at home, 3.56 percent of the population speak Southeast Asian languages at home, 2.24 percent Northeast Asian languages, 1.02 percent South Asian languages, and 1.94 percent Northwest or Central Asian languages.

3. Here I refer to Christians in Australia with a Chinese cultural heritage, which may include migrants from China, Taiwan, Hong Kong, or other Southeast Asian countries such as Singapore and Malaysia. They are by no means a homogenous group, yet as this paper will demonstrate, certain commonalities exist in ideologies relating to cultural issues.

4. As Roland Boer indicated, Australian biblical studies is "caught in-between" Asia (the Pacific) and the West. Boer, "Caught in Between," 232.

5. Australian Chinese Christian churches often have multilingual congregations under one roof, including Cantonese, Mandarin, and English. The focus of this paper will be on those who read the Chinese Bible, i.e., Cantonese and Mandarin congregations. There are, of course, Christians of Chinese heritage attending multicultural English-speaking churches, who may find resonances in some aspects of the discussion.

6. Brenner-Idan contends that a valuable exercise of biblical scholarship in contextual interpretations should go beyond the concern of how a community would read a text. Instead, with the tools of trades of biblical criticism, one should illuminate back and forth between the text and the context. This would in turn bring contributions to other communities. Brenner-Idan, "Where Are We?"

7. The translation context is also a key component of my reading strategy in *Who Is to Blame for Judges 19*, but due to the limitation of the scope of this paper this will not be considered here. See Tsoi, *Who Is to Blame*.

rhetorical message of the text for its ancient readers."[8] This in turn may contribute to the reading of communities beyond the Chinese context.

The encounter of Saul with the necromancer in Endor in 1 Samuel 28 is chosen here as a test case. This has been a controversial passage since the early church, with the center of the debate on the identity of the "being" raised by the woman. Some contend that it is truly the ghost of Samuel, while others consider it an evil spirit in disguise. For those who advocate the authenticity of Samuel, there remains disagreement in whether it was the God of Israel or the woman (and the presumed demonic power behind) who raise him from the dead.[9] In much of the discussions thus far, the attention of scholarship has been focusing on dogmatic and logical consideration, such as views of the afterlife and the power of the evil over the righteous.[10] Seldom is the social perception of the practice of necromancy in the ancient Near East considered, though it may play a significant role to the rhetoric of the narrative. In fact, as Frederick Cryer observes, there has previously been a general lack of interest to the issue of divination in Old Testament studies.[11] He attributes this phenomenon to modern Western scholarship, which considers divination that falls into the realm of magic primitive and superstitious, hence in opposition to religion.[12]

The reading interest of Chinese Christians is rather different in this regard. As the practice of communicating with the dead has continued to exist in China since ancient times, Chinese readers of the Bible would be well alert to the use of necromancy in 1 Samuel 28, and their interpretation of the narrative would inevitably find resonance in their own culture.[13] Combined with an investigation of the social implication of necromancy

---

8. Tsoi, *Who Is to Blame*, xvii.

9. For a comparison of the various early Rabbinic and Christian exegesis in each of these views, see Smelik, "Witch of Endor," 160–79.

10. For a detailed analysis of critical early Christian exegetes reflecting these considerations, see Greer and Mitchell, *Belly-Myther*, and Edwards, "Review," 723–24.

11. Cryer, *Divination*, 235–37.

12. Cryer, *Divination*, 237. This may explain why spiritualism and psychics that exist in Western cultures are rarely considered in relation to the interpretation of the account of Endor.

13. This is not to claim, of course, that the practice is unique in Chinese among all cultures. For example, consulting the dead or the medium is still commonly practiced in Africa today, see Ngundu, "Necromancy." Brison also describes the commonplace occurrence of divination in contemporary Israel as a context of interpreting 1 Sam 28. Brison, "Medium of En-Dor," 124–47.

in the ancient Hebrew context, this contextual interpretation may in turn contribute to the classic debate on the authenticity of Samuel.

I will begin with an overview of the history of communicating with the dead in Chinese culture, and my experience in reading the passage with Australian Chinese Christians. Interestingly, although necromancy is a familiar social practice, the vast majority are inclined to reject the possibility of the appearance of Samuel. I will then examine the ancient Hebrew context through historical and literary criticisms, which both point to a view that supports the authenticity of Samuel. This finding will then be brought into comparison to the Chinese reading, and a new interpretative direction will be proposed for Chinese readers.

Communicating with the Dead in Chinese Culture

The Chinese practice of communicating with (or literally, summoning) the soul is termed *zhaohun* (招魂),[14] and its history can be traced in classical literature dated from the Zhou Dynasty (1100–256 BC). It was part of a funeral ritual *fu* (復), where the soul that was believed to be wandering outside the corpse, was "summoned" to return to the body in the hope of resurrection.[15] The summoner would go through a series of maneuvres originated from witchcraft, sometimes with props such as the clothing of the person, which was considered as a means of controlling the soul.[16] As the ritual in reality did not successfully bring back the dead, gradually its

---

14. In the pre-Qin period, the Chinese concept of the spirit of a person consists of *hun* (魂) and *p*[set ayin before o]*'o* (魄). For the difference between the two, see 沈曉柔 (Shen), 〈黃泉歸來〉, 10–12. Yu, "O Soul, Come Back." The distinction gradually faded in history and *hun-p*[set ayin before o]*'o* became an expression referring to the spiritual being of a person as opposed to the physical body, and includes both the living and the dead, see 胡新生 (Hu), 《中國古代巫術》, 379–80. I use the English translation of *hun* as "soul" here for communication purposes, noting that there are complex nuances in the concept.

15. 胡新生 (Hu), 《中國古代巫術》, 380. For archaeological evidence of *fu*, see Yu, "O Soul, Come Back," 365–69.

16. 胡新生 (Hu), 《中國古代巫術》, 379. *Zhaohun* also includes calling upon the soul of the living as a means of healing sickness, which has a long history in China and continues in regional areas till today. See 王國旭、胡亮節 (Wang & Hu), 〈烏蒙山區的叫魂儀式管窺〉; 王杰文 (Wang), 〈一个巫婆的招魂唱詞及相關分析,〉 44. 陳瑤 (Chen), 〈魯東南農村民眾叫魂習俗淺析〉. As this category of *zhaohun* is not in the same realm as the incident of Endor, it will not be included in the discussion.

meaning was shifted towards an act of remembrance from the living and continued in various forms and expressions till today.[17]

The practice of *zhaohun* through witchcraft also existed in forms other than funeral rituals. Some were recorded in legendary stories as a means of reconnecting with a loved one or an ancestor,[18] and a particular incident resembling the biblical account of Endor was recorded in *bei qi shu*(北齊書): in the course of a war the emperor enquired of a diviner, who claimed to recall a famous dead warrior and lead the army in combat.[19] Some other practices extend to the category of divination and are termed *fuji* (扶箕/乩), where the purpose of consultation is to foretell the future or acquire supernatural knowledge. The target was not restricted to the dead, but also includes all kinds of gods and demons in folk religion.[20] The gods or the souls may come into the body of the medium and speak through him/her, or it may come to a subject such as a pen to convey messages.[21]

While the prevalence of *fuji* seemed to have temporarily declined in the Republican era due to modernization of the country and, in particular, the New Culture Movement that advocated science over superstition,[22] the practice continued to exist in various parts of China and even experienced a growth in the 1930s.[23] Written during WWII, the pioneering work by Xu-Dishan in academic studies of *fuji* attested that *guanwang* (關亡), a form of

---

17. The changes of *zhaohun* as a part of the funeral ritual from the pre-Qin period (before 221 BC) through to Qing (1644–1912 AD) is seen in 何先成 (He), 〈從長時段看中國傳統社會的招魂葬〉; 李梅田、李童 (Li & Li), 〈魂歸於墓〉. There are also numerous studies of contemporary funeral ceremonies in regional China that have retained a similar concept in their funeral rituals, see 徐海波 (Xu), 〈甘肅省會寧縣丁溝鄉南門村一次喪葬活動的考察及闡釋,〉 199; 曹端波 (Cao), 〈招魂與送靈〉.

18. 胡新生 (Hu), 《中國古代巫術》, 385–92.

19. 據《北齊書·恩倖傳》記載，北齊薛榮宗自稱能夠 '使鬼'.北周來攻北齊，薛對齊後主高緯說，我已派名將斛律光帶大兵上前抵擋.此時斛律光已死多年，而高緯對薛的話竟很信服. See 胡新生 (Hu), 《中國古代巫術》, 396.

20. The distinction here is not always clear, as often the gods in Chinese folk religion are people believed to be deified after death. 歐大年 (Overmyer), 〈神明、聖徒、靈媒和邊境,〉 8.

21. 胡新生 (Hu), 《中國古代巫術》, 392–93. For a comprehensive study on *fuji* in Chinese classical literature, see 許地山 (Hsu), 《扶箕迷信的研究》.

22. Written in 1920, Lewis Hodous, an American missionary in China, was rather optimistic about a progressive diminishment of *fuji* and other forms of folk religion. 何樂益 (Hodous), 〈基督教以外的中國宗教,〉 70–72. Though it might have been driven by an agenda to promote Christianity in China, the report that results from extensive survey retains credibility in its observations.

23. 侯亞偉 (Hou), 〈民國學者的扶乩研究,〉 113.

witchcraft that called upon the spirit of the dead for consultation, remained popular in China.[24] In recent years, despite the promotion of a materialistic ideology by the Communist government, reports of the practice of *fuji* persisted in various parts of China, especially in rural regions and ethnic minority groups.[25] In regions outside of mainland China, such as Taiwan, *fuji* and other forms of divination also continues to be a familiar social ritual, and there is even an increase in the phenomenon in recent years.[26]

Reading 1 Sam 28 in Australian Chinese Christian Communities

Given the prevalence of the practice of communicating with the dead in various forms in Chinese culture, it is logical to anticipate that Chinese Christians find resemblance in their cultural background with the necromancer of Endor. Considering the heterogeneity in the composition of the Australian Chinese Christian community, with members originating from rural and metropolitan regions of mainland China, Hong Kong, Taiwan, and other parts of Southeast Asia, it is possible that in any local church community some members will be familiar with the rituals of *zhaohun* or *fuji*, and subsequently be more inclined to acknowledge the authenticity of Samuel in the narrative. However, this has not been the case in my experience of reading the passage with various groups of Australian Chinese Christians.

A few years ago, I studied 1 Sam 28 with a group of about sixty Chinese Christians in a local church in Sydney, and I asked the question, "Who thinks this being raised by the necromancer is truly Samuel?" To my surprise, only one person raised his hand! Similarly, every time when I discussed the topic with Bible college students in my class, who are mostly Chinese migrants, the vast majority would reject the authenticity of Samuel in the account. And the reasons they give for this view are often related to the teaching that they have received in the church: the social practice of *zhaohun* and *fuji*, or any form of communicating with the dead in Chinese culture is against Christian belief, and they should reject such customs once

24. 許地山 (Hsu), 《扶箕迷信的研究》, 4.
25. 吳重慶 (Wu), 〈民間信仰中的信息溝通與傳播〉; 徐義強 (Xu), 〈客家薩滿的通靈途徑、儀式及與台灣的比較,〉.
26. Though the practice is more commonly in communicating with deities of folk religion than with the spirit of the dead, see 林美容, 〈從乩童到通靈人〉, 6–8.

converted to Christianity. Being raised by the necromancer must therefore be a disguise from evil power.

Similar concerns originating from the social context can also be observed in popular Chinese Christian reading. An article published in *Golden Lampstand*, a well-received bimonthly loose-leaf pamphlet,[27] places the discussion of 1 Sam 28 within the context of concerns for Chinese Christians who might participate in practices of communicating with the dead.[28] After surveying biblical evidence that rejects the return of the soul of a dead person to the living, Ng dismisses 1 Sam 28 as a possible exception and argues vigorously that "the ghost definitely can't be Samuel."[29] He provides a list of ten reasons for support, one of which is, "If God sends Samuel to reply to Saul in this occasion, how could God himself be glorified? Wouldn't that reinforce the concept of necromancy?"[30] Concluding with a warning to readers in avoiding necromancy which might lead to doubts in their faith, the apprehension towards Chinese Christians following the example of Saul is quite explicit.

It is not surprising if the teachings that Australian Chinese Christians received have been influenced by views of a similar nature: in order to warn Chinese Christians against their cultural practice of spiritualism, the efficacy of the necromantic rite in the passage must be falsified and rejected. However, is denying the authenticity of Samuel in the narrative a necessary response against a culture that practices necromancy? As Ko Ming-Him suggests, the effectiveness of the necromancer does not necessarily legitimize the action in view of biblical laws and accepting the authenticity of Samuel is not equivalent to welcoming the practice of necromancy.[31] And more importantly, if the ancient Hebrew culture is also familiar to such acts of divination, how was the identity of "Samuel" intended to be received by the ancient audience?

---

27. It is printed in Hong Kong with international readership including Australia, see Golden Lampstand, "Info."

28. 吳主光 (Wu), 〈鬼魂的正解〉.

29. 「那鬼魂絕不可能是撒母耳」, my translation.

30. 「如果神在這場合差撒母耳來回答掃羅，豈能叫神自己得榮耀？豈不是加強人們對交鬼法術的觀念？」, my translation. The other reasons mostly refer to consistency within biblical teaching and theological considerations.

31. Ko contends for the authenticity of Samuel and based his arguments on the literary features of the passage, which I shall turn to in the later section of this article. 高銘謙 (Ko), 《釋經釋出禍》, 82–87.

Necromancy in the Ancient Hebrew Context

In order to discuss the possible social perception of the narrative in the ancient Hebrew context, one shall need to first identify the nature of the activity in 1 Sam 28. The instruction of Saul to the woman is rather direct: "Consult a spirit for me and bring up for me the one whom I name to you" (v. 8). As verse 3 reminds the readers that Samuel has died (which was first reported in 25:1), and that the purpose of Saul bringing up Samuel is clearly in seeking direction from him in relation to the battle crisis (v. 15), this fits into the category of necromancy, which is defined as "the art or practice of magically conjuring up the souls of the dead . . . to obtain information from them, generally regarding the revelation of unknown causes or the future course of events."[32] Moreover, the narrator places the incident within a context that Saul is ultimately seeking guidance from YHWH: "When Saul inquired of the Lord, the Lord did not answer him, not by dreams or by Urim or by prophets" (v. 6), which is again confirmed in the request of Saul himself: "God has turned away from me and answers me no more, either by prophets or by dreams so I have summoned you to tell me what I should do" (v. 15). Therefore, the incident in Endor should be considered as a form of divination with YHWH, though performed indirectly through a double media, first by the woman, then by the prophet Samuel.

Divination as "actions culturally understood to allow acquisition of knowledge otherwise restricted to the divine realm" takes various forms in the Hebrew Bible.[33] Some are legitimate in the laws (such as Urim and Thummim in Lev 8:8), others are implied in the narratives (such as the dreams of Jacob and Solomon in Gen 28:10–17 and 1 Kgs 3:5–15), and yet some are considered unacceptable in ancient Israel, including necromancy, which is prohibited in both the legal corpora (Lev 19:31; Deut 18:10–11) and prophetic reference (Isa 8:19).[34]

According to Cryer, the phenomenon of divination was much neglected in early Jewish tradition, and studies on Israelite divination have

---

32. Bourguignon, "Necromancy." It is noted that some propose a more inclusive definition where divinatory purpose is not a decisive factor; see Tropper, *Nekromantie: Totenbefragung im Alten Orient und im Alten Testament* AOAT 223 (Neukirchen-Vluyn: Neukirchener Verlag, 1986), 14–15, quoted by Nihan, *1 Samuel 28*, 24. Yet for the context of discussing the event of Endor it is more appropriate to consider the practice in the more restricted sense.

33. Hamori, *Women's Divination*, 4.

34. Cryer, *Divination*, 229–30.

also been scarce in modern times.[35] There are only two aspects of Israelite divination that have attracted some attention of scholarship, namely prophetic oracles and dream interpretations.[36] With the evolutionary schemes of nineteenth-century social science, scholars assumed that prophecy, being a more advanced form of divination, has replaced other practices and therefore downplayed the role of the rest of the spectrum. However, this seems to have neglected the fact that "divination is, at least in primitive societies, indicative of an entire pattern of behavior which entails a number of corollaries for the ways such societies understand cause and effect, deal with illness, uncertainties, social tensions, and so on."[37] In other words, divination described within a context that performs these actions should be interpreted, at least primarily, in its own right.

Having recognized such necessity, practices of divination such as necromancy have become topics of interest in recent scholarship.[38] Discussions of necromancy in the ancient Hebrew context have often revolved around two related issues: 1) whether it existed; and 2) if it did, when and where was the origin of the practice. These will be examined respectively below.

The Existence and Origin of Necromancy in Ancient Israel

Necromancy and worship of dead ancestors is closely related in many ancient cultures including Mesopotamia.[39] The funerary cult, which is a body of rituals including funeral rites, rites for supplying the dead with food and water, and rites of commemoration, is well attested in all of the ancient Near East. Archaeological studies of interments from Judah also support the existence of this cult in Judahite society throughout the monarchy.[40]

---

35. Cryer, *Divination*, 231.

36. For an overview of these studies, see Cryer, *Divination*, 235–41. Although scholarship previously placed prophecy in opposition to divination, there is increasing consensus now that prophecy is simply one type of divination. Hamori, *Women's Divination*, 4.

37. Cryer, *Divination*, 242. Regrettably, however, Cryer does not investigate the practice of necromancy in many details in his studies and focused on other forms of divination instead.

38. Schmidt, *Beneficent Dead*, 1–2.

39. Nihan, *1 Samuel 28*, 25. For archaeological evidence of the practice of necromancy in Mesopotamia, see Finkel, "Necromancy."

40. Bloch-Smith provides detailed discussions of both archaeological and biblical

The virtue of the rituals indicates a belief that the dead could survive both the underworld and in the memory of the descendants and the clan.[41] Moreover, some sort of supernatural knowledge is often attributed to the dead due to "their proximity to, and acquaintance with, the deities of the underworld," which becomes beneficial to their lineage.[42] Archaeological evidence also supports the notion that the gods are believed to play a decisive role in evoking the spirit of the dead in revealing divine knowledges: in the fragment of the Mesopotamian ritual BM 36703 (col. 2, 11.1–6), Finkel makes the observation that the deity "has the power and the authority to bring up a ghost from the Underworld, and the whole operation is put under his auspices."[43] It is with such cultural background that necromancy is practiced in ancient Near East for divinatory purposes. Although the evidence directly associated with necromancy in Syria-Palestine is limited, scholarship often confers that it is likely for preexilic Israel to adopt necromantic divination as per their neighboring regions.[44]

This *opinio communis* is recently challenged by Brian Schmidt in the monograph rewritten from his Oxford dissertation. Based on his interpretation of a range of extrabiblical textual evidence from Syria-Palestine of the late third to the early second millennium BCE, Schmidt argues that ancestor cults and necromancy are not attested in the historical context of Israel before the time of Manasseh. Instead, it is under the influence of neo-Assyrian power, where ample archaeological evidence points to the practice of ancestor cults, that necromancers became active in Israel thereafter. He then dismisses the historicity of necromancy in early Israel, claiming that texts that proposed a Canaanite origin of necromancy from antiquity is a rhetorical strategy by exilic or postexilic redactors to enhance Deuteronomistic ideology.[45] His argument, however, attracted much disagreement from experts in the area. For example, Dennis Pardee considers it "essentially an argument from silence" in a field that is rapidly evolving and he disagrees in much of his interpretations;[46] and Marvin Pope also cautions against the presumption that "beliefs about the dead in ancient

---

evidence of the cult, see Bloch-Smith, "Cult of the Dead," 213–24.

41. Nihan, *1 Samuel 28*, 26.
42. Nihan, *1 Samuel 28*, 27.
43. Finkel, "Necromancy," 5.
44. Hamori, *Women's Divination*, 117–18.
45. Schmidt, *Beneficent Dead*, 134–40.
46. Pardee, "Brian B. Schmidt," 362.

Israel differed radically from those of their neighbors and kin."[47] Nihan convincingly argues against the deduction of Schmidt, which is the core of the issue to note here: although archaeological evidences point towards an expansion of necromantic divination during the neo-Assyrian period, this does not render such practice nonexistent prior to this time.[48] Moreover, the rhetorical strategy of the Deuteronomist in discouraging the readers from participating in necromancy does not rely on an imaginary nature of necromancy prior to exilic Israel: it could well be reframing a tradition from ancient Israel with new perspectives.

It is therefore reasonable to contend that necromancy is a familiar social practice in the context of 1 Sam 28.[49] Questions remain, however, on the origin of the practice as to whether it is considered "foreign ritual" or native to ancient Israel. Commentators often presume that the woman of Endor is either Canaanite or an idolatrous Israelite practicing rites from a foreign origin,[50] yet when examined closely evidence does not seem to sufficiently support such assertion. There is no direct reference to the ethnic background of the woman within the text, and the location of Endor is uncertain and therefore unhelpful in this consideration.[51] The prohibition of Lev 19:31 and 20:6 does not specify a Canaanite origin of necromancy, and Deut 18:9–14 is the only occasion in the legal corpora that attributes the practice to foreign influence.[52] With the possible influence of Deuteronomistic ideology, where a Canaanite origin may enhance the rhetorical force of prohibiting the practice, it is therefore debatable to rely on this passage alone in defining its origin.

47. See Pope, "Review," 92.

48. Nihan, *1 Samuel 28*, 28.

49. The dating of the passage is controversial, with some postulating an ancient oral tradition or pre-Deuteronomistic document behind the present account, and others advocating a post-Deuteronomistic composition (see Nihan, *1 Samuel 28*, 32–33, for a summary of the reasonings). As the focus in this paper is on the rhetorical effect of the narrative, where the anchor of the argument is a context in which readers are familiar with the practice of necromancy in their social setting, suffice to say that since necromancy has existed in the ancient Hebrew context, readers would be well aware of the social connotations regardless of the dating of the passage.

50. Such as Reis, "Eating the Blood, 5–6; Beuken, "1 Samuel 28," 10.

51. Hamori, *Women's Divination*, 112. In fact, if the woman was living within the land where mediums are expelled by the command of Saul, it is more likely that she was an Israelite.

52. Cryer, *Divination*, 231–32. Although, as Cryer points out, the foreign origin could be presupposed in the priestly documents and not explicitly mentioned.

Scholars therefore resort to etymology in search for an answer. The meaning and etymology of the Hebrew term בוא referring to necromancy has been much of a debate, with proposals ranging from Hittite to Ugarit, Assyrian, and Sumerian, and some consider this as possible evidence of a foreign origin of the rite.[53] Nihan argues against such a view and contends that "the most satisfying solution consists of linking the בוא mentioned in the context of necromantic practices with the Hebrew term referring to the 'father' or the 'ancestor,' which has the same root." The בוא in this view refers to a dead ancestor, which is consistent with the social understanding of necromancy. While scholarship has not yet reached consensus on this matter, with the possibility that the term may in fact have a Hebrew origin, the evidence for a foreign origin of necromancy is therefore inconclusive.[54]

One could then put the incident of Endor back to its ancient Hebrew context. Necromancy, being part of a funerary ritual for divinatory purposes, is familiar to the Israelites. Though we cannot be certain of its origins, it has possibly been practiced from antiquity. This is apparent in the narrative of 1 Sam 28 itself, where the servants of Saul immediately point him to Endor upon the king's enquiry (v. 7), almost as if it is common knowledge. It is not surprising, therefore, when Saul is desperate for divine guidance, he would resort to a customary funerary ritual. If other spirits of the dead were deemed to have access to divine knowledge, it is even more convincing that Samuel would have such ability: after all, he was already a prophet of YHWH when he was alive! Moreover, if the evoking of the spirit is understood to be directed by the gods, then it is quite possible that the appearance of Samuel is considered to be instructed by YHWH, who would no doubt have the ability to command the spirit of the prophet. It is therefore not a question at all, to the audience in this context, that the "being" could truly be the ghost of Samuel.

This reading potential that points to the authenticity of Samuel is yet to be confirmed with the rhetorical strategy of the text, which will be the focus in the next section.

---

53. For a detailed discussion of the various proposals, see Hoffner, "Second Millenium," 385–401.

54. Hamori also contends that "there is no indication in the text that she is anything other than a Yahwistic diviner providing her services of religious access for the king." Hamori, *Women's Divination*, 114.

The Identity of "Samuel" through the Eyes of the Characters: A Literary Analysis

In this section the literary features of the text will be investigated, in order to discern the rhetorical strategy of the text that shapes the readers' perception of the act of necromancy and the identity of Samuel. The characters involved in the scene, including the narrator, the woman, Saul, and Samuel will be examined respectively.

The Narrator

The view of the narrator is rather straightforward. The "being" is consistently addressed as "Samuel" by the narrator throughout the narrative, first in verse 12 when he appeared to the woman, then twice in the reference of the speech in verses 15 and 16; and again, in verse 20. There is not the most subtle hint in any of these occasions that the narrator ever doubts the identity of Samuel, and if the being is in fact a disguise by the devil, or a staged act of the medium, the "omniscient narrator" would not have been deceived by either of these tricks and would be able to inform the readers.[55] Moreover, in all of the references in the narrative there is no additional detail to his identity, and phrases such as "the ghost of Samuel" are not used at all. He is, to the narrator, simply Samuel. This results in a rhetorical impression to the readers that this is indeed Samuel who has come and spoken to Saul.

The Woman

The diviner is usually the focus of attention in a divinatory act, as both the appearance of the spirit and the reception of a message anchor on the actions of the diviner. However, the woman of Endor plays a relatively passive role in the scene in verses 12–19. There is no description of her performance or actions in the narrative,[56] as would be expected of any necromancer, and when she saw Samuel in verse 12, she cried out in a loud voice, which does not seem to be a normal response if she had expected the appearance

---

55. For the literary theory behind the omniscient narrator, see Alter, *Biblical Narrative*, 155–57.

56. This has also been understood to be due to lack of interest of the author, or lack of familiarity of the practice. Hamori, *Women's Divination*, 118.

of Samuel through her "professional performance." It is quite possible, as scholars have speculated, that Samuel appeared before she had done any of her necromantic maneuvres.[57] In other words, instead of coming upon her summoning as per necromantic activity, the prophet came on his own accord, and this is extraordinary even to an experienced necromancer. In a reading context that believes in the deity's control in the appearance of the dead, this may well be perceived as the proactive action of YHWH, the Lord of the prophet.

The speech of the woman in the following verses is consistent with this interpretation. She describes her vision as "a divine being coming up out of the ground" (v. 13), which emphasizes the supernatural nature of his appearance. It is noticeable that she does not directly calls him "Samuel," which could again be an emphasis on his "self-invited" nature: she does not have control upon his coming, unlike the normal necromantic act where a specific target is summoned. And when she describes him as an "old man wrapped in a robe," it is clear that the being is independent and outside of her body, unlike certain occasions where the spirit may dwell inside the body of the diviner. She also seems to play no role in the divinatory speech, as verses 15–18 portray direct conversation between Saul and Samuel.[58]

There is also evidence that supports the passive role of the woman of Endor in the book of Samuel outside the current passage. Matthew Michael provides an extensive list of intertextual associations that establishes a link between the representation of Hannah, the first woman in the life of Samuel, and the woman of Endor, the last woman that appeared with him

---

57. For example, Beuken, "1 Samuel 28," 9. Plenty of proposals have been made to explain the reaction of the woman and her subsequent recognition of the king. For example, Reis suggests that Samuel would only allow himself to be summoned by Saul, and the woman is afraid of the king, not Samuel, see Reis, "Eating the Blood," 9–10. On the contrary, Hamori attempts to resolve the interpretive tension by suggesting a defective spelling for the word ותרא at the beginning of v. 12, rendering a translation "and the woman feared Samuel" instead of "and the woman saw Samuel" (Hamori, *Women's Divination*, 121). This interpretation, however, does not explain why Saul subsequently asks the woman, "Have no fear; what do you see?" in v. 13. In my opinion, it is logical that the sudden appearance of Samuel puts the woman in fear, and knowing that something extraordinary is happening, she reflects upon the promise of the client that no punishment will come upon her. She in turn realizes only the king has the authority to do so as it was his own command to cast out mediums.

58. Contrary to Pigott who considers the prophetic speech as coming from the woman (Pigott, "1 Samuel 28," 438), there is no indication from the text that this actually happened. In fact, scholars such as Beuken suggest that she could not hear the prophetic speech at all, see Beuken, "1 Samuel 28," 7.

in the book.⁵⁹ The literary artistry encourages the readers to bring the two characters together, and 1 Sam 2:6 declares: "The Lord kills and brings to life; he brings down to Sheol and raises up." The song of Hannah forms the framework for interpretating the event at the very end of the life of Samuel: it is the Lord who raises him up from Sheol.

Overall, the woman of Endor is not acting like a necromancer at all in the narrative. She did not summon the spirit, the Lord raises him up; the spirit did not dwell upon her, he stood outside of her body; she did not convey the message, he spoke for himself. As the only character who sees Samuel in the narrative, her role is to testify for his appearance and acknowledge his supernatural origin from a power higher than herself.

Saul

There is no doubt in the narrative that Saul is familiar with the practice of necromantic divination. Verse 3 records retrospectively that he has expelled all mediums from the land, which indicates that he is well aware of the existence of the practice. And when he cannot find an answer from YHWH, "by dreams or by Urim or by prophets" (v. 6), he turns to the medium as his last resort. He would have to believe in the efficacy of the rite, at least to a certain extent, to take the trouble to travel to Endor at the brink of war.

Therefore, it is fair to say that Saul expects, or at least wishes, to be connected with Samuel through the medium. Upon the woman's description of her vision and before Samuel starts speaking, Saul already identifies him and bows down to him (v. 14). Regardless of the reason that allows him to recognize Samuel,⁶⁰ that the king adopts this humble gesture demonstrates his belief in his authenticity. The direct conversation between the prophet and the king in verses 15–19 further confirms his belief, as the prophet refers to the incident against Amalek at 1 Sam 15, in which the warning was probably private between the two (1 Sam 15:30–31). There is no reason for Saul to publicize the verdict from Samuel, and when he hears about it again, he knows for sure that it is the prophet himself speaking.

---

59. Michael, "Narrative Conjuring," 478.

60. Some suggest that it is due to the garment that is characteristic of the prophet (Beuken, "1 Samuel 28," 10). However, as Hamori accurately points out, it was not Saul, who would have been the one familiar with Samuel's clothing, who saw Samuel, but the woman of Endor. Hence, there is no evidence from the text that points to the recognition of the prophet by his clothing. Hamori, *Women's Divination*, 122.

Saul responds to the speech by falling to the ground with fear (v. 20), which again reflects his firm belief that the prophecy is truly from Samuel, and in turn, from YHWH.

Samuel

While the character Samuel does not identity himself throughout the narrative, his prophecy in verses 16–19 is sufficient to demonstrate his authenticity. Not only is his warning consistent with the prophecy that he made during his lifetime (1 Sam 15), his prophetic message on the fate of Saul and his army is realized in 1 Sam 31, which is the ultimate test for a true prophet (Deut 18:21–22). Moreover, the sacred Tetragrammaton is repeated seven times in his speech,[61] which emphasizes the role and authority of YHWH in the message.

Reading in this context, the initial words of Samuel, "Why have you disturbed me by bringing me up?" need not be understood literally in that the prophet was indeed raised by the medium. It could be a conversation breaker for the prophet to acknowledge that Saul's visit to the necromancer indeed initiated his appearance. However, the prophet's reply to Saul's enquiry trumps the possibility that he is here to answer to the demand of the king: contrary to the wish of the desperate king for guidance to victory, Samuel announces his imminent death and defeat. It is not the typical beneficiary blessing that Saul has hoped for through divination, as the prophet acts according to the will of YHWH, in life, and in life after death.

Rhetorical Message on Necromancy

It is clear from the above literary analysis that Samuel is authentic to all the characters in the narrative, and there is no reason to doubt that the rhetorical intent is otherwise. It does not, however, lead to a necessary conclusion that the passage endorses necromancy. In fact, there is ample evidence from the text that readers are warned against the practice.

Firstly, the framework of the narrative is written in the awareness that necromantic divination is forbidden in Israel. Saul himself has enacted this prohibition and expelled mediums from the land, and this sets the tone for

---

61. Beuken, "1 Samuel 28," 5.

interpretating the entire event.[62] The readers are reminded twice of this background, first in verse 3, and again through the mouth of the medium in verse 9. And Saul himself is well aware that he is breaking his own decree, as he puts on a disguise so that others won't recognize him (v. 8). This becomes even more sarcastic when he promises the woman amnesty in the name of the Lord (v. 10). The irony in the self-defeating behavior of Saul certainly brings negative judgment to his divinatory action.

Secondly, necromancy did not take place in Endor. The woman did not perform any maneuvres to summon Samuel, and for the ghost of prophet to appear, it could be due to no other supernatural power but that of YHWH. By the sovereignty of YHWH, Samuel is sent to give a final warning to Saul, and the necromancer had no role in the entire scene apart from witnessing to the mighty power of YHWH in awe.

Thirdly, the intertextual connection between 1 Sam 15:23 and 28:18 acts as a subtle reminder to the readers of the seriousness of the sin of divination.[63] As the prophet recalls the verdict at Gilgal, the words of 1 Sam 15:23 come to mind: "For rebellion is no less a sin than divination." The sin of Saul at Endor is almost foreshadowed in this warning.

And finally, though Samuel did not explicitly condemn Saul for consulting a medium, he literally pronounced a death sentence to Saul and his sons (v. 19). As the outcome of the only attempt of necromantic divination in the Hebrew Bible, is this not sufficient warning for all?

Reflections for Australian Chinese Christians and Beyond

It is clear from the above analysis that denying the authenticity of Samuel is not a necessary response in a reading context that exercises necromancy. To the ancient Hebrew readers, the prophet genuinely came and spoke to Saul, and yet they were given more than sufficient warning against following the example of the king through the literary artistry of the narrative. It is not the interest of the author to examine, or even contemplate the efficacy of necromancy: it has simply been submitted to the sovereignty of YHWH, who consistently forbids the practice through the laws and the prophetic voices.

---

62. The dating and relationship of the passage in relation to Deut 18:10–11 is therefore not crucial here. Regardless of when and where Saul gets the idea, his action in forbidding the practice sets the tone for interpretation.

63. Michael, "Prophet," 323.

The incident of Endor is therefore intended to be a negative example against engaging in necromantic divination, even if the enquiry is towards YHWH. The implication to Chinese Christians is clear: any forms of necromancy, such as *fuji*, are not the way to seek divine guidance even when you are desperate. Necromantic divination is forbidden even in enquiry to God, let alone towards any other supernatural power. And this is the core of the message of 1 Sam 28, across generations and cultures.

Bibliography

Alter, Robert. *The Art of Biblical Narrative*. New York: Basic, 1981.
Beuken, Willem A. M. "1 Samuel 28: The Prophet as 'Hammer of Witches.'" *Journal for the Study of the Old Testament* 3, no. 6 (1978) 3–17.
Bloch-Smith, Elizabeth M. "The Cult of the Dead in Judah: Interpreting the Material Remains." *Journal of Biblical Literature* 111, no. 2 (1992) 213–24.
Boer, Roland. "Caught in Between: Australian Biblical Studies between Asia, the Pacific, and the West." *The Future of the Biblical Past: Envisioning Biblical Studies on a Global Key* (2012) 223–36.
Bourguignon, Erika. "Necromancy." In *Encyclopedia of Religion*, edited by Mircea Eliade and Charles J. Adams, 6451–54. Detroit: Macmillan Reference, 2005.
Brenner-Idan, Athalya. "So Where Are We? Some Reflections on Contextual Interpretations as Practiced." 2016 SBL International Meeting, Seoul, 2016.
Brison, Ora. "The Medium of En-Dor (בוא תלעב תשא) and the Phenomenon of Divination in Twenty-First Century Israel." In *Samuel, Kings and Chronicles 1: Texts @ Contexts*, vol. 5, edited by Athalya Brenner-Idan and Archie C. C. Lee, 124–47. London: Bloomsbury, T. & T. Clark, 2017.
曹端波 (Cao, Rui Bo). 〈招魂與送靈：川黔滇苗族「解簸箕」儀式研究.〉《貴州師範學院學報》32, no. 11 (2016) 40–45.
陳瑤 (Chen, Yao). 〈魯東南農村民眾叫魂習俗淺析.〉《黑龍江史志》, no. 5 (2014) 277.
Cryer, Frederick H. *Divination in Ancient Israel and Its Near Eastern Environment: A Socio-Historical Investigation*. London: A&C Black, 1994.
Edwards, M. J. Review of *The "Belly-Myther" of Endor: Interpretations of 1 Kingdoms 28 in the Early Church*, by Rowan A. Greer and Margaret M. Mitchell. *The Journal of Ecclesiastical History* 59, no. 4 (2008) 723–24.
Finkel, Irving L. "Necromancy in Ancient Mesopotamia." *Archiv für Orientforschung* 29 (1983) 1–17.
Golden Lampstand. "Info." https://www.goldenlampstand.org/info/info.php?highlights.
Greer, Rowan A., and Margaret M. Mitchell. *The "Belly-Myther" of Endor: Interpretations of 1 Kingdoms 28 in the Early Church*. Atlanta, GA: Society of Biblical Literature, 2007.
Hamori, Esther J. *Women's Divination in Biblical Literature: Prophecy, Necromancy, and Other Arts of Knowledge*. New Haven: Yale University Press, 2015.
何先成 (He, Xian Cheng). 〈從長時段看中國傳統社會的招魂葬.〉《西部學刊》, no. 4 (2016) 18–22.

何樂益 (Hodous, Lewis D. D.). 〈基督教以外的中國宗教.〉 In 《中華歸主：中國基督教事業統計（1901–1920）》, 70–81. 北京: 中國社會科學出版社, 1987.

Hoffner, Harry A., Jr. "Second Millenium Antecedents to the Hebrew'ōḇ." *Journal of Biblical Literature* (1967) 385–401.

侯亞偉 (Hou, Ya Wei). 〈民國學者的扶乩研究.〉《世界宗教研究》, no. 5 (2017) 113–20.

許地山 (Hsu, Ti-Shan). 《扶箕迷信的研究》. 北京: 商務印書館, 1997.

胡新生 (Hu, Xin Sheng). 《中國古代巫術》. 北京: 人民出版社, 2010.

高銘謙. (Ko, Lawrence Ming-him). 《釋經釋出禍：處理難解經文》. 香港: 宣道出版社, 2017.

李梅田、李童 (Li, Mei Tian, and Tong Li). 〈魂歸於墓：中古招魂葬略論.〉《江漢考古》, no. 4 (2019) 95–103.

Liew, Tat-siong Benny, ed. *Semeia 90/91: The Bible in Asian America*. Society of Biblical Literature, 2002.

———. *What Is Asian American Biblical Hermeneutics? Reading the New Testament: Reading the New Testament*. Honolulu: University of Hawaii, 2007.

林美容 (Lin, Mei-Rong). 〈從乩童到通靈人：與神靈溝通媒介的典範轉移.〉《慈濟大學人文社會科學學刊》16 (2014) 1–26.

Michael, Matthew. "Narrative Conjuring or the Tales of Two Sisters? The Representations of Hannah and the Witch of Endor in 1 Samuel." *Journal for the Study of the Old Testament* 42, no. 4 (2018) 469–89.

———. "The Prophet, the Witch and the Ghost: Understanding the Parody of Saul as a 'Prophet'and the Purpose of Endor in the Deuteronomistic History." *Journal for the Study of the Old Testament* 38, no. 3 (2014) 315–46.

Ngundu, Onesimus A. "Necromancy in Africa." In *Global Perspectives on the Old Testament*, edited by Mark Roncace and Joseph Weaver, 76–77. New Jersey: Pearson, 2014.

Nihan, Christophe. *1 Samuel 28 and the Condemnation of Necromancy in Persian Yehud*. Edinburgh: T. & T. Clark, 2003.

歐大年 (Overmyer, Daniel L.). 〈神明、聖徒、靈媒和邊境:從中國文化觀點比較地方民間信仰傳統.〉《台灣宗教研究》2, no. 2 (2003) 1–15.

Pardee, D. "Brian B. Schmidt, Israel's Beneficent Dead: Ancestor Cult and Necromancy in Ancient Israelite Religion and Tradition." *Journal of Semitic Studies* 42, no. 2 (1997) 362–68.

Pigott, Susan M. "1 Samuel 28—Saul and the Not So Wicked Witch of Endor." *Review and Expositor* 95, no. 3 (1998) 435–44.

Pope, Marvin. Review of *Israel's Beneficent Dead: Ancestor Cult and Necromancy in Ancient Israelite Religion and Tradition*, by Brian B. Schmidt. *Jewish Quarterly Review* 88, nos. 1–2 (July–October, 1997) 91–93.

Reis, Pamela Tamarkin. "Eating the Blood: Saul and the Witch of Endor." *Journal for the Study of the Old Testament* 22, no. 73 (1997) 3–23.

Schmidt, Brian B. *Israel's Beneficent Dead: Ancestor Cult and Necromancy in Ancient Israelite Religion and Tradition*. Tübingen: J. C. B. Mohr, 1994.

沈曉柔 (Shen, HsXiao-Rou). 〈黃泉歸來：試探古代中國「死後復甦」的觀念.〉《史穗》2, no. 2 (2009) 1–22.

Smelik, Klaas A. D. "The Witch of Endor: 1 Samuel 28 in Rabbinic and Christian Exegesis Till 800 AD." *Vigiliae Christianae* 33, no. 2 (1979) 160–79.

Tsoi, Grace Kwan Sik. *Who Is to Blame for Judges 19?: Interplay between the Text and a Chinese Context.* Eugene, OR: Wipf and Stock, 2022.

王國旭、胡亮節 (Wang, Guo Xu, and Liang Jie Hu). 〈烏蒙山區的叫魂儀式管窺.〉《大眾考古》, no. 3 (2016) 117–21.

王杰文 (Wang, Jie Wen). 〈一个巫婆的招魂唱詞及相關分析.〉《民俗研究》, no. 1 (2003) 38–50.

吳重慶 (Wu, Chong Qing). 〈民間信仰中的信息溝通與傳播：莆田民間信仰田野調查的思考.〉《東南學術》, no. 6 (2017) 21–18.

吳主光 (Wu, Zhu Guang). 〈鬼魂的正解.〉《金燈台》 no. 12 (1987). https://www.goldenlampstand.org/glb/read.php?GLID=01204.

徐海波 (Xu, Hai Bo). 〈甘肅省會寧縣丁溝鄉南門村一次喪葬活動的考察及闡釋.〉《民俗曲藝》 173, no. 9 (2011) 161–231.

徐義強 (Xu, Yi Qiang). 〈客家薩滿的通靈途徑、儀式及與台灣的比較.〉《宗教學研究》, no. 2 (2008) 128–32.

Yu, Ying-Shih. "'O Soul, Come Back!' A Study in the Changing Conceptions of the Soul and Afterlife in Pre-Buddhist China." *Harvard Journal of Asiatic Studies* 47, no. 2 (1987) 363–95.

5.

Examining Cultural Conflict through the Lens of the Book of Acts

MING LEUNG

Abstract

INTERCULTURAL CONFLICT SEEMS TO be a prevailing topic of discussion amongst the Chinese diaspora churches. Whether it is the intergenerational conflict between the Chinese-speaking first-generation migrants and their English-speaking second generation or, in the Australian context, the newly emerged subcultural conflict of the Cantonese-speaking and Mandarin-speaking congregations, it troubles leadership of ethnic Chinese churches in Australia and threatens unity of the church. The book of Acts encompasses numerous cross-cultural encounter examples which could shed light on the issue. I specially choose 6:1–7 as a test case to explore some principles of managing cross-cultural conflict. The reason for this decision is that its context resembles the ethnic Chinese churches in Australia: most scholars contend that both the Hebrews and the Hellenists in Act 6 present ethnic Jews of different subcultures; likewise, ethnic Chinese churches are mainly comprised of ethnic Chinese with different (Chinese, English) cultures. Through examining the background, process, and consequence of the narrative, this paper seeks to explore Luke's theological intention behind the story. Hopefully, it will contribute to the discussion of cross-cultural conflict in the ethnic Chinese churches in Australia. From the analysis of the text, it is explicit that Luke asserts care for minorities and leadership succession. Moreover, his intention of formulating an ideal inclusive community is conspicuous and I believe it is the wish of most ethnic Chinese church leaders in Australia.

The Context

Intercultural conflict is evident in ethnic Chinese churches in Sydney, Australia.[1] There are two major ones. Firstly, the conflict between the predominantly Chinese-speaking first-generation migrants and the English-speaking second-generation migrants or locally born ethnic Chinese. Most of the ethnic Chinese churches in Sydney were established by first-generation migrants from Hong Kong with Cantonese as their *lingua franca*. They dominate the church especially at the leadership level and are also the main stakeholders of the church financially. With the increase of the second-generation English-speaking population, English congregations within Chinese churches are established.[2] Eventually, English-speaking leaders and pastors come to the scene and intergenerational conflict slowly creeps in.

With the increase of Mandarin-speaking migrants from mainland China and other parts of the world during the last few decades, Mandarin congregations have been established in predominately Cantonese-speaking churches. Due to differences in language and background, the subcultural conflict evolves between the Cantonese-speaking and Mandarin-speaking congregations in the church. To avoid complicating the discussion, this article focuses on the conflict between the English-speaking second-generation congregation and the Chinese-speaking first-generation migrant congregation.

---

1. The term "ethnic Chinese churches" is by no means exclusive to all Australian churches with a Chinese congregation. It refers mainly to Chinese churches formed by ethnic Chinese and the congregation is predominately ethnic Chinese whether they originated from mainland China or the Chinese diaspora. The author's ministry experience is mainly in Sydney where most of the ethnic Chinese reside in Australia and has the most significant number of Chinese churches among different cities in Australia. Therefore, they could be a good representation of ethnic Chinese churches in Australia.

2. Chu provides a brief history of ethnic Chinese churches in Sydney. See Chu, *Intercultural Competence*, 94–139. This book is a recent study of pastoral leaderships' cross-cultural conflict in ethnic Chinese churches in Sydney.

My observation is that the minority groups frequently suffer from the mentality of being a "second-class citizen" and conviction of being treated unfairly both in resources and their opinions. This phenomenon threats the unity of the church.[3] Even though this has been discussed frequently, unfortunately, there is not a lot of study in this area in the Australian context. Certainly, this is an area worthy of further research.

Acts 6:1–7

The beginning of this narrative is very positive—"when the disciples were increasing in number" (v. 1a).[4] With this new Jesus movement, disciples grew in population, and one would expect more good news to be reported. It, however, is followed immediately by an incidence of dissident—"the "Hellenists" complained against the "Hebrews" because their widows were being neglected in the daily distribution of food" (v. 1b). The identity of these two conflicting groups ("Hellenists" and "Hebrews") attracts lots of scholarly interest.[5] Even though there is no consent of the exact meaning of the terms, most commentators identify the "Hellenists" as a group of ethnic Jews with different languages/cultures and possibly different origins from the first batch of Jesus' disciples—Palestinian Jews.[6] Although the term Hellenists could refer to an ethnically non-Jewish origin,[7] the Hellenists mentioned here were most probably ethnic Jews coming from different

---

3. I was invited to join the annual pastors' dinner for the Sydney Chinese Christian Churches Association in 2013. This association represents the majority of the ethnic Chinese churches in Sydney. Since this meeting was organized by the English tract of the association, nearly all the participants were pastors and church leaders of the English congregations in the ethnic Chinese churches. This was the impression I gathered from the discussion. According to my observation, there is little change in the situation in the last decade.

4. Bible verses quoted are from the NRSV unless specified otherwise.

5. Both Longenecker and Pao have a good summary of different proposals. See Longenecker, *Acts*, 802–5, and Pao, "Waiters or Preachers," 127–44n4.

6. See Bruce, *Acts*, 120; Bock, *Acts*, 258. Barrett argues that some Hellenists may assimilate well with the heathen environment and thus have tension with the strictly observant Jews. Barrett, *Acts*, 308–9.

7. Nicolaus is identified as the proselyte of Antioch (v. 5) and there is no mention of the other six regarding their ethnicity and place of origin. This highly suggests that they are not gentile, otherwise they would be specified. For further discussion, see Barrett, *Acts*, 304. Haenchen provides a detailed discussion on this issue and asserts that the Hellenists are Jews from the diaspora. Haenchen, *Acts of Apostles*, 267–68.

places to attend the festival celebration in Jerusalem who became followers of Jesus and stayed at the church in Jerusalem (Acts 2).[8] The deliberate mention of Nicolaus, a proselyte of Antioch (v. 5) indicates that the rest of the Seven could be Jewish in origin rather than gentile, notwithstanding their Greek names.[9] On the other hand, the inauguration of the gentile mission appears later in Acts 10. Hellenists have a hybrid culture of typical diaspora Jews; they may have a different view on the temple and Torah, whereas the predominantly Aramaic-speaking Palestinian Jews adhered more to the Hebrew tradition.[10] The term "Hebrews" may also indicate a sense of superiority or purity in tradition since the other two appearances of it refer to Paul's defense of his Hebrew heritage and purity (2 Cor 11:22 and Phil 3:5). The deliberate use of these highly cultural connoted terms, in verse 1b, in describing both groups alludes that the core of the problem is cross-cultural conflict.[11] Since the "Hebrews" are great in number and hold leadership in the Jerusalem church there may also be a conflict between a majority group and a minority group.

In response to the complaint of the Hellenists, the leaders (the Twelve) of the church called together the congregation to resolve this conflict.[12] Eventually, seven Hellenists were chosen and appointed to manage the problem. Consequently, further expansion of the church was reported

---

8. I use the term "church" to identify the community of followers of Jesus in Jerusalem for the sake of convenience.

9. It is common for Jews to have Greek names, especially Greek-speaking Jews. See Nagel, "Twelve," 119, and Fitzmyer, *Acts*, 350. Both, however, suggest it is highly possible that Hellenists are Diaspora Jews.

10. The accusation to Stephen in Acts 6:11–14 reflects such a probability. In addition, the passing remark "all except the apostles were scattered throughout the countryside of Judea and Samaria" (8:1b) hints that the apostles—Palestinian Jews—survived well in this persecution until Acts 12. The severe persecution of Palestinian Jewish believers started after the inauguration of the gentile mission. The inclusion of gentiles into the community of the "people of God" could be seen as a threat to the privilege of ethnic Jews being "the people of God."

11. Juedes, "Deacons," 274–75.

12. The term "the Twelve" only appears here in Acts and is used in Acts deliberately to refer to a "special group of disciples" in which eleven of them were named in Acts 1:13 and the replacement Matthias was elected and added to fulfill the number of twelve in 2:14. They were directly linked with Jesus. See Barrett, *Acts*, 305, 310–11. Their leadership was also made explicit when they gathered the whole community and proposed the solution.

(Acts 6:7). This forms an *inclusio* structure that defines this narrative as a discrete entity and signifies a new chapter of Christian missions.[13]

Acts 6 has a similar context to the ethnic Chinese church in Sydney. The cross-cultural conflict is evident in the narrative setting—the "Hellenists" and "Hebrews" have the same ethnic origin (Jewish) but distinctive cultures. Similarly, ethnic Chinese churches are predominantly ethnic Chinese with different cultures—the Chinese-speaking first-generation migrants who adhere more to the culture from where they came and the English-speaking second-generation ethnic Chinese group who is highly influenced by and has adopted the Australian culture. The narrative serves well as an example for Chinese churches' leadership in managing the cross-cultural conflict in their congregations. I believe that the strategies employed by the leaders (the Twelve) in Acts could open possibilities for contemporary ethnic Chinese churches in Australia in handling this issue.

Inconsistency in the Narrative

There exist some inconsistencies between this narrative and other parts of Acts. First, the conflict seems to have originated from an unfair treatment of the Hellenist widows in the daily supply of food. However, there is no mention of scarcity of necessity so far in Acts; instead, it is clearly spelled out in the previous chapter that, "There was not a needy person among them, for as many as owned lands or houses sold them and brought the proceeds of what was sold. They laid it at the apostles' feet, and it was distributed to each as any had need" (Acts 4:34–35). "To hold goods for common" is one of the characteristics of the nascent Christian community. In addition, different cultures and languages do not appear to be barriers to the development of the church but rather something to be celebrated implicitly in Acts (Acts 2). There is also no detail of this conflict described here. Luke just abruptly introduces the Hellenists and their complaints.[14] As Spencer puts it,

---

13. For further discussion, see the following sections.

14. I concur with most scholars to use Luke in identifying the author of Luke-Acts for convenience and by no means argue the authenticity of authorship since the identity of the author does not impact the discussion here. On the other hand, the common authorship of the Gospel of Luke and Acts is assumed in line with major scholarly consent. It is hard to deny the literary connection between the two.

Acts 6:1 marks an abrupt shift in the Lucan account of the developing church of Jerusalem. A community characterized by extraordinary unity and generosity in the face of external persecution suddenly exhibits signs of internal division and deficiency.[15]

It is certainly an anti-climax to the narration so far.

Second, this narrative has been frequently considered as an inauguration and justification for the office of the deacon. The noun διάκονος for deacon does not appear here. Instead, the related noun διακονία (serving, service) and verb διακονέω (to serve at the table) are used to describe the task of fulfilling the needs of the Hellenists' widows and as a resolution to the conflict. It is hard to imagine the inauguration of the office of deacon without mentioning the term διάκονος.[16]

Third, since the task of administration is put in contrast to the ministry of the word in Luke-Acts (v. 2 and Luke 10:38–42), it is reasonable for other people, apart from the Twelve, to be appointed to serve at the table (administer distribution of resources) in response to the complaint. Consequently, seven people who all bear Greek names are elected. Barrett suggests that they are from the group of Hellenists.[17] One would expect more deliberation on the consequence of this appointment and the fate of Hellenist widows. They, however, are not mentioned anymore in Acts but are abandoned again! This is not good storytelling.[18] Subsequently, only two, Stephen and Philip, out of the Seven are mentioned, they continue to play a major role in the narrative but more as preachers and evangelists rather than administrators of the resources. Is it not the aim of appointing the Seven to relieve the administrative role of the Twelve and allow them to concentrate on the ministry of the word?

Finally, the selection criteria for the Seven are explicit: "good standing, full of Spirit and Wisdom.." When describing Stephen, Luke retaliates the quality of "a man full of faith and the Holy Spirit." Some argue that these are important qualities for people managing "ministry of practical

---

15. Spencer, "Neglected Widows," 715.

16. Barrett, *Acts*, 304.

17. Barrett argues that a Greek name is not conclusive proof for the Seven to be Hellenists since Greek names were also popular in Palestine because of Hellenization. He, however, agrees that the possibility of the Seven coming from the Hellenists is high. Barrett, *Acts*, 314.

18. Barrett, *Acts*, 306.

care in the life of the church."[19] However, in comparison with the criteria of electing Matthias—a replacement of the Twelve, Luke only mentions "accompanied them from the beginning and a witness to Jesus' resurrection" (Acts 1:21–26). Certainly, the office of the Twelve is a higher authority in leadership in this narrative corresponding to the Seven. Why are the criteria for electing Seven higher than that of the Twelve? To resolve these difficulties, some argue that there is no clear delineation of duties between these two groups.[20] It is, however, not evident in this narrative. In contrast, the Twelve always take the lead.

Are these inconsistencies a consequence of Luke's careless recording?[21] Or an imperfect redaction of different sources?[22] Or does Luke have something to say that goes beyond the narrative?

The Function of Acts 6:1–7 in Acts

Marshall argues that Luke is not only a historian but also a theologian. He has the intention of exploring/evangelizing the nature of God and the church in his writings. Thus, the narrative in Acts is not only a record of the development of the Jesus movement, but also serves Luke's special theological intention.[23] This section seeks to explore how Luke utilizes Acts 6:1–7 to illustrate two of his theological intentions, hoping that may shed light on the above inconsistencies.

1. Care for the Minority

Despite facing persecution of some prominent leaders (Acts 4) and an incidence of sin (Acts 5),[24] there is no record of disagreement among disciples

19. Peterson, *Acts*, 233. See also Bruce, *Acts*, 120–21, and Brock, *Acts*, 260.
20. Witherington, *Acts*, 250. Krodel, *Acts*, 6134.
21. As Pao observes, "Almost all proposed explanations appear to assume, however, that this seeming inconsistency is the result of Luke's careless writing." Pao, "Waiters or Preachers," 129.
22. Barrett asserts multiple sources of Acts. The two main ones are from the Jerusalem tradition and the Antiochene tradition. The appointment of the Seven falls into the Antiochene tradition. Barrett, *Acts*, 52.
23. Marshall, *Acts*, 34–42. A detailed treatment of this discussion can be found in Marshall, *Luke*, 21–52.
24. The Ananias and Sapphira incident may be regarded as a minor hiccup of evil that exists in the community. The church, however, reacts swiftly. No disagreement in

of Jesus. The church is united and the number of Jesus's followers increased. Abruptly, Luke paints a picture of disaccord. A little error in administration led to a sharp confrontation between the two groups, the Hellenists and Hebrews. Is this a disparity in theology/practice? Or Luke's deliberate purpose of illustrating something deeper? It is worth investigating the incident in more detail.

Regardless, some well-off widows, like Judith in the apocryphal book of Judith, bear the connotation of being poor, underprivileged, victims of violence, and being exploited in the Jewish tradition.[25] God, however, always specially cares for and protects them. At the same time, doing justice for the widows reflects the just nature of God. As Spencer says, "Into a deprivation of economic, practical, social, or emotional assistance created by either absent or abusive male's steps God the 'father of orphans and protector of widows' (Ps. 68:5; cf. 146:9; Prov. 15:25; Jer. 49:11)."[26] Therefore, in the Jewish tradition, the responsibility of care for the widows who have not had family support rests upon the shoulder of the "People of God."[27] Similarly, the Lukan Jesus frequently interacts with and cares for widows. Simultaneously, they also play a role in his ministry (e.g., Luke 2:36–38;7:11–17;18:1–8; 21:1–4). There were Jewish widows from the diaspora who returned to Jerusalem to spend the rest of their lives, hoping they could be buried there. Despite their inculturation with gentile culture (mainly Greek), they have a strong sense of Jewishness and are in close contact with the temple.[28] Since they have no support from the family locally, the responsibility of care and support for them would be taken up by the Jerusalem community via the temple. When these widows come to faith in Jesus, the ambiguous relationship between the church and temple may jeopardize their support. Then, the church would inherit the responsibility of caring for them. These diaspora widows constitute the Hellenist widows in Acts 6. On the other hand, caring for the needy is depicted as one of the primary distinctions of the church in line with "devot[ing] themselves to the apostles' teaching and fellowship" and worship (Acts 2:40–42).

---

handling the issue is recorded.

25. Spencer, "Neglected Widows," 720.

26. Spencer, "Neglected Widows," 721. Galpaz-Feller has a detailed discussion on widows in the Bible and the responsibility of the Jewish community. Galpaz-Feller, "Widow," 231–53.

27. Aung provides a concise summary of the history of care for widows in the Jewish community. Aung, "Abandoned Widows," 161–74.

28. Marshall, *Acts*, 126.

Unexpectedly, the Hellenist widows are neglected by the Hebrew leadership. The problem may arise from the rapid growth of the congregation that the leaders are unable to administer support equally, or the cultural gap between the Hellenists and Hebrews breeds miscommunication and eventually neglect. This is a classic case of cross-cultural conflict. The complaint could be seen as a rebellious action against the existing leaders. As Keener explains, "those with political power generally repressed complaining minorities,"[29] and a disastrous consequence that splits the community could result. Fortunately, the Hebrew leadership does not go down this path. Instead, they treat the complaint seriously and react swiftly to resolve it. Even though a happy ending, "and what they said pleased the whole multitude ... and the word of God increased; and the number of the disciples multiplied greatly ..." (vv. 5, 7), concludes the narrative, there are, however, some riddles that remain unresolved.

First, the Twelve's attitude towards the neglected widows' needs was ambiguous. In verse 2, "it is not right that we should give up preaching the word of God to serve tables," they seem to trivialize the widows' needs. Second, the neglected widows are unheard of afterward. Lastly, there is no mention of the Seven's work of administration but instead Stephen and Philip are depicted as apologists and evangelists like the Twelve. Highly plausible, Luke's interest rests on other things rather than the neglected widows.[30] I suggest that Luke is more focused on the attitude of the leadership rather than the needs of the widows. One would observe that the majority of the narrative is devoted to the reaction of leadership and the consequence of their actions (vv.2–7) and the only speech is from the Twelve (vv. 2–4), whereas the neglected widows remain silent. It is unusual for an organization to focus on the needs of a minority group, especially if they have been labelled as dissenting. It is always the needs of the majority that come first. The Twelve depicted in this narrative, however, do not neglect their complaint, but instead recognize their need and hand "the whole system over to the offended minority that had felt marginalized."[31] This action not only affirms the importance of the Hellenists but also delegates power to their leaders. From this point onward, the Hellenists (Stephen and Philip)

---

29. Keener, *Bible Background*, 334.

30. Reactional critics suggest numerous reactional intentions of Luke, such as he wants to whitewash the conflict between two streams of early Christianity, introducing Stephen, and a turning point to the gentile mission. See Spencer, "Neglected Widows," 715–17.

31. Keener, *Bible Background*, 334.

take the stage to become the main characters of the narrative. This is also a turning point from Jerusalem to Samaria and onto the world (Acts 1:8) and fulfills the commission and prediction of Jesus. I suggest one of Luke's theological intentions is to accentuate the church as an inclusive community and that the needs of the minority should be taken care of. This intention is also explicit in view of the table fellowship motif in the narrative.

Acts 6:1–6 is set in the silhouette of an eating scene. Even though one may argue that τῇ διακονίᾳ τῇ καθημερινῇ does not specifically allude to table fellowship but rather to the distribution of food/necessities; it is about helping the poor financially since τραπέζαις in διακονεῖν τραπέζαις (v. 2) is used to refer to a banker's counter. Luke, however, utilizes the term τραπέζαις in meal settings frequently (Luke 16:21; 22:21; 22:30; Acts 16:34); he only uses it once to refer to a banker's counter (Luke 19:23).[32] Will the core problem of Acts 6:1–7 be an issue of table fellowship and acceptance of the Hellenist widows? Are they not welcomed in the table fellowship of the church? If one looks at Luke-Acts, the theme of table fellowship emerges recurrently. The Lukan Jesus always eats with the wrong sort of people (sinners, tax collectors, and prostitutes) and is rebuked by the Hebrew authority (Luke 5:30; 7:36; 15:2). They regard Jesus's action as a trespass to the Hebrew custom of boundary reinforcing through table fellowship.[33] The underlying issue is exclusiveness against inclusiveness. The Hebrew authority uses a choice of meal companions as a boundary marker to exclude gentiles and exert their identity as people of God,[34] whereas Jesus invites all those outcasted, marginalized, and unworthy people to the meal table, illustrating the inclusiveness of the eschatological kingdom of God. As Kelley states,

> In various cultures underlying the New Testament, dining with someone indicated solidarity with that person. To eat with is to identify with. To take a meal with another was to offer that individual the right hand of fellowship in the deepest sense of the term. Meal fellowship—what an appropriate image for an incarnational Christianity."[35]

---

32. Pao thoroughly discusses this point and concludes that Acts 6 refers to a meal setting. Pao, "Waiters or Preachers," 135–37.

33. Both Neyrey and Finger provide a good discussion on meals as a cultural symbol and the significance of table fellowship in boundary making, especially in reference to the purity code of the Jews. Neyrey, "Ceremonies," 361–87. Finger, *Widows and Meals*, 169–82.

34. This is also reflected in the rebuke of the religious leaders to the Lukan Jesus's wrong choice of meal companions (Luke 5:30; 15:2).

35. Kelley, "Meals with Jesus," 123.

On the other hand, table fellowship and teaching are invariably linked together in Luke. Jesus teaches during mealtime (Luke 5:27–39, 7:36–50, 22:14–30).[36] Thus the ministry of the "word" intertwines with table fellowship. The reason for the Hellenists' widows to be excluded from the table fellowship or teaching of the Hebrew leadership remains unsolved. It may be the difference in eating culture or even theology that divides the Hellenists and Hebrews,[37] or the Hellenist widows have not had the language or knowledge to understand the teaching of the Twelve. There is no further information provided in the text. It seems Luke is not interested in what happens to them later! I suggest that the real issue at stake here is the exclusion of the minority (Hellenists' widows) in the fellowship of the disciples rather than the needs of the Hellenists' widows. The narrative juxtaposes two uneven groups, the Hebrews being the majority and the Hellenists the minority. The Hebrew leadership (the Twelve) has a closer relationship with the founder of the faith—Jesus—and is depicted as the authority bearer. They make the final decision. The Hellenists, the minority, are dissident and unsatisfied with the situation. Instead of fostering a picture of power struggle, through selecting the Seven, Luke asserts the leadership accepts and cares for the needs of the minority. It is further accentuated by using the widows as the minority of the minority, underprivileged and neglected ones. The whole narrative conveys Luke's theological intention of care for the minority. This assertion is in line with the Lukan Jesus who always cares for the marginalized.

2. Leadership Succession

Whether the Seven are appointed as "waiters at the table" or "preachers" attracts lots of scholarly attention since Stephen and Philip are depicted more as preachers and evangelists after Acts 6 rather than administrators. Panning suggests that the Seven are appointed to the task of "relieving work" just as Acts describes, whereas the Twelve retain the ministry of the word. Stephen's preaching and Philip's evangelistic work are only circumstantial, and both ministries are not mutually exclusive.[38] Similarly, Nagel argues

---

36. It is common for ancient philosophers to utilize mealtimes to teach. See Kelley, "Meals with Jesus," 128.

37. Haenchen provides a good summary of scholarship development in identifying the two groups and the rivalry theology. Haenchen, *Acts of Apostles*, 264–69.

38. Panning, "Acts 6," 17.

that Luke's theological focus in Acts is "the spreading of the word." The administrative work of the Seven is not outside this primary responsibility of the church.[39] The question, however, to be asked is why there is no further mention of the administrative duties of the Seven, which is supposed to be their primary task. To answer this question, it may be worthwhile to investigate the differences and similarities between the Twelve and the Seven.

The Twelve is a closed group selected by a higher authoritative figure—Jesus. They have a special relationship and knowledge of the earthly Jesus. They are not only the witnesses to the event of salvation but also "their teaching and piety constituted for him the rule which continued to guide the faith and life of that community in whose history the salvation of God is worked out (Acts 2:42)."[40] The selection process and criteria for them are not mentioned, it totally relies on the sovereignty of Jesus, it is a once-off historical event, and could not be repeated. So, their special status and "privilege in the history of God's salvation" is undeniable.[41] The election of Matthias to make complete the Twelve, thus, becomes an urgent task for them (1:16–26), whereas the Seven are elected via a democratic process and based on their merits (6:3). Despite their difference, there exist numerous similarities between the two. The Twelve are chosen by Jesus and promised the coming and filling of the Holy Spirit (1:4–5). Likewise, one of the qualifications of the Seven is "full of the Spirit" (6:3), while Stephen, the main character, is described explicitly as "a man full of faith and the Holy Spirit" (6:5) straight after this. The Twelve are given the power and authority over all demons and to cure diseases, and Jesus sent them out to preach the kingdom of God and to heal (Luke 9:1–2). The same pattern of ministry is repeated in the narrative of Philip in Samaria (Acts 8). Considering the narrative flow of Acts, a clear direction of change of locality is depicted. From Jerusalem to all Judea and Samaria, and to the ends of the earth (1:6). This move is accomplished by different main characters. In Jerusalem, it is the Twelve, whereas in Samaria, it is the Seven or at least two of the Seven.[42] Regardless of the different personages, the mission, however, remains the same—"be Jesus'

---

39. Nagel asserts, "Luke's emphasis on the Word of God as the primary doer in the Acts of the Apostles may help to explain why the Seven are not outside the ministry of the Word by their designation 'to serve tables,' any more than the Twelve had been, as is confirmed by what we are later told of Stephen and Philip." Nagel, "Twelve," 119.

40. Wall, "Successors," 630–31.

41. Wall, "Successors," 631.

42. Except for Cornelius's incident (Acts 10), Peter's escape (Acts 12), and the Jerusalem council (Acts 15).

witnesses" (1:8). From the above discussion, it is evident that the Twelve and the Seven are two different distinct groups with different origins and occupy different stages of the development of the church, however, they carry out the same ministry in sequence, thus forming a continuum of the grand narrative of Acts. This is a familiar pattern of leadership transition from first-generation leaders to second-generation leaders in a movement. First generation leaders are appointed/ordained by a special authoritative figure/deity whereas second-generation leaders are appointed/elected based on their merits. Regardless of their difference in formation, they carry the same mission and form a continuum of the movement. In addition, there are numerous similarities between Acts 6 and the Old Testament succession stories (Exod 18:13–27; Num 11:1–30; Deut 1:9–18). Vocabularies like "appoint καταστήσομεν," "chose ἐξελέξαντο," and "laid their hands ἐπέθηκαν αὐτοῖς τὰς χεῖρας" in Acts 6 are reminiscent of a delegation/commissioning/ordination scenario.[43] As Barrett argues, "it is however probably true that the story embodies the method of appointing ministers that was familiar to Luke himself: popular choice, approval by those already ministers, and the laying on of hands."[44] I suggest it is a succession story of church leadership in disguise. Luke utilizes this conflict story to disguise a succession narrative in the propagation of salvation history.[45]

From the above analysis of the text, we conclude that two of the functions of Acts 6 are care of the marginalized and succession of ministry to the Hellenists. How do these shed light on the ethnic Chinese church in Australia?

What Is That to the Ethnic Chinese Churches in Australia?

1. Care for the Minority

Since most of the ethnic Chinese churches in Australia were established by first-generation migrants from Hong Kong in the eighties and nineties of last century, they form the majority of the congregation. Comparatively, the second-generation or newly arrived members from mainland China

---

43. Nagel, "Twelve," 118–19.
44. Barrett, *Acts*, 304.
45. As Timothy-Johnson puts it, "The very disjointedness of the account is, therefore, the best evidence that Luke's main preoccupation was in establishing this transition of leadership." Timothy-Johnson, *Acts*, 111.

are the minority. The leadership usually remains in the majority group and the leadership style resembles their place of origin, despite some adaptations to the Australian context that have been made. Most of the ministries are geared toward the needs of this majority group and, consequently, the needs of the minority may be neglected. The situation is accentuated by the cultural differences and language barrier. The minority group may have the feeling of being a second-class citizen. Considering Acts 6, leaders should address the needs of the minority group and equip themselves to work in a cross-cultural context. The language barrier is always the first obstacle in cross-cultural communication. In the case of the ethnic Chinese churches in Sydney, Cantonese is the most popular language. Leadership, however, needs to familiarize themselves with the language of the minority group—English or Mandarin. In addition, leaders should enhance their metacognition which consists of understanding of their own cognition and culture and, at the same time, the differences with the minority group, for example, the preference of collective and individual personality, class and equality, honor and shame culture, openness and closeness of communication style, and differences in facing conflict.[46]

Table fellowship emphasized in Acts 6 connotes acceptance. With the enhancement of cultural competency, leaders could have more understanding of the uniqueness of the minority group's culture or subculture. Concurrently, they could recognize the differences between themselves and the minority group. It, however, does not automatically resolve the cross-cultural conflict between groups. Leaders should have the determination of accepting the differences of the minor group while not giving up their own culture uncritically. They should emphasize a common culture—Christian culture—and celebrate their differences in love and acceptance. As Richardson puts, "As leaders of all backgrounds are working in increasingly diverse settings, organizations are being challenged to ensure that they reflect the diversity of the communities that they serve and are equitable and inclusive to all stakeholders."[47]

---

46. After interviewing both first-generation Chinese-speaking migrant pastors and second-generation English-speaking pastors regarding cross-cultural conflict, Chu suggests that enhancement of metacognition is a possible way forward for managing cross-cultural conflict. Chu, *Intercultural Competence*, 242–57.

47. Richardson, "Ethics of Inclusion," 59.

2. Succession of Leadership

From Chu's observation, it is not uncommon for second-generation English-speaking pastors, usually younger, to feel that the first-generation migrant leaders have not empowered them, and this leads to much frustration and conflict.[48] The problem could be on both sides. The younger second-generation English-speaking pastors growing up in a Western culture get used to open dialogue and positive reinforcement culture. They tend to be more adventurous and willing to try new strategies in ministries but, at the same time, lack experience that makes them unaware of the possible negative side of the move. In contrast, first-generation migrant leaders have grown up in a predominantly Chinese culture. They tend to be more reserved and conservative, with open encouragement and praise not familiar to them. Consequently, cultural differences between these two groups lead to conflict at church. The younger pastors may think that they have not been trusted as lots of their new ideas are banned by the senior leaders. They see that senior leaders do not dare to try new strategies but always focus on the negative side of them. Besides, they are looking for open dialogue when their opinions differ, which, unfortunately, is usually not the case with senior leaders. Eventually, they feel their voices unheard and their efforts unrecognized. Without open dialogue, they see the church leadership operating in a black box with the senior leaders grasping tightly to power.

The first-generation migrant leaders may feel that the younger leaders are inexperienced and cannot foresee the potential danger of new moves which could be detrimental to the well-being of the church. Additionally, the Chinese culture tends to be more reserved, rather than open, and these leaders treasure a harmonious working relationship. In order not to make another party "lose face," they tend to use non-verbal hints, for example, gestures and tones, rather than open dialogues. This difference may make the senior leaders feel they have not been respected and pushed to make decisions when the younger leaders insist on having an open discussion.

In Acts 6, the apostles are willing to pass on the leadership to the Hellenists despite their cultural differences. They, however, clearly define the core of the church's mission—prayer and preaching the word. This action could be risky since the Hellenists may have a different attitude toward the Hebrew tradition (place of the temple, Torah, and Jerusalem in their faith)

---

48. Chu, *Intercultural Competence*, 1–3.

that may destroy the harmony of the nascent Christianity, however, they are willing to take the risk for the continued propagation of the gospel. Following this narrative, the focus of Acts turns to the Hellenist leaders, and they are doing exactly what the Hebrew leaders are doing—being a witness to the Lord through preaching and teaching. The consequence is that "the word of God continued to increase, and the number of the disciples multiplied greatly in Jerusalem" (6:7). This narrative encourages first-generation migrant leaders to pass on the baton to second-generation predominately English-speaking leaders or newer Mandarin-speaking migrant leaders despite the risks that may accompany the decision. However, for the continuation of the mission of the church, it is worth trying.

Bibliography

Aung, James Ha Tun. "Caring for Abandoned Widows: Reading Acts 6.1–7 Afresh." *Asia Journal of Theology* 29, no. 2 (2015) 161–74.
Barrett, C. K. *A Critical and Exegetical Commentary on the Acts of the Apostles Volume 1*. The International Critical Commentary. Edinburgh: T. & T. Clark, 1994.
Bock, Darrell L. *Acts*. Baker Exegetical Commentary on the New Testament. Grand Rapids: Baker, 2007.
Bruce, F. F. *The Book of the Acts*. New International Commentary on the New Testament. Grand Rapids: Eerdmans, 1988.
Chu, Michael K. *Intercultural Competence: Cultural Intelligence, Pastoral Leadership, and the Chinese Church*. Sydney: Morling, 2019.
Finger, Reta Halteman. *Of Widows and Meals: Communal Meals in the Book of Acts*. Grand Rapids: Eerdmans, 2007.
Fitzmyer, Joseph A. *The Acts of the Apostles*. Anchor Bible Commentary. New York: Doubleday, 1997.
Galpaz-Feller, Pnina. "The Widow in the Bible and in Ancient Egypt." *Zeitschrift für die alttestamentliche Wissenschaft* 120, no. 2 (2008) 231–53.
Haenchen, Ernst. *The Acts of Apostles*. Translated by R. McL. Wilson. Oxford: Blackwell, 1971.
Juedes, John P. "Deacons on a Mission—The Pivotal Place of Acts 6." *Lutheran Mission Matters* 26, no. 2 (2018) 273–81.
Keener, C. *The IVP Bible Background Commentary: New Testament*. Downers Grove: IVP, 1993.
Kelley, Robert L. "Meals with Jesus in Luke's Gospel." *Horizons in Biblical Theology* 17, no. 2 (1995) 123–31.
Krodel, Gehard A. *Acts*. Augsburg Commentary on the New Testament. Minneapolis: Augsburg, 1986.
Longenecker, R. N. *Acts*. The Expositor's Bible Commentary. Grand Rapids: Zondervan, 2007.
Marshall, I. Howard. *Acts*. Tyndale New Testament Commentary. Leicester: IVP, 1980.
———. *Luke: Historian and Theologian*. Leicester: IVP, 1998.

Nagel, Norman. "The Twelve and the Seven in Acts 6 and the Needy." *Concordia Journal* 31, no. 2 (2005) 113–26.
Neyrey, Jerome H., ed. "Ceremonies in Luke-Acts: The Case of Meals and Table Fellowship." In *The Social World of Luke-Acts: Models for Interpretation*, 361–87. Peabody, MA: Hendrickson, 1991.
Panning, Armin J. "Acts 6: the Ministry of the Seven." *Wisconsin Lutheran Quarterly* 93, no. 1 (1996) 11–17.
Pao, David W. "Waiters or Preachers: Acts 6:1–7 and Lukan Table Fellowship Motif." *Journal of Biblical Literature* 130, no. 1 (2011) 127–44.
Peterson, David G. *The Acts of the Apostles*. The Pillar New Testament Commentary. Grand Rapids: Eerdmans, 2009.
Richardson, Leopold A. Kimo. "The Ethics of Inclusion: A Social and Cultural Analysis of Acts 6:1–7." *Journal of Biblical Perspectives in Leadership* 11, no. 1 (2021) 59–66.
Spencer, F. Scoot. "Neglected Widows in Acts 6:1–7." *Catholic Biblical Quarterly* 56, no. 4 (1994) 715–33.
Timothy-Johnson, Luke. *The Acts of the Apostles*. Sacra Pagina. Collegeville: Liturgical, 1992.
Wall, Robert W. "Successors to 'the Twelve' According to Acts 12:1–17." *Catholic Biblical Quarterly* 53, no. 4 (1991) 628–43.
Witherington, Ben, III. *The Acts of the Apostles: A Socio-Rhetorical Commentary*. Grand Rapids: Eerdmans, 1998.

6.

Church Ministry in Light of *Munus Triplex Christi*

Wally Wang

Abstract

IF THE CHURCH IS founded upon Christ and gathered together by the Spirit, then in whatever cultural context the local church is situated, her ministry, whose sole purpose is to serve the people of God as well as to serve the Lord of the church, should be able to witness to the fact that Christ is the head of the church. Therefore, one of the fruitful ways to delineate the principle behind responsible church ministry is to explore the meaning of *munus triplex Christi*. This is because the church is called by the Spirit not only to submit to the authority of her head but also to participate in Christ's eternal threefold offices. In this article, we will start by examining the historical development of *munus triplex Christi*, including the formation of the doctrine, as well as its relationship to the Christian life. Then we will explain why this doctrine can be a good way to understand the principles behind church ministry. After that, we will explore *munus triplex Christi* in detail. From Christ's priestly office, church ministry is shown to be characterized as *for* God and *for* the world. From Christ's kingly office, church ministry is demonstrated to be a humble service serving God and serving the world.

From Christ's prophetic office, church ministry is required to be *to* the world as well as faithful *to* the Word.

Introduction

The classical marks of the church—one, holy, catholic, and apostolic—from the Nicene Creed do not provide a clear prescription for one to distinguish which church activities can be truly classified as a church ministry.[1] During the Reformation era, the marks of the church were reduced to two: preaching and sacrament.[2] However, these two marks create a tendency to reduce all other church ministries to a subservient position. Similar to the classical marks of the church, it cannot supply a clear direction for one to know what form a church ministry should take.

In the last century, Barth integrated, in his discussion of "The Doctrine of Reconciliation," Christology, soteriology, hamartiology, pneumatology, and ecclesiology into a unified whole. Central to the whole discussion is *munus triplex Christi*.[3] In recent years, Greggs has used Christ's priestly office as a means to discuss its implications for church ministry.[4] In this paper, we will follow Greggs's lead. We will first discuss the relationship between *munus triplex Christi* and church ministry. Then we will discuss the threefold office—priest, king, and prophet—in detail and draw out its implications for church ministry.

Munus Triplex Christi

Munus triplex Christi is not a Reformation invention from the sixteenth century. There is an indication that in the middle of the second century, Justin had already described Jesus as "King and Christ and Priest and

---

1. At most, one can say that negatively, church ministry should not destroy the oneness and holiness of the church, and positively, church ministry should be the same everywhere (catholicity) and agree with the apostolic teachings. This does not give a sufficient indication of what a church ministry should look like.

2. In his discussion on the visible church, Calvin asserted that "[w]herever we see the Word of God purely preached and heard, and the sacraments administered according to Christ's institution, there, it is not to be doubted, a church of God exists." Calvin, *Institutes*, IV.1.9.

3. Busch, *Great Passion*, 53.

4. Greggs, *Dogmatic Ecclesiology*.

Messenger" in his dialogue with Trypho the Jew.[5] In the fourth century, Eusebius, in his magnum opus *Ecclesiastical History*, also described Jesus as "the only high priest of all, and the only King of every creature, and the Father's only supreme prophet of prophets."[6] Besides, Peter Chrysologus and John Chrysostom mentioned Christ as king, priest, and prophet in their sermons, respectively.[7] According to Guyette and Sherman, these church fathers have no intention of developing the inner logic of Christ's threefold office or discussing it within the context of soteriology. Their main purpose is to show that Christ is the perfect fulfillment of the Old Testament types: priests, kings, and prophets.[8]

In the high Middle Ages, Thomas Aquinas mentioned in his *Summa Theologica* that ". . . Christ, as being the Head of all, has the perfection of all graces. Wherefore, as to others, one is a lawgiver, another is a priest, another is a king; but all these concur in Christ, as the fount of all grace."[9] Thomas used this as an answer to the objection that Christ could not be a priest and lawgiver at the same time. He does not elaborate further on Christ's kingly office and "prophetic office." His main concern was to discuss the high priesthood of Christ in detail because this would provide a theological foundation for his later discussion on the sacrament. Particularly in Question 63, Article 3, Thomas stated: "Now the whole rite of the Christian religion is derived from Christ's priesthood. Consequently, it is clear that the sacramental character is especially the character of Christ, to Whose character the faithful are likened by reason of the sacramental characters, which are nothing else than certain participations of Christ's Priesthood, flowing from Christ Himself."[10] Although Thomas does not fully develop the threefold office of Christ, he indicates that there is a close connection between the sacramental practices of the church and the priesthood of Christ.[11]

    5. Guyette, "Jesus," 88.
    6. Guyette, "Jesus," 89.
    7. Guyette, "Jesus," 90; Sherman, *King*, 64.
    8. Guyette, "Jesus," 88–90; Sherman, *King*, 64.
    9. Aquinas, *Summa Theologica*, III, q. 22, a. 1, ad 1.
    10. Aquinas, *Summa Theologica*, III, q. 63, a. 3.
    11. Calvin rejects the connection between the sacraments and Christ's priesthood. "The papists use these names, too, but coldly and rather ineffectually, since they do not know that each of these titles contains." Calvin, *Institutes*, II.15.1. Later on, in concluding his discussion on Christ's priesthood, Calvin states: "The more detestable is the fabrication of those who, not content with Christ's priesthood, have presumed to sacrifice

During the Swiss Reformation, Martin Bucer is the one who not just mentions *munus triplex* in his commentary but also associates the benefits of salvation with Christ's threefold office.[12] However, only in Calvin's hands does *munus triplex* become "a characteristically Reformed way of unpacking theologically the various works of the one Mediator, Christ."[13] Indeed, in the final edition of the *Institutes*, Calvin spent the whole chapter discussing Christ as prophet, king, and priest. According to Peterson, this discussion "forms a bridge between preceding and subsequent chapters of *Institutes* II," and it "was one of Calvin's ways of telling his readers not to separate the person and work of Christ."[14] Calvin uses *munus triplex Christi* to summarize the one mediator Christ and his atonement works *pro nobis*. Furthermore, in *Institute* III.1.1, Calvin stated, "the Holy Spirit is the bond by which Christ effectually unites us to himself. To this, also, pertains what we taught in the previous book concerning his anointing." By the work of the Spirit, we are united with Christ, and through this union, all the benefits of Christ's atonement work are imparted to us. This implies that who we are and what we should do as Christians is inextricably linked to Christ and his works. If *munus triplex Christi* is a summary of Christ and his works, it will have a close connection with the Christian life.

This understanding finds its clear expression in the Heidelberg Catechism, which is influenced by Calvin's Geneva Catechism.[15] In the Lord's Day 12 of the Heidelberg Catechism, question thirty-one and its answer read:

> *Why is he called "Christ," meaning "anointed"?*
>
> Because he has been ordained by God the Father and has been anointed with the Holy Spirit to be
>
> our chief prophet and teacher . . .
>
> our only high priest . . .
>
> our eternal king . . .

---

him anew! The papists attempt this each day, considering the Mass as the sacrificing of Christ." Calvin, *Institutes*, II.15.6. In other words, instead of using Christ's priestly office to inform what ministry should look like, Thomas uses it to justify the traditional practices of the church.

12. Sherman, *King*, 65.

13. Sherman, *King*, 66.

14. Peterson, *Calvin*, 60.

15. Butin, "Reformed Catechisms," 198. For a detailed discussion on the formation of the Heidelberg Catechism, please see de Boer, "Christology," 1–8.

The following question thirty-two and answer immediately turn its attention to Christians:

But why are you called a Christian?

Because by faith I am a member of Christ and so I share in his anointing.

I am anointed

to confess his name

to present . . . as a living sacrifice of thanks . . .

to reign with Christ over all creation for eternity.[16]

These two articles not only clearly explain the threefold office of Christ but also link directly to what a Christian should do. Although it does not mention the Spirit directly in question thirty-two, the implication is clear. Through the work of the Spirit, one can become a member of the body of Christ. Because of one's union with Christ, a Christian can participate in Christ's threefold office. Yet it also makes it clear that, unlike Christ, a Christian's participation is derivative and has no saving significance. Corresponding to Christ's office of prophet, a Christian is anointed to confess Christ's name, or better yet, to hold onto Christ's teachings. Corresponding to Christ's priestly office, a Christian should be anointed to live as a living sacrifice of thanks. Corresponding to Christ's kingly office, a Christian should have hope that, on Christ's return, he/she will reign with Christ.

If there is a close connection between *munus triplex Christi* and Christian living, can one say the same for church ministry? Can it provide a guide for the church to determine what shape her ministry should take? To begin with, we need to have a proper understanding of how Christ relates to his church. Traditionally, there exist two extremes. The first extreme believes that the church is completely identical to Christ. This understanding eliminates the uniqueness of Christ and elevates the church to become the sole mediator between God and people in this world. It confuses Christ and his church. The second extreme says that the church has nothing to do with the risen Christ, who is now sitting at the right hand of the Father. The church is a creation of the Spirit. Yet this view has a hard time distinguishing between the Spirit and human spirits.[17] In the end, the church is simply

---

16. "Heidelberg Catechism."
17. According to John 15:26–27, the work of the Spirit is to lead people towards

the result of human works. Both extremes fail to express clearly the close and yet asymmetric relationship between Christ and his church—Christ is the foundation on which his church builds. For our purpose, following Paul's use in his Epistles, we employ "the body of Christ" as a proper description of the church.[18]

This concept—the church as the body of Christ—has the following implications. First, just as the body cannot live without its head, this concept expresses the close relationship between Christ and his church—the church cannot *be* without her Lord. At the same time, just as the head is distinct from and superior to the body, this clearly expresses Christ's superiority over his church. The church is absolutely dependent upon Christ. Second, as we have cited before, Calvin states the church can be seen as the result of applying the saving work *pro nobis* via the Spirit. By the work of the Spirit, we are not only united with Christ vertically but also united with each other horizontally. Therefore, the church is the creature of the Word and the Spirit.[19] Third, because the church is joined to her Lord through the Spirit, the benefits of Christ's work of atonement flow naturally to her. In other words, the church participates passively in the life of Christ. Therefore, the church is called "one, holy, and catholic" in the Nicene Creed. Fourth, the church is also called "apostolic" in the creed. She, as the body of Christ, is commissioned by Christ and sent out in the power of the Spirit to be a faithful witness of her head. This does not mean that she can replace Christ and do Christ's own works. Rather, as Christ continues to carry out his threefold office at the right hand of the Father, she is given the right to actively participate in Christ's own works through the power of the Spirit.[20] If this is the case, and if the church wants to be a faithful witness to her head, her ministry must be regulated and shaped by the *munus triplex Christi*.[21]

Christ; hence, it becomes the Reformed teaching that Christ and his Spirit are inseparable in God's economic work. By eliminating Christ, one loses the way to differentiate the Spirit from other spirits.

18. Ladd, *Theology*, 590–92. Pace Ladd, we consider this not just a metaphor but a proper theological concept.

19. Webster, *Holy Scripture*, 44–46.

20. For a detailed discussion, please see Greggs, *Dogmatic Ecclesiology*, 82–92.

21. A word of caution: *munus triplex Christi* is a theological construct. It cannot become an abstract principle standing on its own. Its meaning must be bound with Scripture. "[I]t offers considerable resources to the church for understanding the relationship of Christ to the people and history of Israel. The key to its use lies in resisting the temptation to over-schematise this concept." Johnson, "Servant Lord," 173. For the modern objections to use this concept and their responses, please see Stroup, "Relevance," 22–32.

Before discussing the *munus triplex Christi* and its implications for church ministry, two things need to be clarified. First, according to *The Westminster Larger Catechism* question forty-two and its answer,[22] Christ's threefold office is not limited to his earthly ministry. Christ is forever to be priest, king, and prophet. Second, one cannot treat Christ's threefold office as three separate offices independent from each other. Even though they can be distinguished from each other, they also depend upon each other. However, this does not imply the threefold office has an internal logical order. Rather, they provide three different angles for us to look at the richness of Christ's works. Similarly, as the church participates in Christ's threefold office, she will not have three different independent ministries. Rather, she will have one single ministry—witnessing—expressible in three distinguishable aspects.

Priestly Office of Christ

The Westminster Larger Catechism question forty-four and its answer read as:

> *How doth Christ execute the office of a priest?*
>
> Christ executes the office of a priest, in his once offering himself a sacrifice without spot to God, to be a reconciliation for the sins of his people; and in making continual intercession for them.

It teaches that on the cross, Christ, as the priest, offers himself up as the perfect sacrifice to be the expiation of our sins. Furthermore, Christ's priestly work is not terminated on the cross. He forever becomes our intercessor before the Father.[23]

The uniqueness of Christ's priestly office can be seen in comparison to the Old Testament priesthood.[24] In the Old Testament, the whole sacrificial system has to be understood from the perspective of the covenant relationship between God and Israel. When God enters into a covenant relationship with Israel, he provides them with this sacrificial system so

---

22. "Q. 42. *Why was our Mediator called Christ?* A. Our Mediator was called Christ, because he was anointed with the Holy Ghost above measure; and so set apart, and fully furnished with all authority and ability, to execute the offices of prophet, priest, and king of his church, in the estate both of his humiliation and exaltation." "Westminster Larger Catechism."

23. For a detailed biblical description, see Greggs, *Dogmatic Ecclesiology*, 54–68.

24. For a detailed discussion, see Sherman, *King*, 181–86.

that sinful Israel can live in front of the Holy God. It is a gracious provision from God for his people. Within this sacrifice system, the priest is playing the role of mediator between God and his people. The priest represents the people offering sacrifices to God, and God blesses the people through him. However, the Old Testament priest is not the perfect mediator; he is a member of sinful Israel. Before he can be the priest for the people, he has to offer up a sacrifice for his own sin (Lev 16:6, 11; Heb 7:27). In comparison, Christ Jesus is the Son incarnate—the very man and the very God. He does not need to offer a sacrifice for himself because he is sinless. Instead, he offers himself up as the perfect sacrifice for all humanity. He is the priest and the sacrificial lamb at the same time. Most importantly, after he has finished the atoning work on the cross, he does not leave us alone. He becomes our "everlasting intercessor: through his pleading we obtain favour."[25]

It is obvious that no one, including the church, will be able to do the priestly work of Christ. Yet Calvin maintains that Christ "receive[s] us as his companions in this great office" and we "are priests in him . . . freely enter the heavenly sanctuary that the sacrifices of prayers and praise that we bring may be acceptable and sweet-smelling before God."[26] As we are made accessible to the heavenly sanctuary through our everlasting intercessor, our priestly works, according to Calvin, consist of offering up praise and thanksgiving to God. As a result, if the church participates in Christ's priestly office, her ministry should always be marked by praise to God. Besides this vertical dimension, does the church's participation in Christ's priestly work have a horizontal dimension?

After Gregg has done a detailed study of how Christ as the priest is described in the New Testament, he proceeds to single out the ontological mode of Christ's priesthood. Gregg states that:

> The essence of this form is the full (and obedient) orientation towards God simultaneous to a life lived for the sake of the world: priesthood is the simultaneity of, and the meeting point of, the twofold commandment of Christ, which rests on loving God and neighbour simultaneously . . . His priestliness is the non-competitive

---

25. Calvin, *Institutes*, II.15.6. Beyond Calvin's twofold work—reconciliation and intercession—of Christ the priest, Greggs identifies the following: mediation, sacrifice, bearing iniquity, intercession, oblation, blessing, and holiness *for*, not *from*. Greggs, *Dogmatic Ecclesiology*, 68–78.

26. Calvin, *Institutes*, II.15.6.

meeting of those two orderings, as a life lived not towards itself (in the *cor incurvatum in se*) but outwards beyond itself."[27]

Therefore, in the liberating power of the Spirit, the church's participation in Christ's priestly office means that negatively she is not living for its own sake, and that positively she participates in these two orderings: *for* God and *for* the world. The implications for church ministry are unmistakable. If the church performs certain activities, and if her purpose or goal is to preserve her own existence or to serve her own interests, these activities can never be called church ministry. Positively, on the one hand, her ministry should be oriented towards God. As Calvin taught us, whatever she does should be characterized by praise and thanksgiving. Her ministry, on the other hand, should be entirely for the benefit of the world. This means that whatever she does or says should be a faithful witness of the Father's love toward the world.

Kingly Office of Christ

The Westminster Larger Catechism question forty-five and its answer read as:

How doth Christ execute the office of a king?

Christ executes the office of a king, in calling out of the world a people to himself, and giving them officers, laws, and censures, by which he visibly governs them; in bestowing saving grace upon his elect, rewarding their obedience, and correcting them for their sins, preserving and supporting them under all their temptations and sufferings, restraining and overcoming all their enemies, and powerfully ordering all things for his own glory, and their good; and also in taking vengeance on the rest, who know not God, and obey not the gospel.

Christ's reign consists of the following. First, He rules over His people (or His church), who are called out from the world. Second, He rules over His church via two means. On the one hand, He governs her via visible means: scripture and ministers. On the other hand, He intervenes via His Spirit directly in His people's hearts. Third, He leads, preserves, and protects His church through dangers and toils. Fourth, His ruling is for the sake of His own glory as well as for the benefit of His church. Implicit in this teaching, Christ is the sovereign Lord of the whole world.

27. Greggs, *Dogmatic Ecclesiology*, 68.

To unpack the significance of Christ's kingly office, we need to review the Old Testament understanding of Israel's kingship.[28] In Moses's speech before Israel entered the promised land, he laid out what Israel's kingship should look like (Deut 17:14–20). This king should be one of the Israelites. His rule should not serve to advance his own wealth and interests. He should rule according to God's commands laid down in the *Torah*. He should not consider himself above his people. The implications are clear. Yahweh is the true king of Israel. Israel's king is not an autonomous king, ruling according to his own wishes. He is the deputy of the true King Yahweh.[29] He has to rule under God's commands. Therefore, he has to rule his people with justice. Particularly, he has to show kindness toward the poor, the widows, and the foreigners within Israel. Moreover, he has the duty to maintain the proper worship of Yahweh.[30] It is obvious that none of the kings of Israel are able to live up to this standard set by Moses.

However, Christ's kingly office transcends even the ideal Old Testament kingship. According to Calvin, Christ's kingly office is eternal, not temporal like that of an earthly king. Further, it consists of two aspects. First, Christ is the eternal protector of his church. Even the archenemy, "the devil, with all the resources of the world, can never destroy the church."[31] Second, Christ is the generous ruler over each individual Christian. "He rules . . . more for our own sake than his."[32] By his Spirit, he "will never leave us destitute, but will provide for our needs until, our warfare ended, we are called to triumph. Such is the nature of his rule, that he shares with us all that he has received from the Father."[33] Through Christ our King, all of God's riches will be given to us, enabling us to live a life pleasing to the Father. Most significantly, Christ, together with the Father, is the sovereign Lord of the whole world. Calvin states: "And surely, to say that he sits at the right hand of the Father is equivalent to calling him the Father's deputy, who has in his possession the whole power of God's dominion."[34] On the one hand, "Christ's kingship is not absolute,"[35] because he rules with the Father.

---

28. For a brief survey of the history of Israel's kings, see Sherman, *King*, 132–35.
29. Sherman, *King*, 136.
30. Sherman, *King*, 137.
31. Calvin, *Institutes*, II.15.3.
32. Calvin, *Institutes*, II.15.4.
33. Calvin, *Institutes*, II.15.4.
34. Calvin, *Institutes*, II.15.5.
35. Sherman, *King*, 68.

On the other hand, unlike an earthly king ruling under God's commands, Christ rules with the Father's full authority. Even though Christ's lordship is deeply hidden at present, Calvin believes that its "full proof will appear at the Last Judgment, which may also be properly considered the last act of his reign"[36] before Christ hands the lordship back to the Father (1 Cor 15:24, 28). In response to this, Calvin suggests that either as an individual or as the church, we should have "hope for blessed immortality,"[37] that we should live a fruitful life to glorify God,[38] and that we should "direct our obedience with the greatest eagerness to the divine will."[39]

Even though Christ's kingship is unique, Christians can participate in Christ's rule through the power of his Spirit. This does not mean that we can do what Jesus does. We cannot be the protectors of the church. We will never be able to give spiritual blessings to others. We will never have the Father's authority. To understand what participation in Christ's kingly office entitles us to, we need to discover the ontological mode of Christ's kingly office. In Christ's teaching, he redefined leadership in terms of servanthood (Mark 9:35) and he described his ministry as serving (Mark 10:45). From this, we infer that Christ's kingly office consists of twofold service. Christ serves God faithfully so that he can serve people without reserve. In the vertical dimension, Christ serves God faithfully by obedience to the divine will, even to death on the cross. In the horizontal dimension, Christ serves people without reserve: He washed his disciples' feet (John 13:5), healed the sick, and befriended sinners. Ultimately, he died on the cross so that they could be reconciled with God. Participating in Christ's kingly office entails engaging in this dual service in the power of the Spirit.

By the power of the Spirit, we are not just liberated from our *cor incurvatum in se* so that we can live *for* God and *for* others but we are also granted the freedom to love, so that whether as an individual or as the corporate body of the church, we can serve God and serve others. Vertically, as taught by Calvin, church ministry should be characterized by obedience to the divine will. Negatively, this implies that church ministry is not seeking approval from society or from the civil government. Positively, the church should have a quiet confidence that God will preserve her life as she serves God faithfully. Horizontally, church ministry should not just minister to

---

36. Calvin, *Institutes*, II.15.5.
37. Calvin, *Institutes*, II.15.3.
38. Calvin, *Institutes*, II.15.4.
39. Calvin, *Institutes*, II.15.5.

people's spiritual needs but also to their physical well-being. Church ministry should show compassion and care for marginalized people.

Prophetic Office of Christ

The Westminster Larger Catechism question forty-three and its answer read as:

How doth Christ execute the office of a prophet?

Christ executes the office of a prophet, in his revealing to the church, in all ages, by his Spirit and Word, in diverse ways of administration, the whole will of God, in all things concerning their edification and salvation.

Christ executes His prophetic office in His church by revealing the entire will of God to His people in the power of the Holy Spirit through Scripture and various teaching offices, so that they can perceive the Father's heart for humanity as well as how to live a life that brings glory to the Father.

To bring out the uniqueness of Christ's prophetic office, we turn again to the prophetic office depicted in the Old Testament. Again, Moses's teaching about the prophetic office in *Deuteronomy* set up the norm for evaluating a prophet. Within the context of discussing covenantal faithfulness to Yahweh,[40] Israel was taught that even though the oracle of a prophet is fulfilled, this prophet was a false prophet if he/she incited Israelites to rebel against Yahweh (Deut 13:1–2). This implies that the main task of a prophet is not to predict the future but to urge Israel to follow Yahweh faithfully. Later in Deut 18:15–19, Moses elucidated what a true prophet of Yahweh should be. First, like Moses himself, a prophet is a mediator between God and his people.[41] Second, if a person can be a prophet, this is not based upon his lineage or upon other people's choices but is totally based upon Yahweh's commission.[42] Third, this prophet is not proclaiming his/her own words, but the words of God given to him/her by God himself. In other words, the authority of a prophet does not come from who he is but from the fact that he is faithfully proclaiming God's words. Fourth, the main purpose of the prophetic office is to call Israel to listen to God's words.

---

40. McConville, *Deuteronomy*, 234.
41. McConville, *Deuteronomy*, 302–3.
42. "As for Yahweh's 'raising up' of the prophet, this contrasts with the 'choosing' of the priest and king (17:15; 18:5)." McConville, *Deuteronomy*, 302.

Therefore, a true prophet is the one sent by God to proclaim his words to his people.[43] Two more aspects of the prophetic office need to be noticed. First, a prophet is not just a mouthpiece for Yahweh, his/her message also dictates how he/she will live (Hos 1–3). Second, just like Jeremiah was persecuted by his kinsmen, a prophet will suffer for his/her message.

What then is the uniqueness of Christ's prophetic office? As expressed clearly in the Gospel of John, just like the prophets of old, Christ is sent by God the Father into this world. Yet unlike them, Christ is not another human agent. Christ is the Son, the second person of the Triune God. He is the very God himself. This leads to a very important point: Christ is not just God's messenger sent to the world but also God's message for the world.[44] In him, God reveals fully who he is and what humanity should be. Unlike those prophets of old, whose messages were given by God, Christ himself is the Word (Heb 1:1–3, ESV). Christ's authority is not derived from anything outside of himself. No wonder Calvin believed that "the perfect doctrine he has brought has made an end to all prophecies," and "outside Christ there is nothing worth knowing."[45] Moreover, Christ's ascension does not terminate his prophetic office. Today, in the power of the Spirit, the church can still participate in this teaching office by faithfully preaching the gospel.[46]

To elaborate further on how Christ's prophetic office can inform church ministry, we have to distinguish the ontological mode of this office. We will use "being sent" to describe the twofold dimension of Christ's prophetic office. First, Christ is sent by God, and he is faithful to his sender. This means that he is faithful to the message entrusted to him. Second, Christ is sent into the world so that he can express this message clearly in his deeds and words. In the power of the Spirit, the church today participates in Christ's prophetic office. She is sent by God into the world not just to proclaim the message entrusted to her by God but also to submit to the same message. Therefore, church ministry should be characterized by this twofold dimension. On the one hand, every church ministry should express its faithfulness to the word of God. This implies that every aspect of the ministry, including its purpose, its goal, and its way of doing things,

---

43. Sherman, *King*, 229.

44. Sherman, *King*, 234.

45. Calvin, *Institutes*, II.15.2.

46. "[H]e received anointing, not only for himself that he might carry out the office of teaching, but for his whole body that the power of the Spirit might be present in the continuing preaching of the Gospel." Calvin, *Institutes*, II.15.2.

has to be regulated and judged by the word of God.[47] On the other hand, church ministry should have an outward dimension because she is sent into the world.

Conclusion

In this paper, we have demonstrated that *munus triplex Christi* is more than a theological concept summarizing Christ's soteriological works. Since the church participates in *munus triplex Christi* in the power of the Spirit, this theological concept also informs us what shape church ministry should take. By studying Christ's threefold office in detail, we infer from it three general guidelines for church ministry.[48] Church ministry should be characterized as "for God and for the world," it should reflect the character of "serving God and serving others," and it should be "to the world as well as faithful to the word of her sender."

They are distinct but not independent from each other. If church ministry can reflect her love for the world, this can only be expressed in her ministry of serving others according to the truth revealed by the word of God. Otherwise, either the world will never know the love of the church, or the church just tries to fulfill what the world desires. If a church's ministry is to truly serve the world, it must stem from her love for others and knowledge of those others' true needs as informed by God's words. Otherwise, the service can become cold and inhuman. In the end, it will not be different

---

47. Here, we use the generic term "the word of God" in place of the Holy Scripture. There are two reasons. First, we are trying to avoid the endless issues concerning biblical hermeneutics. Especially after Gadamer's works, we know that the interpretation of a text cannot be done in a purely objective fashion. This leads to endless debates on what is the correct reading of a text. Second, we want to use this phrase to denote the church's reading of the Holy Scripture under the grace of the Spirit. As John Webster points out (see Webster, *Holy Scripture*, 86–106), faithful reading is always done in the power of the Spirit. This consists of the following. First, with the help of the Spirit, we can turn away from our self-interest and concentrate on God's clear words in the Scripture. (This presumes the Reformed understanding that God's word is self-authenticated.) Second, we understand that we are always pupils under the Scripture. We will never exhaust the meaning of the text. Therefore, the church's present reading will not be the final reading. It can contain errors. When we say that church ministry is regulated by the word of God, we mean that it is guided by our present reading of the Scripture in the power of the Spirit. Since our reading is never sufficient, this also means that church ministry is done under the forgiveness of God.

48. Our treatments should not be considered final. We have only indicated three possible directions for further study and reflection.

from the social services provided by the civil government. If a church can effectively proclaim God's words to the world, it has to arise from her love for others, expressed in her ministry of serving. Otherwise, proclaiming the truth becomes just another exercise of authority over others. Instead of God's gracious words leading to life, it becomes a set of legal requirements leading to death. Finally, these three guidelines can be fleshed out differently within different cultural contexts.[49] They will provide the local ethnic church with a useful way to reflect on her ministry within her particular social setting.

Bibliography

Aquinas, Thomas. *Summa Theologica*. 5 vols. Translated by Fathers of the English Dominican Province. Allen: Thomas More, 1981.
Busch, Eberhard. *The Great Passion: An Introduction to Karl Barth's Theology*. Grand Rapids: Eerdmans, 2004.
Butin, Phil. "Two Early Reformed Catechisms, the Threefold Office, and the Shape of Karl Barth's Christology." *Scottish Journal of Theology* 44 (1991) 195–214.
Calvin, John. *Institutes of the Christian Religion*. 2 vols. Edited by John T. McNeill. Translated by F. L. Battles. Louisville: Westminster John Knox, 2006.
De Boer, Erik A. "Christology and Christianity: The Theological Power of the Threefold Office in Lord's Day 12." *In die Skriflig* 47 (2013) 1–8.
Greggs, Tom. *Dogmatic Ecclesiology: The Priestly Catholicity of the Church*, Vol. 1. Grand Rapids: Baker Academic, 2019.
Guyette, Fred. "Jesus as Prophet, Priest, and King: John Wesley and the Renewal of an Ancient Tradition." *Wesleyan Theological Journal* 40 (2005) 88–101.
"The Heidelberg Catechism." https://www.crcna.org/sites/default/files/HeidelbergCatechism.pdf.
Johnson, Adam J. "The Servant Lord: A Word of Caution Regarding the *munus triplex* in Karl Barth's Theology and the Church Today." *Scottish Journal of Theology* 65, (2012) 159–73.
Ladd, George E. *A Theology of the New Testament*. Revised ed. Edited by Donald A. Hanger. Grand Rapids: Eerdmans, 1993.
McConville, J. G. *Deuteronomy*. Apollos Old Testament Commentary. Downers Grove: InterVarsity, 2002.
Peterson, Robert A. *Calvin and the Atonement*. Fearn: Geanies House, 2009.
Sherman, Robert. *King, Priest, and Prophet: A Trinitarian Theology of Atonement*. London: T. & T. Clark International, 2004.
Stroup, George W., III. "The Relevance of the *Munus Triplex* for Reformed Theology and Ministry." *Austin Seminary Bulletin* 98 (1983) 22–32.
Webster, John. *Holy Scripture: A Dogmatic Sketch*. Current Issues in Theology. Cambridge: Cambridge University Press, 2004.
"The Westminster Larger Catechism." http://www.freepresbyterian.org/uploads/Larger_Catechism.pdf.

---

49. The discussion of this is totally beyond the scope of this paper.

7.

What Does "Indigenization of a Religion" Mean? An Investigation of Methodological Issues on Sinicization of Christianity in China and Diaspora

Hung-En (Tallis) Tien

Abstract

THE AUTHOR OF THE paper identifies four categories of approaches in methodology for understanding Christianity in China. Approaches of the hermeneutics overlook God's choice of specific historical and cultural contexts for the incarnated Christ and the development of the church. The approaches of cultural studies mainly integrate Confucianism and Christian doctrines but usually forget the gospel is the ultimate judge and redeemer of all cultures. Approaches of empirical religious studies are worth continuing to develop as are the approaches of indigenous Chinese theology. The author of this paper proposes adopting the canonical-linguistic approach as the principal methodology and constructing indigenous Chinese theology from the dimensions of discovery and expression. In the process of discovering the truth, it requires us to refer to the historical and cultural background of the Bible, focusing on biblical text and respecting church traditions, thereby developing theology in Chinese language and indigenous Chinese theology context under the guidance of the Holy Spirit. Moreover, this truth-pursuing journey should not only focus on indigenous issues and applications, but also share the fruits of indigenous Chinese theology with global churches.

Introduction

In the Chinese Christian community, indigenization has always been a popular topic. It seems that Sinicization of Christianity is inevitable to Chinese Evangelicals, which has also aroused extensive discussion.[1] It has been also widely discussed on how Chinese churches can be indigenized recently.[2] However, there is no systematic studying on the definition of the Sinicization of Christianity, which has led to a fact that divergent perspectives regarding the definition and contents of the Sinicization of Christianity have been formed by different researchers. In addition, some scholars have begun discussing how to research indigenization, that is, the methodology;[3] however, there is still no comprehensive solution for it. This paper focuses on the methodology of researching the Sinicization of Christianity and Chinese indigenous theology from the perspectives of hermeneutics, studies of culture, and religious studies (including studies of sociology and anthropology). Selective methodologies which have been adopted in published research on the Sinicization of Christianity will be analyzed in terms of definitions and contents, as well as their strengths and disadvantages. This paper will then point out the future direction of researching the Sinicization of Christianity and Chinese indigenous theology.

Methodology

This paper defines Sinicization as: assimilating or even merging something with the world view and value systems of the Han Chinese (漢人), especially Confucianism,[4] and expressing it in Chinese. This paper will focus

---

1. For example, 林金水、郭榮剛 (Lin & Guo), 《基督教中國化研究初探》. However, there are only a few academic papers in this collection of essays.

2. For example, 劉家峰 (Liu) (編), 《離異與融會》.

3. For example, 陳胤安 (Chen), 〈從社會的觀念談基督教「本色化」的假設——以人類學理論反思文化概念的使用〉, 147-71; 溫偉耀 (Wan), 《生命的轉化與超拔》; 郭鴻標 (Kwok), 《基督信仰漢語神學芻議》 (香港: 建道神學院出版社, 2011); 賴品超 (Lai), 《廣場上的漢語神學》.

4. This definition is formulated with reference to Standaert, *Handbook*, 98. In

on exploring the methodologies of the ideas of Sinicization; therefore, the relationship between Chinese Christianity and imperialism and politics in China, which is not the purpose of this paper and has been widely researched in historical studies, will not be discussed. Secondly, the Sinicization of the institution of Chinese churches and para-church organizations, that is, the control and executive authorities of denominations, local churches, and Christian institutions, will also not be discussed.

Regarding the selective methods or representative figures that have been presented in previous studies of Sinicization, this paper will only discuss the direction of their methodology rather than investigating their contents or thoughts in details due to limited space of this paper. In addition, since mission to Chinese people is always an intention of Sinicization of Christianity, this paper will also address this concern and point out a possible way of methodology which is associated with mission.

The Meaning and Direction of Sinicization of Christianity in China

Before discussing the four methodological approaches of Sinicization, we need to understand the origin of this concept and its development and trend. The development of the idea of Sinicization has always been linked with missions. Some scholars point out that Sinicization was promoted by Chinese churches after the "anti-Christianity movement" (非基運動) in China in the 1920s.[5] At that time, apart from the fact that both Christianity and imperialism were originated from foreign countries,[6] Chinese Christians started to reflect on the main reasons why Christianity was not accepted by Chinese people: (1) the organization and funds were controlled by foreigners, and Chinese churches should be independent, self-propagating and self-supporting; (2) most Chinese did not adapt to Christian rituals introduced by foreigners; and (3) the alienation of Christianity

---

addition, because most Chinese or people who live in Chinese culture do not differentiate between original Confucianism and neo-Confucianism, this paper does not distinguish between original Confucianism, neo-Confucianism, or any other branches of Confucianism.

5. For example, 王治心 (Wang), 《中國基督教史綱》, 236–37; 趙天恩 (Chao), 《中國教會本色化運動 (1919–27)》, 297–300.

6. 王治心 (Wang), 《中國基督教史綱》, 238–40.

from Chinese culture.[7] These are what we need to pay attention to when researching the idea of the Sinicization of Christianity.

Approaches of Hermeneutics

First of all, it needs to be clarified that "hermeneutics" here does not just refer to general Christian hermeneutics, but the hermeneutics with a philosophical attention, that is, the (philosophical) understanding of a thing.[8] All methodologies adopted in the hermeneutic approach to the Sinicization of Christianity assumes that there is a "pure" Christianity, and thus in order to remove the Western or any existing interpretations, Chinese Christians must reinterpret Christianity. In this realm, it involves the local Chinese churches who advocate restorationism, as well as the approach of Liu's (劉小楓) "Sino-Christian theology" approach in the academic circle. Although those two methodologies seem to be two extremes, both utilize hermeneutic approaches.

1. Restorationism: Reinterpreting Christianity by Oneself

Fundamentalists in China believe that there is pure Christianity and thus they advocate restorationism.[9] These people are generally active within church circles. They advocate that Chinese churches should go back to the Bible directly and should not accept any preexisting teachings, which means "anti-traditional." For example, Wang (王明道) opposed any kind of existing teachings, theology, church traditions, and canon laws,[10] but only relied on his own interpretation of the Bible. He stated: "When I stayed at home and read the Bible in those years, I completely put aside the teachings I had heard previously from the church but just studied the Bible myself . . . I never read any commentaries since I despise that kind of books most . . . I am reluctant to accept any church traditions and human-made rules . . ."[11] They opposed any form of indigenization, maintaining that it would pollute

---

7. 王治心 (Wang), 《中國基督教史綱》, 236–37.

8. As Richard E. Palmer said, Hermeneutics is about "what is the nature of understanding itself." He also mentioned "a theory of understanding is most relevant to hermeneutics." Palmer, *Hermeneutics*, 66, 68.

9. 梁家麟 (Leung), 〈中國近代教會史裡的本色化與福音化討論〉, 114.

10. 王明道 (Wang), 《五十年來》, 61.

11. 王明道 (Wang), 《五十年來》, 71–72.

the pure teachings of the Bible. However, scholars suggest that these Chinese fundamentalists, who are most against the indigenization of Christianity, have established the most indigenized Chinese church.[12] Even Ming-Tao Wang himself admitted that the Bible and *the Four Books* are the most inspiring to him personally.[13]

For some scholars who believe that Western culture can be detached from Christianity, which can then return to the core of the gospel, the perspective categorized as "regarding Christianity as culture" proposed by Chen (陳胤安)[14] is not accurate enough. This is because the goal of restorationism is to remove any cultural elements from Christianity, and they believe that there exists a "pure" idea without any cultural colors. Therefore, restorationists should not be regarded as a group of people adopting approaches of cultural studies. The perspective of advocating that Christianity should dialogue and even integrate with Chinese culture is opposed to the approach of "pure Christianity" and anti-indigenization proposed by fundamentalists.[15] Approaches of cultural studies are also completely different in terms of their starting point and methodology compared to those of fundamentalists, and this will be discussed later.

2. Liu's "Sino-Christian Theology"

The "Sino-Christian theology" initiated by Liu also adopts a hermeneutic approach. He believes that there is an "ideal form" of Christianity (Christian theology)[16] that is like systematic theology,[17] and which can be used in different cultures and situations. Liu emphasized that Jesus Christ is an "event,"[18] and people can encounter Jesus Christ in the context of Chinese culture and language,[19] and they will eventually "accept, state the event of

12. 梁家麟（Leung）,〈中國近代教會史裡的本色化與福音化討論〉, 115.

13. 王明道（Wang）,〈新年來信〉, 2.Publishers may use different methods in translating Chinese names. "Mingdao Wang" and "Ming-Tao Wang" refer to the same person 王明道（Wang）.

14. 陳胤安（Chen）,〈從社會的觀念談基督教「本色化」的假設〉, 150.

15. 邵玉銘（Shao）,〈基督教與中國論集序〉, 於林治平,《基督教與中國論集》, 序 23.

16. 劉小楓（Liu）,〈現代語境中的漢語基督神學〉, 41–42.

17. 劉小楓（Liu）,《這一代人的怕和愛》, 177.

18. 劉小楓（Liu）,〈現代語境中的漢語基督神學〉, 40, 42.

19. 劉小楓（Liu）,〈現代語境中的漢語基督神學〉, 42, 47; 劉小楓（Liu）,《聖靈降臨的敘事》, 290.

Christ and reflect on the confession of Christ" in "the language experience of Chinese ideology."[20] Liu intends to break away from Western dominant Christianity, which he calls "historical,"[21] and "incidental"[22] Christianity. His method is to abstract pure "Christian theology" from any historical and cultural background, including historical and cultural context of the Bible,[23] because "Ethnicity . . . may distort and alter the words of Christ."[24] Liu explains that Chinese Christianity "is not based on the integration of the event of Christ and the ontology of various existing thoughts (whether Judaism, thoughts of ancient Greece and Rome, Confucianism, Taoism, or Buddhism) or the construct of various modern philosophies, but the encountering with the original individual survival experience in the ethnic-regional texture of language."[25] Liu himself opposes any indigenization of Christianity,[26] since Jesus Christ challenged all cultures, including the Chinese one.[27] Furthermore, if Christianity is indigenized in China, it will become another "historical" Christianity, thereby being unable to face the events of Christ directly. He also believes that the traditional Chinese culture, dominated by Confucianism with nationalism and political agenda, cannot merge with the Christianity clothed in Western culture.[28]

Approaches of Cultural Studies

Another approach to construct Sinicization is from the perspective of cultural studies with the contribution of sociology, anthropology, and communication studies. This approach regards Christianity as a kind of culture.[29] There are three models explaining the encountering of Chris-

20. 劉小楓 (Liu), 〈現代語境中的漢語基督神學〉, 42.
21. 劉小楓 (Liu), 〈現代語境中的漢語基督神學〉, 41–43.
22. 劉小楓 (Liu), 《這一代人的怕和愛》, 183.
23. 劉小楓 (Liu), 〈現代語境中的漢語基督神學〉, 47; 劉小楓 (Liu), 《這一代人的怕和愛》, 183, 185–86.
24. 劉小楓 (Liu), 《這一代人的怕和愛》, 184.
25. 劉小楓 (Liu), 〈現代語境中的漢語基督神學〉, 47.
26. 劉小楓 (Liu), 《這一代人的怕和愛》, 175, 180, 189–90.
27. 劉小楓 (Liu), 〈現代語境中的漢語基督神學〉, 46–47; 劉小楓 (Liu,), 《這一代人的怕和愛》, 184.
28. 劉小楓 (Liu), 《聖靈降臨的敘事》, 29–42.
29. 陳胤安 (Chen), 〈從社會的觀念談基督教「本色化」的假設〉, 149, 151.

tianity and Chinese culture: (1) Jacques Gernet's "cultural conflict"[30]; (2) Nicolas Standaert's "accommodation and inculturation"[31]; and Pan's (潘鳳娟) "circulation of interpretation of cultural exchanges."[32] From approaches of cultural studies, Sinicization is "re-experiencing" the Bible[33] after Christianity met Chinese culture, and then utilizing Chinese cultural "symbols" and "contextual systems" as a vehicle of spreading the message.[34] In other words, Sinicization of Christianity is "to establish indigenised 'missiology' . . . through Chinese cultural background with utilization of all cultural media."[35] The definition of indigenization in this approach is that Christianity is no longer regarded as a foreign religion,[36] and Christianity is widely spread within the places where Chinese live.[37] This approach takes Sinicized Buddhism as its goal.[38] It is evident that there is a strong motivation for evangelism in approaches of cultural studies in Sinicization of Christianity.

The rationale that indigenizing Christianity must take place in any situation is twofold: theology and history. From a historical aspect, Christianity has been indigenized in Greek and Roman culture in the progress of evangelism,[39] and many customs and Christian etiquette were developed within these two cultures.[40] From a theological perspective, "incarnation" and harmonizing with the environment is the principle of indigenization. For example:

1. Promoters quote John 1:14 and Hebrews 2:17 and maintain that Christianity needs to identify with people in the context. It is because:

    the descending of [the] Son provides the perfect model of indigenization for today's church. As in history, Jesus Christ . . . adopt

---

30. 潘鳳娟 (Pan,), 《西來孔子艾儒略》, 221–24.
31. 潘鳳娟 (Pan,), 《西來孔子艾儒略》, 224–26.
32. 潘鳳娟 (Pan,), 《西來孔子艾儒略》, 226–29, 234–37.
33. 楊森富 (Yang,), 《中華基督教本色化論文集》, 172.
34. 林治平 (Lin,), 《基督教與中國論集》, 56–58, 72–73.
35. 楊森富 (Yang,), 〈唐元兩代基督教興衰原因之研究〉, 57–61, 68.
36. 林治平 (Lin,), 〈基督教在中國本色化之必要性與可行性〉, 6.
37. Please refer to the discussion in 梁家麟 (Leung), 〈中國近代教會史裡的本色化與福音化討論〉, 118–20.
38. 王治心 (Wang), 《中國基督教史綱》, 236; 邵玉銘 (Shao), 〈基督教與中國論集序〉, 序23.
39. 林治平 (Lin,), 《基督教與中國論集》, 59–60.
40. 楊森富 (Yang), 《中華基督教本色化論文集》, 174–81.

indigenous Jewish social, economic and political environment, deeply immersing in the Old Testament, and sharing everything in Jewish culture. In the same way, the church preaching the Gospel should try its best to be born into every culture as fully and closely as possible like what Jesus Christ did. The church, like Christ, also brings the gospel of salvation to people belonging to this culture in indigenous ways.[41]

2. Because Jesus utilizes illustrations from daily life,[42] and in Acts 2:8 disciples use "native language" to preach the gospel;[43] Christianity, therefore, should utilize indigenous languages and convey the message in a way that indigenous people can understand.

3. Since the contents of the four Gospels varies for different audiences,[44] and because of Paul's practice of "I have become all things to all people" in 1 Corinthians 9:22,[45] Christianity should adjust the emphasis of its message adapting to the needs of audiences from various backgrounds.

4. As Jesus challenged the Jewish laws,[46] similarly, the message of Christianity also needs to adapt to the environment, focusing on contemporary Chinese issues[47]; as such the theology must keep pace with the times.

In terms of practice, there are four ways Christianity is seen the Chinese context: integration with Confucianism; as a supplement to Confucianism; utilizing Christianity to build a strong China; and against Confucianism.[48] Integration is the most common among them.[49] Those who promote Sinicization believe that missionaries come to China with their own "cultural ideas and symbol systems,"[50] making Chinese people

---

41. My translation. 輔仁神學著作編譯會〈Fu Jen Theological Publications Association〉,〈教會與文化〉, 827.

42. 王志希（Wang）,〈「如果基督生活在今日之中國」〉, 31–32.

43. 王志希（Wang）,〈「如果基督生活在今日之中國」〉, 33–35.

44. 王志希（Wang）,〈「如果基督生活在今日之中國」〉, 32–33.

45. 王志希（Wang）,〈「如果基督生活在今日之中國」〉, 35–37.

46. 王志希（Wang）,〈「如果基督生活在今日之中國」〉, 32.

47. 林治平（Lin）,《基督教與中國論集》, 76.

48. Please refer to 邢福增（Ying）,《文化適應與中國基督徒》, 117–43.

49. 邢福增（Ying）,《文化適應與中國基督徒》, 142.

50. 林治平（Lin）,〈奠下一塊堅固的磐石〉, 序2.

think Western culture is equal to Christianity,[51] which makes it difficult for Chinese people to accept Christianity.[52] The first step to resolve this issue is cultural exchange which finds "conflicting points" between Confucianism and Christianity, and then finding common grounds for both parties.[53] This is quite similar to Ching's (秦家懿) "Inculturation."[54] The second step is to integrate Christianity with Chinese "traditional culture,"[55] that is, to "merge with . . . Confucian and Taoist culture."[56] Some scholars maintain that the reason Christianity died out in China after the end of the Yuan Dynasty was that it was not Sinicized and was regarded as a foreign religion.[57] Wang (王治心) adopted Jesus's parable of the sower as his rationale, proposing Christianity needs to be rooted in a culture as a seed to soil,[58] and Christianity must "absorb the nourishment of Chinese culture,"[59] which "allows ancient Chinese culture to be integrated with Christian truth, so that [the] spiritual life of Chinese Christian[s] can fit into [the] Chinese context without estrangement."[60] Wang even suggests that the goal of Sinicization is to "marry the church and Chinese culture."[61] Ching points out this requires the Chinese to intentionally incorporate "Christian thought and Chinese culture."[62]

Approaches of Religious Studies

Understanding indigenization of Christianity from the perspective of religious studies mainly adopts research methods from anthropology and sociology. They study the "travel" of a religion from one context to another[63]

51. 陳馴 (Chen), 《當代中國的基督教神學方法》, 6–7.
52. 林治平 (Lin), 《基督教與中國論集》, 83–84.
53. 林治平 (Lin), 《基督教與中國論集》, 83–84.
54. 秦家懿 (Ching), 〈本位化神學及其普世性〉, 13.
55. 林治平 (Lin), 《基督教與中國論集》, 76.
56. 邵玉銘 (Shao), 〈基督教與中國論集序〉, 序23.
57. Standaert, Handbook, 94–97; 楊森富 (Yang), 〈唐元兩代基督教興衰原因之研究〉, 57–61, 68.
58. 王治心 (Wang), 〈中國本色教會討論〉, 12.
59. 王治心 (Wang), 〈中國本色教會討論〉, 12.
60. 王治心 (Wang), 〈中國本色教會討論〉, 14.
61. 王治心 (Wang), 《中國基督教史綱》, 236.
62. 秦家懿 (Ching), 〈本位化神學及其普世性〉, 13.
63. Leopold, "General Introduction,"), 8–9.

and the "transforming religious symbolic systems."⁶⁴ Some scholars suggest that the fusion of two religions follows four processes:

1. Amalgamation: at this stage, the two religions can still be clearly distinguished
2. Assimilation: the two religions in contact would gradually come together consciously
3. Symbiosis: the synthesis of two religions
4. Identification: to their believers two religions are identical.

Confucianism, Buddhism, and Taoism "fusing into functions of a great whole" in Chinese history is an example.⁶⁵ What deserves our attention is that when religions are introduced into China, it has been quite common for "cultural integration" (inculturation) to occur. When it comes to Christianity, its Scriptures, teachings, and rituals were expressed in a non-Christian (other religious or cultural) way.⁶⁶ When Chinese culture was comparatively dominate, "syncretism" was observed; Christianity in the Tang Dynasty is an example.⁶⁷

Approaches of Indigenous Theology（本土神學）

There are other methodologies under the name of "Sino-Christian theology,"⁶⁸ although the major emphasis is philosophical,⁶⁹ distinguished from that of Liu. He (何光滬) mentioned, "the so-called indigenous theology is a theology based on the materials of the living experiences of an indigenous community with homogeneous culture and the cultural resources derived from these experiences, utilizing indigenous language as a vehicle,

64. Droogers, "Syncretism," 8.
65. Kamstra, "Religie en Syncretisme," 217.
66. 陳馴 (Chen), 《當代中國的基督教神學方法》, 21.
67. 陳馴 (Chen), 《當代中國的基督教神學方法》, 23–25. This group of Christians, the Assyrian Church of the East, has been mistakenly regarded as heretical "Nestorian" by many modern Christian scholars. However, it has been demonstrated that they were orthodox Christians using different languages (Assyrian and Persian) to express their faith, and their languages were unfamiliar to Catholic, Eastern Orthodox or Oriental Orthodox churches. Please see Brock, *Fire from Heaven*, esp. 14, 79–80, 176–77.
68. 賴品超 (Lai), 〈漢語基督教神學對宗教分歧的論述〉, 82–83.
69. 賴品超 (Lai), 〈漢語基督教神學對宗教分歧的論述〉, 82; 賴品超 (Lai), 《廣場上的漢語神學》, 29–33.

and with the purpose of reflecting, clarifying and serving the faith of the indigenous group."[70] He also emphasizes "since indigenous theology is a theology, it cannot lack other basic elements of theology, such as revelation, reason, tradition and the Bible, etc."[71] His comprehension of "Sino-Christian theology" is significantly different from Liu's. Furthermore, he prefers "indigenous theology" rather than "indigenized theology." He explains:

> The biggest difference between the concept of "indigenous theology" and the one of "indigenised theology" is that the latter implies the "transforming" something "non-indigenous" for our own purpose and use, whilst the former implies seeking theological implications from indigenous living experience and culture. It enriches the spiritual life of indigenous people and adds something new to global theology at the same time.[72]

From this perspective, his indigenous theology is not much different from general systematic theology. The difference between general systematic theology and indigenous theology is that there is more emphasis on doing theology in an indigenous context and serving the people in the indigenous context.

Evaluation of the Methodology of Sinicization of Christianity and Future Direction of Research

In the next section, the advantages and limitations of these methodologies will be discussed with suggestions about the implications and directions for future research on indigenous theology and the development of its methodology.

1. History, Culture and Christ

Liu wants to develop "Sino-Christian theology" and to break away from Western dominance over Christianity. Liu's methodology, however, is still Western, especially Søren Kierkegaard's theology emphasizing the complete duality between God and the world, which was adopted by Karl Barth to combat liberal theology, and Dietrich Bonhoeffer's ideas rejecting Nazi

70. 何光滬 (He),〈「本土神學」管窺〉, 161.
71. 何光滬 (He),〈「本土神學」管窺〉, 161.
72. 何光滬 (He),〈「本土神學」管窺〉, 161.

control over the church under a special circumstance.⁷³ As such, God has nothing to do with the world,⁷⁴ and even the historical event of the incarnation of Christ is reductively interpreted as "the word of God became flesh and suddenly broke into this place with the help of a certain historical and cultural body."⁷⁵ What kind of Christ, therefore, will be in this "Christian theology" that is abstracted from history and culture? Can anyone "meet" Christ in his/her own context? For example, Raimon Panikkar maintains that "transcendent divine reality" is the core of religion, which is not limited by any forms of religions.⁷⁶ Then Panikkar claims that "Christ is not just Jesus"⁷⁷ and concludes that "the unknown Christ" can be found in any religion, including Hinduism.

Liu believed that both Jesus and Paul opposed their own culture and used this as the rationale for his "Sino-Christian theology"; however, this view is somewhat mistaken. Both Jesus Christ and Paul opposed the Jewish concept that "only superior Jews will be saved by the blood of Abraham, whereas inferior Gentiles cannot be saved" since God's love extends to the whole world. However, Jesus and Paul did not deny the fact that God's revelation is through the Israelites.⁷⁸ Therefore, knowing Jewish history and culture is the starting point of understanding God's revelation. It is inappropriate to assume that we have a better understanding of God in the Chinese context but bypassing Jewish history and culture. Galatians 4:4 mentions, "When the time was fulfilled, God sent His Son, born of a woman, and born under the law." God the Father chose Jewish history and culture as the domain for the incarnation of Jesus Christ, and these two are the spheres in which "the events of Christ" happens. When facing Liu's "Christian theology" detaching from history and culture, we need to take Karl Rahner's suggestion into account: "what sense the formal horizon for 'ontological Christology' could be discovered in this connection, inasmuch as God's promise of himself to the world has its apex in Jesus Christ in whose humanity—as being and history—it reaches *ultimate* eschatological appearance."⁷⁹

73. 劉小楓 (Liu), 《這一代人的怕和愛》, 184.
74. 劉小楓 (Liu), 《這一代人的怕和愛》, 188, 190.
75. 劉小楓 (Liu), 《這一代人的怕和愛》, 186.
76. Panikkar, *Unknown Christ*, 15.
77. Panikkar, *Unknown Christ*, 14.
78. For example, Matt 5:17–18; Rom 9:4–5.
79. Rahner, *Hearers*, 146n3.

2. Text and "the Event of Christ"

Jesus Christ has lived in the world, and people can know Christ because of the testimony about him, which was transmitted to today's people in different contexts through the Bible (text)[80] and church traditions[81] (many of which are also preserved in the form of text). As scholars have pointed out: Liu's most fundamental problem is that he asserts the Christ event as "extralinguistic."[82] If the Christ event is extralinguistic, modern people will not be able to grasp the content of the Christ event. Therefore, we must start with the interpretation of the Bible (text) to understand Jesus Christ, and this is one of the focuses of indigenized or indigenous theology.

3. Context and Interpretation of Texts

Christianity must be conditioned by the text and its interpretation.[83] To interpret a text, we must consider four categories of contexts: literary, historical, theological, and social contexts. George Lindbeck believes that the interpretation of the Bible should adopt the "cultural-linguistic approaches"[84] and the "intratextuality" principle.[85] Christians should not interpret the Bible extratextually, that is, understand the Bible through a non-biblical background (another text),[86] especially modern culture.[87] It is methodologically infeasible to understand Jesus Christ without biblical theology, that is, an interpretation without an informed biblical history, geography, and cultural context.

People live in a sphere of society, language, and tradition from a sociological perspective. As David Tracy mentioned, "there is no such thing as an unambiguous tradition; there are no innocent readings of the classics. We are who we are because of the traditions that form us. Our lives are shaped by the preconscious effects of all the traditions whose narratives and ways of envisioning the world have forged our memories and consequently

---

80. Please refer to Watson, *Text*, 2–3.
81. Please refer to Watson, *Text*, 5–7.
82. 關瑞文 (Kwan), 〈評劉小楓的漢語基督神學〉, 225, 228–29.
83. Please refer to the discussion in Vanhoozer, *Meaning*, 49–59, 105–6, 427–29.
84. Lindbeck, *Nature of Doctrine*, 32–42, 79–84, 112–14.
85. Lindbeck, *Nature of Doctrine*, 113–24.
86. Please refer to Thiselton, *Thiselton*, 445–46.
87. Treier, *Theological Interpretation*, 82.

our actions."[88] And "Christian religion is like a culture that operates with a system of signs."[89] "Relevance theory" also points out that the author, who usually has something in common with the readers, assuming that the readers have certain knowledge, will skip some specific content in the text and expect readers to "fill in the necessary mental gaps."[90] For example, the Bible does not mention many details about worshipping God, because God's people were assumed to attend services and should have known the practice extensively. In this sense, ecclesiastical tradition is indispensable for understanding Christ. Liu insists that Sino-Chinese theology is "ontic;"[91] however, it is an existentialist[92] Christianity for individuals,[93] detaching from the theological and social context of the church. Furthermore, Liu and his followers are mostly active in academic circles, labelling themselves "cultural Christians"[94] and have little connection with churches. Therefore, it is doubtful that such practice can achieve the goal of "Sino-Christian theology," and it should not become the mainstream methodology for indigenized or indigenous Chinese theology.

4. Church History and Indigenized Theology

Neither fundamentalists nor Liu reject the influence of history on the development of Christianity; fundamentalism denies the concept of "development" of Christianity. However, the development of Christianity is apparent as the knowledge of God is inevitably influenced by historical factors, which also shapes expressions of faith in different time and space. The Bible itself emphasizes time and space greatly.[95] In its early development, although Christianity departed from an inadequate Jewish understanding of God, it inherits their correct understanding of God and expressions of faith (worship). Therefore, Christianity developed in the knowledge of God and in faith expression.

---

88. Tracy, *Plurality*, 36–37.
89. Treier, *Theological Interpretation*, 81.
90. Treier, *Theological Interpretation*, 135.
91. 劉小楓 (Liu), 〈現代語境中的漢語基督神學〉, 46–47.
92. 劉小楓 (Liu), 《這一代人的怕和愛》, 174, 177.
93. 劉小楓 (Liu), 《這一代人的怕和愛》, 189.
94. 劉小楓 (Liu), 《聖靈降臨的敘事》, 83–94.
95. For example, "*the day of the Lord*" was mentioned many times in the Bible.

Rejecting Jewish liturgy does not mean refusing to understand God's revelation through Jewish culture and history, but rather opposing a Jewish narrow-minded interpretation of salvation. Similarly, while opposing Western dominance and arbitrary interpretations of Christianity, one cannot deny the fact that God chose Europe, Africa, and America, and their cultures and history, as the field for the development of the church. In other words, it will be an overly confident statement to think that we would acquire the same level of understanding of God by bypassing them and church history.

It would be a big mistake to think that "Christ" can be found in every culture and one can come to God the Father through the "Christ" in one's own culture whilst omitting "Jesus of Nazareth" in history. Similarly, it is equally dangerous for us to create a new doctrine of God denying the Trinity, or to invent a theory regarding the Trinity ourselves, without being informed of the early church traditions.[96]

5. Potential Methodological Problems of Approaches to Cultural Studies: Circular Argument and Problematic Rationale

Leung criticizes the idea that "Christianity needs to be Sinicized because Chinese do not accept the gospel," and says it is a circular argument, pointing out that those who support Sinicization of Christianity believe that the reason Chinese do not accept Christianity is because it has not been Sinicized. These promoters first claim the failure of spreading the gospel in a Chinese context, and then use this to justify their agenda or actions. Therefore, the principle of Sinicization of Christianity has been continuously mentioned for more than a hundred years.[97] Furthermore, Chen points out that Sinicization of Christianity seems to be a pseudoproposition:

> When we discuss "whether Christianity should be indigenized," we are "reconstructing" the "objectiveness" of Christianity—that is, we have presumed the nature of non-indigenized Christianity before the question of "whether" being indigenized is discussed. This is the premise leading to the conclusion, and the discussion

---

96. Please refer to Osborne, *Hermeneutical Spiral*, 393, 401.

97. 梁家麟（Leung）,〈中國近代教會史裡的本色化與福音化討論〉, 118–20.

under the framework of this premise will only see Christianity as a foreigner.⁹⁸

Another methodological problem is that Wang uses Jesus's parable of the sower as the basis of his theory, requiring for the seeds of Christianity to be rooted in the soil of Chinese culture.⁹⁹ Leung, however, sharply points out that Jesus's point is to highlight the problem of the soil, instead of emphasizing that the seeds must adapt to the soil.¹⁰⁰

In addition, it is problematic to measure the degree of Sinicization of Christianity by the degree of acceptance of Christianity and the proportion of Christian population in China, since there are many reasons why Chinese people do not accept Christianity.¹⁰¹ It is unreasonable to expect that Christianity is received by Chinese people like Buddhism, considering the history of Christian mission in China is relatively short.¹⁰² Besides, most Buddhist masters were invited to China to teach out of the interest of Chinese people, whereas Christian missionaries were self-invited.¹⁰³ The above are the methodological problems of the approaches of cultural studies.

6. Concerns about and Limitations of Approaches to Cultural Studies: The Relationship between Culture and the Gospel

There are many potential problems in the Sinicization of Christianity from approaches of cultural studies. A scholar who advocates the Sinicization of Christianity points out syncretism is its potential problem.¹⁰⁴ Ching, taking the process of Sinicization of Buddhism as an example, indicates that Christianity may also be conquered just like Buddhism was transformed by Confucianism.¹⁰⁵ We need to understand the limitations and relativity of indigenous theology.¹⁰⁶ "Regarding indigenous elements as the ultimate

98. 陳胤安 (Chen), 〈從社會的觀念談基督教「本色化」的假設〉, 152.
99. 王治心 (Wang), 〈中國本色教會討論〉, 12.
100. 梁家麟 (Leung), 〈中國近代教會史裡的本色化與福音化討論〉, 116.
101. 梁家麟 (Leung), 〈中國近代教會史裡的本色化與福音化討論〉, 125–36.
102. 梁家麟 (Leung), 〈中國近代教會史裡的本色化與福音化討論〉, 123.
103. 秦家懿 (Ching), 〈本位化神學及其普世性〉, 12.
104. 楊森富 (Yang), 《中華基督教本色化論文集》, 58–62.
105. Julia Ching even describes it as "Chinese conquest of Buddhism." 秦家懿 (Ching), 〈本位化神學及其普世性〉, 17–19.
106. 何光滬 (He), 〈「本土神學」管窺〉, 161–63, 167.

goal and standard of judgment is not only absurd and exclusive, but also sinful and catastrophic."[107]

Furthermore, the so-called Sinicization of Christianity promoted by some Chinese Christians advocates experiencing God without referencing two thousand years of church history, emphasizing personal emotions rather than doctrine, and expressing faith in Chinese ways. This type of Christianity is categorized as "liberal experiential-expressivism"[108] according to Lindbeck's analysis. It may not be the thing which promoters of approaches of cultural studies to Sinicization of Christianity would like to see.

Thirdly, to what extent is Sinicization of Christianity considered to achieve the goal? One scholar points out: "Christianity came into China expecting China to be evangelised (中華歸主). However, what Chinese people expected was that Christianity should be sinicised (主歸中華) . . . Chinese people . . . always view Christianity as a foreign religion unconsciously, and Christianity has to be sinicised before many people follow[ing] it."[109] One of the reasons advocating the Sinicization of Christianity is to evangelize Chinese. Even though Christianity is Sinicized, Wang believes that it is still difficult to find corresponding concepts of Christian "resurrection and eternal life" in Chinese culture, and thus it is hard for Chinese people to understand and thereby accept them.[110] As a scholar in missiology suggests, the "incarnation of the Word" does not guarantee that the "Word" will be accepted, as Jesus was rejected by his own people.[111] The "Word" exposes people's sins, and it is even "outrageous."[112] Therefore, it is obvious that even if Christianity is Sinicized in its expression, it may not be accepted by the Chinese.

How can we determine if indigenization of Christianity in a culture is successful or not? A missionary scholar proposes a criterion: "in relation to the particular culture in which the church is contextualized we expect the gospel to make a dynamic impact on their design for living equivalent to the impact that the biblical people of God made on their societies."[113] To respond to the concern of the Sinicization of Christianity for evangelizing

---

107. 何光滬 (He), 〈「本土神學」管窺〉, 161–62.
108. Lindbeck, *Nature of Doctrine*, 31–32, 38, 42, 47, 112–13.
109. 張開沅 (Zhang), 〈序一：「中華歸主」與「主歸中華」〉, 序一1.
110. 王治心 (Wang), 《中國基督教史綱》, 21.
111. Peskett and Ramachandra, *Message of Mission*, 80–81.
112. The authors mention "the message of the cross is scandalous." Peskett and Ramachandra, *Message of Mission*, 81–83.
113. Nicholls, *Contextualization*, 64.

Chinese, we need to consider some deeper issues, namely the relationship between the gospel and culture. A scholar in missiology points out that there are supracultural entities, such as God and Satan, affecting people in every culture.[114] Moreover, "the gospel is never the guest of any culture; it is always its judge and redeemer."[115] This is why Paul, who preached to the gentiles in Athens, exhorted the church to testify to "both Jews and Greeks about repentance towards God and faith in our Lord Jesus Christ" (Acts 20:21).[116] Gentiles cannot be exempted from hearing the testimony about Jesus Christ because of their own culture; likewise, no ethnic groups can be exempted from hearing Jesus Christ for the same reason.

7. Future Direction of Research on Methodology: Approach of Sociology and Pneumatologically Ecclesiological Approach

Chen believes that the previous research on Sinicization of Christianity paid too much attention to cultural studies, and thus he proposed a methodology that regards Christianity as a "society."[117] However, such a methodology has its limitations. For example, there were not many churches or Christians for sociological studies when Christianity was introduced into China and therefore the result from the sociological research at that time was limited; however, Christianity had already entered China at that time.

In addition, the pneumatologically ecclesiological approach is also to be considered. Since the Holy Spirit is present in the church, the church is empowered by the Holy Spirit and shares the fellowship of the Holy Spirit,[118] and Pentecostalism is developed in marginal groups in society in its beginning,[119] Pentecostalist ecclesiology would accommodate various churches and reflect "church unity." A scholar suggests that:

> The Spirit poured out on all flesh enables the miracle of human communications—so that was once far off is brought near (cf. Eph. 2:13) and what was strange is now intelligible (cf. 1 Cor. 14:21). All of these combine to conform the missiological principle of

---

114. Nicholls, *Contextualization*, 13–15.

115. Nicholls, *Contextualization*, 15.

116. Please also see Peskett and Ramachandra, *Message of Mission*, 239.

117. 陳胤安（Chen）,〈從社會的觀念談基督教「本色化」的假設〉, 159–66.

118. Yong, *Spirit Poured Out*, 127.

119. Yong, *Spirit Poured Out*, 138.

independence . . . except that it demands extension of this principle in the twenty-first century from the realm of culture to the realm of the religion.[120]

Scholars in missiology indicate that in its early days the Pentecostal movement did progress towards mutual acceptance; however, there were still divisions and a refusal to accept one another,[121] and they are not always united. Therefore, the pneumatologically ecclesiological approach can be adopted to study the Sinicization of Christianity; nevertheless, it should not become its principal methodology.

8. Possible Future Direction of Research on Indigenous Theology: Discovery and Expression

The two major categories of Augustine's hermeneutics, "discover" and "express,"[122] were borrowed in this paper to construct indigenous theology in the Chinese context. According to previous discussion, it can be found that the methodologies of anthropology and religious studies are helpful for constructing indigenous Christian theology. However, the theological hermeneutic approach, especially the canonical-linguistic approach, is a better methodology for it.[123] That is, the interpretation of the canon (text and established theological ideas) is led by the Holy Spirit, and is expressed in an indigenous language within the indigenous context.[124]

In terms of "discovering," flexibility should be allowed since the interpretation will by no means be the same as text,[125] whilst the interpretation cannot bypass church traditions either. Theories in missiology tend to believe that God's revelation is equal in amount across all ethnic groups, and thus we cannot use any one of the cultures as the principle to interpret Christianity, which is tantamount to declaring the superiority of a certain culture. Although cultures are equal before God, we must admit certain cultures are in "priority" in understanding Christianity as God chooses

---

120. Yong, *Spirit Poured Out*, 247.

121. Peskett and Ramachandra, *Message of Mission*, 216–17.

122. Augustine, "Argument," 1. See books 1–3 for interpretation of the Scriptures and book 4 for expression and communication of the truth. The English translations were adopted from Augustine, "On Christian Doctrine," 522.

123. Treier, *Theological Interpretation*, 149–50.

124. Please refer to Vanhoozer, *Drama of Doctrine*, 189–99, 203–20, 231–37.

125. Weinsheimer, *Philosophical Hermeneutics*, 87.

certain groups of people, their history, and culture in history as vehicles for his revelation and a stage for revealing himself. We must not confuse cultural equality with the priority of understanding Christianity. In terms of expression, Christians can refer to church traditions to find a solution that is suitable for an indigenous context. However, the direction and purpose of the expression must not conflict with church traditions. This is because "beyond merely setting boundaries, the Rule of Faith grants us true freedom by guiding us to pursue particular directions of interpretation."[126]

Sino-Christian theology attaches great importance to the translation of Western Christian humanistic classics[127] as well as contributing to the academic circle. The church needs academia to assist in terms of "community of formation."[128] From a social perspective, each religious tradition has its boundary. Even though this boundary may move when being introduced in a new situation, if the religion has changed to the extent of crossing the boundary, it would then be regarded as a different religion.[129] Therefore, religious traditions are usually defined and guarded by religious professionals.[130] Lindbeck argues that the second theology (doctrine) should become the rule of faith and help the practice of the first theology (rituals and liturgy),[131] that is, "doctrine helps Christians to inhabit the faith of the church as a culture and to pass on the meaning of its signs and symbols with integrity."[132] Furthermore, empirical research has also found that rituals strengthen a Christian's understanding of "the signed reality," that is, an understanding of an object which doctrine refers to.[133] For this reason, if development of indigenous theology is desired, we should advance academic research and train indigenous professionals, especially pastoral workers with theological literacy and understanding of the ecumenical traditions, by which the first theology and the practice of faith are regulated and Christian community is shaped. It would excel indigenous theology with "discovering" and "expressing."

---

126. Treier, *Theological Interpretation*, 63.
127. 劉小楓 (Liu) ，《聖靈降臨的敘事》, 65–77.
128. Fowl, *Engaging Scripture*, 179.
129. Shils, *Tradition*, 96.
130. Shils, *Tradition*, 97.
131. Lindbeck, *Nature of Doctrine*, 79–84.
132. Treier, *Theological Interpretation*, 81.
133. Lombaert, "Religious Symbolization," 291–318.

9. Other Possible Directions of Future Researching and Developing of Indigenous Chinese Theology

In the dimension of cultural studies in indigenous Chinese theology, some achievements are worth noting. For example, Milton Wan's (溫偉耀) research, starting from Confucian philosophy of mind and humanity and being grounded on epistemology[134] and the doctrine of God,[135] analyzes Confucian idealism of the heart-nature and dialogues with it from the perspectives of philosophy, Christian spirituality, and systematic theology. Wan highlights that self-transformation requires "an ultimate Being" as the reference point, so that transformation pursued by Confucianism can be "actualised."[136] More academic research results of this kind are needed.

From the dimension of time, Chinese society is changing rapidly, and thus research on the Sinicization of Christianity and indigenous Chinese theology should not just stay in the past,[137] but also needs to look forward.[138] Looking at the development of indigenous Christian theology in terms of research scope, Lam (林子淳) adopting Hans Frei's theory discusses the direction of the development of Sino-Christian theology,[139] especially participation in the public domain, and is worthy to be considered.

The relationship between indigenous theology and ecumenical tradition is also worth exploring.[140] We should understand the development of Christianity, especially Christianity in China, from both aspects of globalization and contextualization.[141] In the light of this framework, we will then be able to understand the development of Christianity from two dimensions: catholicity and indigenization. Nowadays, the interpretation of the Bible should be "Glocal," which means indigenous Chinese theology with publicity should start from the interpretation of the Bible,[142] focusing on the

---

134. 溫偉耀（Wan），《生命的轉化與超拔》，359-461；《成聖之道——北宋二程修養工夫論之研究》，125-56.

135. 溫偉耀（Wan），〈論基督教與中國信仰中的超越體驗〉，113-62.

136. 溫偉耀（Wan），《生命的轉化與超拔》，134-42，312-57；〈論基督教與中國信仰中的超越體驗〉，211-20；《成聖之道》，125-56.

137. 秦家懿（Ching），〈本位化神學及其普世性〉，22-23；何光滬（He），〈漢語神學的方法與進路〉，18.

138. 秦家懿（Ching），〈本位化神學及其普世性〉，22-23.

139. 林子淳（Lam,），《多元性漢語神學詮釋》，102-5.

140. Please refer to Kim, "World Christianity," 51-53.

141. 陳馴（Chen），《當代中國的基督教神學方法》，10-16, esp. 16.

142. 謝品然（Chia），《開放的文本——聖經學和公共神學關係的初探》

text of the Bible. It should be the principal element of the development of theology, whilst relating the fruits of exegesis to the readers' context and developing proper applications.[143] Because indigenous theology also "add[s] something new to global theology,"[144] it should go beyond an indigenous context.[145] He states that "a genuine indigenous theology should go beyond the concept of 'indigeneity' and point towards the universal concept that is always above and stays ahead of indigenous theology. This is the paradox of indigenous theology and of all theologies."[146] We should not oppose other theologies with indigenous theology but rather develop indigenous theology in a way of "cooperating and complementing" the existing theology instead of "separating and competing" with them.[147] For "every local church is the only place where Jesus Christ presents and acts, and the realisation of the whole mystical body of Christ in a particular situation. From this perspective, the indigenisation of a local church is not only for its own benefit, but also for the benefit of other churches. In fact, [the] universal church will be nourished by the indigenisation of a local church. Because of indigenisation of local churches, it is more evident it is one Church, with diversity in unity, and the diversity does not diminish the unity."[148]

Another goal of indigenous Chinese theology could be that Chinese culture develops better because of Christian input.[149] Chinese Christians should also testify to the incarnate Word,[150] which may be presented as "the life experience and self-reflection of Chinese Christians" and "proclaiming the meaning of Christian universal salvation to people."[151] Therefore, "the church will be living in love and generosity, spreading the good news to all who will hear it, in their own languages, and growing upwards, downwards, outwards and in numbers."[152] Pan further suggests that the church should

---

, 79.

143. 謝品然 (Chia), 《開放的文本》, 121–22.

144. 何光滬 (He), 〈「本土神學」管窺〉, 161.

145. Please refer to Balasundaram, *Contemporary Asian*, ii.

146. 何光滬 (He), 〈「本土神學」管窺〉, 163.

147. 何光滬 (He), 〈「本土神學」管窺〉, 163, 167–68.)

148. 輔仁神學著作編譯會〈Fu Jen Theological Publications Association〉, 〈教會與文化〉, 827.

149. 余達心 (Yu), 〈本色神學初探〉, 198–99.

150. Peskett and Ramachandra, *Message of Mission*, 83–85.

151. 楊慶球 (Yeung), 〈從文化角度看本色化神學〉, 140.

152. Peskett and Ramachandra, *Message of Mission*, 223.

shift the mission paradigm from a propagation mode emphasizing church growth in numbers to a hermeneutic mode promoting dialogues and the exchange of ideas.[153]

Conclusion

Sinicization of Christianity in China has always been a topic attracting heated discussion, and its concern is to evangelize Chinese people. There are four categories of methodological approach for understanding Christianity in China. Approaches of hermeneutics overlook God's choice of specific historical and cultural contexts for the incarnated Christ and the development of the church. The approaches of cultural studies mainly try to integrate Confucianism and Christian doctrines. However, they usually forget the gospel should be the ultimate judge and redeemer of all cultures, and sometime underestimate the level of syncretism. Approaches of empirical religious studies are worth continuing to develop, as are the approaches of indigenous Chinese theology. In order to continue developing indigenous Chinese theology, the author of the paper proposes adopting the canonical-linguistic approach as the principal methodology and constructing indigenous Chinese theology from the dimensions of discovery and expression. In the process of discovering the truth, it requires us to refer to the historical and cultural background of the Bible, focusing on biblical text and respecting church traditions, thereby developing theology in Chinese language and in an indigenous Chinese theology context under the guidance of the Holy Spirit. Moreover, this truth-pursuing journey should not only focus on indigenous issues and applications, but also share the fruits of indigenous Chinese theology with global churches.

Bibliography

Augustine. "On Christian Doctrine." In *A Select Library of the Nicene and Post-Nicene Fathers of the Christian Church*, First Series, vol. 2, *Augustin: The City of God, On Christian Doctrine*, edited by Philip Schaff, trans. Marcus Dods and J. F. Shaw, 513–97. Peabody, MA: Hendrickson, 1994.

Balasundaram, Franklyn. *Contemporary Asian Christian Theology*. Delhi: Indian Society for Promoting Christian Knowledge, 1998.

Brock, Sebastian Paul. *Fire from Heaven: Studies in Syriac Theology and Liturgy*. Aldershot, Hampshire: Ashgate, 2006.

---

153. 潘鳳娟（Pan），《西來孔子艾儒略》，271–77.

趙天恩（Chao, Johnathan Tien-en）.《中國教會本色化運動（1919-27）：基督教會對現代中國反基督教運動的回應》.台北：橄欖，2019.

陳胤安（Chen, Yin An）.〈從社會的觀念談基督教「本色化」的假設——以人類學理論反思文化概念的使用〉.《道風》第32期（2010春）：147-71.

陳馴（Chen, Xun）.《當代中國的基督教神學方法》.北京：宗教文化，2010.

謝品然（Chia, Philip P.）.《開放的文本——聖經學和公共神學關係的初探》.修訂版.聖經與公共生活叢書：神學與理論系列.香港：研道社，2009.

秦家懿（Ching, Julia）.〈本位化神學及其普世性〉.於《基督教與中國本色化國際學術研討會論文集》10-24.林治平（編）.台北：宇宙光，1990.

Droogers, Andre. "Syncretism: The Problem of Definition." In *Dialogue and Syncretism: An Interdisciplinary Approach*, edited by Jerald D. Gort et al., 7–25. Amsterdam: Editions Rodopi, 1989.

Fowl, Stephen E. *Engaging Scripture: A Model for Theological Interpretation, Challenges in Contemporary Theology*. Oxford: Blackwell, 1998.

輔仁神學著作編譯會〈Fu Jen Theological Publications Association〉.〈教會與文化〉.於《神學辭典》825-27.增修版.台北：光啟文化，2012.

何光滬（He, Guanghu）.〈「本土神學」管窺」〉.《道風》第2期（1995春）152-68.

———.〈漢語神學的方法與進路〉.《維真學刊》第4期（1996年3月）16-24.

Kamstra, Jacques H. "Religie en Syncretisme." In *Inleiding tot de Studie van de Godsdiensten*, edited by D. J. Hoens et al., 210–23. Kampen: Kok, 1985.

Kim, Kirsteen. "World Christianity Curricula: A Perspective from Missiology/Mission Studies." In *World Christianity: History, Methodologies, Horizons*, edited by Jehu J. Hanciles, 49–60. Maryknoll, NY: Orbis, 2021.

關瑞文（Kwan, Simon Shui-man）.〈評劉小楓的漢語基督神學〉.《道風》第4期（1996春）220-39.

郭鴻標（Kwok, Benedict H.）.《基督信仰漢語神學芻議》.普及神學叢書.香港：建道神學院出版社，2011.

賴品超（Lai, Pan-chiu）.《廣場上的漢語神學——從神學到基督宗教研究》.漢語基督教文化研究所叢刊45.香港：道風，2014.

———.〈漢語基督教神學對宗教分歧的論述〉.《道風》第28期（2013春）65-86.

林子淳（Lam, Jason Tsz-shun）.《多元性漢語神學詮釋——對「漢語神學」的詮釋及漢語的「神學詮釋」》.漢語基督教文化研究所叢刊19.香港：道風，2006.

Leopold, Anita Maria. "General Introduction." In *Syncretism in Religion: A Reader*, edited by Anita M. Leopold and Jeppe S. Jensen, 2–12. London; Equinox, 2004.

梁家麟（Leung, Ka-lun）.〈中國近代教會史裡的本色化與福音化討論〉.《超前與墮後——本土釋經與神學研究》111-70.文化集刊13.香港：建道神學院出版部，2003.

林治平（Lin, Chih-pin）.〈基督教在中國本色化之必要性與可行性——從中國教會歷史發展觀點檢討之〉.於《基督教在中國本色化論文集》，1-34.林治平（主編）.北京：今日中國，1998.

———..〈奠下一塊堅固的磐石——紀念宇宙光創設廿週年出版基督教與中國歷史文化叢書總序〉.《基督教與中國論集》.台北：宇宙光，1993，序1-12.

———..《基督教與中國論集》.台北：宇宙光，1993.

林金水（Lin, Jin-shuei）、郭榮剛（Guo, Rong-gang）.《基督教中國化研究初探》台北：以琳，2014.

Lindbeck, George A. *The Nature of Doctrine: Religion and Theology in a Postliberal Age*. Philadelphia: Westminster, 1984.

劉小楓（Liu, Xianfeng）.〈現代語境中的漢語基督神學〉.《道風》第2期（1995春）: 9–48.
———.《這一代人的怕和愛》.增訂版.北京：華夏，2007.
———.《聖靈降臨的敘事》.增訂版.北京：華夏，2008.
Nicholls, Bruce J. *Contextualization: A Theology of Gospel and Culture.* Outreach and Identity: Evangelical Theological Monography 3. Exeter: Paternoster, 1979.
Osborne, Grant R. *The Hermeneutical Spiral: A Comprehensive Introduction to Biblical Interpretation.* 2nd ed. Downers Grove, IL: Inter-Varsity, 2006.
Palmer, Richard E. *Hermeneutics: Interpretation Theory in Schleiermacher, Dilthey, Heidegger, and Gadamer.* Evanston, IL: Northwestern University Press, 1969.
潘鳳娟（Pan, Feng-chuan）.《西來孔子艾儒略——更新變化的宗教會遇》.台北：聖經資中心，2002.
Panikkar, Raimon. *The Unknown Christ of Hinduism: Towards an Ecumenical Christophany.* Maryknoll, NY: Orbis, 1981.
Peskett, Howard, and Vinoth Ramachandra. *The Message of Mission: The Glory of Christ in All Time and Space.* The Bible Speaks Today: Bible Themes Series. Leicester: Inter-Varsity, 2003.
Rahner, Karl. *Hearers of the Word.* Revised by J. B. Metz. Translated by Michael Richards. New York: Herder and Herder, 1969.
Shils, Edward. *Tradition.* London: Faber and Faber, 1981.
邵玉銘（Shao, Yu-ming）.〈基督教與中國論集序〉.於林治平《基督教與中國論集》序19–26.台北：宇宙光，1993.
Standaert, Nicolas. *Handbook of Christianity in China. Volume 1: 635–1800.* Leiden: Brill, 2001.
Thiselton, Anthony C. *Thiselton on Hermeneutics: The Collected Works and New Essays of Anthony Thiselton.* Aldershot, Hampshire: Ashgate, 2006.
Tracy, David. *Plurality and Ambiguity: Hermeneutics, Religion, Hope.* San Francisco: Harper & Row, 1981.
Treier, Daniel J. *Introducing Theological Interpretation of Scripture: Recovering a Christian Practice.* Grand Rapids, MI: Baker Academic, 2008.
Vanhoozer, Kevin J. *The Drama of Doctrine: A Canonical Linguistic Approach to Christian Doctrine.* Louisville, KY: Westminster John Knox, 2005.
———. *Is There a Meaning in This Text?: The Bible, the Reader, and the Morality of Literary Knowledge.* Grand Rapids, MI: Zondervan, 1998.
溫偉耀（Wan, Milton Wai-yiu）.《生命的轉化與超拔：我的基督宗教漢語神學思考》.北京：宗教文化，2009.
———.〈論基督教與中國信仰中的超越體驗〉.於《基督教與中國文化的相遇》107–220.盧龍光編.崇基學院宗教研究叢書龐萬倫基督教與中國文化系列一.香港：香港中文大學崇基學院出版社，2001.
———.《成聖之道——北宋二程修養工夫論之研究》.比較研究叢刊2.台北：文史哲，1996.
王志希（Wang, Chih-hsi）.〈「如果基督生活在今日之中國」——從《天風》雜誌看基督教「本色化」與「聖經文本」（一九八〇～二〇一三年）〉.《鵝湖月刊》第505期（2017年7月）28–42.
王明道（Wang, Ming-tao）.《五十年來》.十二版.香港：晨星，2005.
———.〈新年來信〉.《福音文宣社通訊》第31期（1981年1至2月）2.
王治心（Wang, Zhixin）.《中國基督教史綱》.上海：上海古籍，2004.
———.〈中國本色教會討論〉.《青年進步》第79冊（1925年1月）11–16.

Watson, Francis. *Text, Church, and World: Biblical Interpretation in Theological Perspective*. Grand Rapids, MI: Eerdmans, 1994.

Weinsheimer, Joel. *Philosophical Hermeneutics and Literary Theory*. New Haven, CT: Yale University Press, 1991.

楊森富（Yang, Sen-fu）.〈唐元兩代基督教興衰原因之研究〉.於《基督教入華百七十年紀念集》29–77.林治平編.台北：宇宙光，1977.

———.《中華基督教本色化論文集》.馬禮遜入華宣教200年紀念文集系列26.台北：宇宙光全人關懷機構，2006.

楊慶球（Yeung, Jason Hing Kau）.〈從文化角度看本色化神學〉.《中國神學研究院期刊》31期（2001年7月）125–44.

邢福增（Ying, Fuk-tsang）.《文化適應與中國基督徒（1860–1911）》.基督教與中國文化研究叢書2.香港：建道神學院出版部，1995.

Yong, Amos. *The Spirit Poured Out on All Flesh: Pentecostalism and the Possibility of Global Theology*. Grand Rapids: Baker Academic, 2005.

余達心（Yu, Carver）.〈本色神學初探〉.於《初熟之果——聖經與本色神學》192–215.陳濟民、馮蔭坤（編）.香港：中國神學研究院出版社，1979.

張開沅（Zhang, Kaiyuan）.〈序一：「中華歸主」與「主歸中華」〉.於《離異與融會：中國基督徒與本色教會的興起》序一1–5.劉家峰編.人文社科新論叢書.上海：人民出版社，2005.

8.

Syncretism and Inculturation: Wang Zheng as an Example

Kai T. Wong

Abstract

INCULTURATION INVOLVES CULTURAL ENCOUNTERS and interpenetrations, as well as borrowing and reconfiguration of concepts. Thus, suspicions of syncretism arise. Wang Zheng, a late Ming Christian literatus, proposed to utilize the concepts of "the Great Parent (*Dafumu*)," "Aweing God and Caring Others," and "Home-coming" to address the Christian God, God-man relationship and redemption. His attempt was criticized by Jacques Gernet, Eric Zücher, and Huang Yi-long as a typical example of syncretism. This paper seeks to illustrate, through Wang Zheng as an example, that inculturation inevitably involves syncretic activities but does not necessarily lead to syncretism. To consider an inculturated theology of syncretism or not, we should take into consideration these factors: definitions of syncretism, the powerplay between "church tradition" and "younger churches," and the interpenetration of theological traditions and cultures.

Introduction

When the gospel reached the Third World, it encountered a more pluralistic environment. In order for the gospel to be firmly planted in new soil, engaging in dialogue with the receiving culture and religions seemed unavoidable. This prompted the process of inculturation. Inculturation is an attempt "to respond meaningfully to the gospel within one's own situation."[1] This process involves dialogue, concept-borrowing, reconfiguration, and incorporation. Syncretism happens in this process.[2] This paper seeks to clarify the phenomena of syncretism and inculturation, which are co-occurring but are not carefully distinguished. Our first finding indicates that syncretism is inevitable but not necessary in the process of inculturation. Although many may think this statement an oxymoron, it is not. When we say syncretism is inevitable, we mean syncretism in terms of incorporation, which is innate to inculturation. When we say it is not necessary, it implies that syncretism is not a logical consequence of incorporation. In this paper, we will attempt to define syncretism through a brief review and classification, to clarify the different connotations of the term. Our second finding shows that syncretism involves power plays behind the scene, between "insiders" and "outsiders," "old churches" and "young churches," and "clerics" and "lay people." These power plays affect how to determine the compatibility of inculturated theologies. The third finding is that inculturation does not only benefit the receiving culture and churches, but also the church tradition. In order to substantiate these findings, we utilize Wang Zheng, a Christian literatus in late Ming China, as a case study to demonstrate the three theses we proposed.

We will, in this paper, firstly provide a brief outlook of syncretism through a brief review. We will also propose way to differentiate the ambiguity of syncretism, which will provide us with a clearer way to address syncretism in our discussion. The second section of the paper will address the relationship of syncretism and inculturation. Wang Zheng, the person and his thought, is a vivid example of the knotty problem of syncretism and inculturation. A study of Wang and his thought will be presented in

---

1. Nicholls, *Contextualization*, 29. It is worth noting that the original term that Nicholls used is contextualization. Contextualization, indigenization, and inculturation are treated as synonymous here, until a clearer differentiation is discussed in the second subsection of the paper.

2. Syncretism is used here as a descriptive term without any value judgment.

the third section. A brief evaluation of his inculturated effort, as well as implications of the study will be offered at the end of the section.

Defining Syncretism

Defining syncretism is a complex matter because it is ambiguous in meaning and the evaluation standards are diverse. For instance, researchers of religious studies and those from Christian theology have different understandings and evaluations. For meaningful discussion on the theses proposed in this paper, we need to define clearly both the meaning and its areas of application.

A Brief Review

Past attempts to define syncretism are numerous but findings are diverse and no consensus has ever been reached.[3] It is beyond the space and scope of a short paper like this to give a conclusive definition. Thus, we will limit our review on the past attempts to a manageable extent which is relevant to our discussion by categorizing their approaches into five groups: 1) etymological; 2) functional; 3) compatibility; 4) process; 5) power play.[4] Through this review, we will identify useful information to substantiate the three findings listed in the introduction.

Etymological Approach

Kraemer noticed at the World Mission Conference in 1928 that "syncretism" frequently appeared in discussions among Protestants. In this conference, "the word 'syncretism' assumed to a very great extent a pejorative character,"[5] although this may not be the meaning of syncretism when it was first used. It is also noteworthy that the prominent persons involved in the discussions were mainly from the "older churches" and representatives

---

3. For a full account of these attempts, see Leopold and Jensen, *Syncretism*; Kane, *Syncretism*.

4. It is worth noting that some researchers in their study on syncretism employ multiple approaches.

5. Kraemer, *Religion*, 388. It is worth noting that syncretism was seen as a descriptive term at the World Missionary Conference in 1910. However, in the 1920s, it began to be constantly deemed negative. See also Kane, *Syncretism*, 39.

from the "younger church" were less vocal.⁶ Leopold and Denmark in their "General Introduction" to *Syncretism in Religions: A Reader* pinpoint that when Plutarch encouraged the Cretans to unite together for self-defence against threats from their enemies that the word used is *syncretismos*, which is a combination of a Greek prefix *syn* and *kretoi* (Cretans) or *kretismos* (Cretan behavior). In this usage, syncretism does not have any pejorative sense.⁷ This positive understanding of syncretism seemed to have been accepted for centuries until the sixteenth century. The fact that Erasmus continued to employ this positive meaning in his *Adagia*⁸ supports this claim. However, the positive current changed in the sixteenth and seventeenth century in the Protestant church. There was a debate among the Lutherans on Lutheran orthodoxy and "syncretists," which may have referred to heretics. It was used to name those who attempted to formulate common religious positions among different Protestant traditions.⁹ Leopold and Denmark point out that this change was based on a new and modern etymological understanding of the terminology of syncretism.¹⁰ They claim that "the modern version of syncretism stems from a neo-etymologist deriving from *synkerannumi* which means to 'mix' things that are incompatible."¹¹ "Incompatible," a value judgment, was then added to the meaning of syncretism. This appears to be the etymological ground for modern Protestants sticking a negative label to syncretism.¹²

The connotation of a term changes with the context of discourse, which is affected by its wider cultural and political contexts. The etymological approach may provide us with insight as to how the terminology evolves but it cannot define the meaning without disputes.

---

6. Kraemer, *Religion*, 387.

7. Leopold and Jensen, "Introduction," 14. See also Kraemer, *Religion*, 392–93; Kane, *Syncretism*, 21.

8. Kraemer, *Religion*, 393; Kane, *Syncretism*, 21.

9. Kraemer, *Religion*, 393. See also, Kane, *Syncretism*, 23–24.

10. However, Kane considers it an invention based on false etymology. Kane, *Syncretism*, 23.

11. Leopold and Jensen, "Introduction," 14.

12. Take Nicholls as an example. He considered syncretism an attempt to synthesize diverse and even conflicting elements into a unified system. See Nicholls, *Contextualization*, 29.

Functional Approach

From an etymological perspective, syncretism can be reckoned as either positive or negative. This difference obviously appears among researchers of religions and Christian theologians. However, this is not only due to the different subscriptions to the etymological origins of the word but also owes more to their different understandings of the function of syncretism.

Kraemer, on the one hand, considered syncretism as a universal religious phenomenon and stated one could find examples in both West and East.[13] On the other hand, he claimed that Christianity was not one of these examples, although, at one point, he also admitted that Christianity demonstrated a certain degree of syncretism in its early stage of formation.[14] However, he argued that Christianity as a prophetic religion, unlike natural religions, was against syncretism. These contradictory sayings reflect the complexity of understanding of syncretism. To solve this complicated issue, Kraemer suggested to distinguish syncretism into two types: phenomenological and theological. He said, "We mean by 'phenomenological': what is syncretism, when we look at it as it functions concretely in religious and cultures? By 'theological' we mean: what is there to say about syncretism in the light of the question of ultimate truth in Christ."[15] Religions frequently borrowed from neighboring religions and cultures in their formation stage. This is how religions function and no religion can be immune. However, certain religions, such as Christianity, Islam, and Judaism, after reaching consensus on doctrinal traditions, tended to avoid any further syncretism.[16] This is the reason why the "older churches" criticized syncretism at the Jerusalem conference in 1928.

Obviously, the differentiation of phenomenological and theological types of syncretism has its merit. It helps by identifying that syncretism is innate to religions. However, it is also a demerit causing confusion because Kraemer failed to distinguish its different usages which address two different aspects of syncretism, namely, functional and appraisal. It is desirable to separate the outcome from the function of syncretism so that we can adequately appreciate the relationship between syncretism and inculturation.

---

13. Kraemer, *Religion*, 389.
14. Kraemer, *Religion*, 397.
15. Kraemer, *Religion*, 392.
16. Kraemer, *Religion*, 397–98.

Compatibility Approach

Kraemer correctly identified that there was a strain of thought viewing and evaluating syncretism from orthodoxy. He named this "theological approach" syncretism. Strictly speaking, Kraemer did not classify all incorporations syncretic. He defined "genuine" syncretism as incorporating or synthesizing contrary elements from two or more religious traditions.[17] In other words, it is the compatibility of the result that matters. Determination of compatibility involves both agents and the standard. This leads to discussions on power play, which we will return to later.

Process Approach

It is valid for Kraemer to employ compatibility as the distinctive defining element of syncretism. However, the process itself is of equal importance to understand syncretism, and in particular, its relation to inculturation. We now turn to the process approach.

Kraemer correctly pointed out that when a religion began to incorporate "foreign elements" into its system, nobody could foresee whether or not the outcome would be legitimate.[18] However, this process is unavoidable when spreading the gospel or when cultures come in contact. The process itself is as important as the result. Vroom, thus, highlights the process as a way to appreciate syncretism. Syncretism is usually deemed as a way of incorporating incompatible religious tradition and practices together. It is this process that involves reinterpretation and reconfiguration or reconception of two different belief systems.[19] This process is indeed hermeneutical in nature and involves reinterpretation and reconfiguration or reconception activities.[20] Through this, new concepts and new practices evolved. These newly reconfigured and reinterpreted concepts or practices may have changed, up to the point where it loses its distinctiveness

---

17. Kraemer, *Religion*, 397–98.
18. Kraemer, *Religion*, 398–99.
19. Vroom, "Syncretism," 103.
20. It is noteworthy that reinterpretation is different from reconfiguration and reconception. Reconfiguration and reconception are "modifications" of concepts which may bring in extraneous elements. These new elements may jeopardize the original unity of elements that the system has. This is perhaps the reason why Christian theologians are so against any form of syncretism.

or original identity.[21] The religions involved will then have to determine whether to adjust their basic insights to accommodate these changes or to reject their assimilation. To limit our understanding to the result of incorporation is not adequate, because overlooking this hermeneutical process may stop us learning from new insights which may bring enrichment to the religions and cultures involved. Syncretism as a hermeneutical process merits appreciation.

Power Play Approach

Determining whether the incorporation is acceptable usually rests on the power of the "older churches" and in particular the clerics or "theologians." They represent the defenders or guardians of the tradition, self-understanding, and "truth." However, it is evidential that syncretism usually happens among general lay persons no matter how subjective and primitive it may be. For instance, Schreiter in discussing syncretism and dual religious systems, points out that in Africa, South America, and Asia, dual-religion practices are common and unlike the Christian leadership, "local members do not see the contradiction."[22] Schreiter's observation informs us that there is a rift between the "powerful" and "powerless," as well as the "outsiders" and insiders."[23] Kraemer had already reported on how the voices of the "older churches" (representing the tradition) nearly monopolized the discussion in 1928. The fact that syncretism is seen as a rising concern in a postcolonial era with reignited interest also demonstrates the power in play behind the scene.[24]

This play or struggle of powers will never end if Christianity endeavors to make itself a universal religion in this pluralistic world. On the one hand, the Western church, in facing the uprising of local theologies developed in the Third World, considers itself the defender and sole interpreter of the "tradition" that would never become outdated. On the other hand, missionaries, local leaders, and lay people of the non-Western churches see themselves as instruments to develop their own theologies which speak

---

21. Vroom, "Syncretism," 103.

22. Schreiter, *Local Theologies*, 148.

23. Outsiders refer to the priests, clerics, and missionaries. Insiders refer to lay persons who participate in dual religious practices. See also discussion on "insiders" and "outsiders" in Leopold and Jensen, "Introduction," 23–24.

24. Leopold and Jensen, "Introduction," 18.

to their local non-Christian people. Despite the "white gaze" that Kane argues,[25] who has the right and authority to determine which local theology is compatible will become an acute issue both now and in the future.

This power play approach reveals another complicated aspect of syncretism. Syncretism is not just a "battle" between false teachings and truth, but power play in cultural, political, traditions, and self-understandings, and most important of all, the authority of discourse and of ideological construction. Deep and thorough discussion on these topics will exceed our scope such that we must stop here.[26] However, the fact that syncretism reflects and involves power play should not be overlooked.

Syncretism Three-In-One

To propose a conclusive definition of syncretism that satisfies everyone seems unrealistic. We will propose an approach that can facilitate the discussion. To discard the terminology completely will not do the job since syncretism seems innate to the formation and spread of religions. Keeping it without qualification is also not an option because of the ambiguity it carries. We will, then, use the same terminology but label them with numbers for differentiation purposes.

The model "Syncretism three-in-one" highlights the three facets of syncretism. "*Syncretism 1*" (*syn1*) denotes incorporation or synthesis occurring in religions contacts. *Syn1* refers to the activity as well as the process of incorporation and does not carry any value judgment. However, the common usage of syncretism among Christian theologians should not be overlooked. Thus, it is rightfully to assign "*syncretism 2*" (*syn2*) to denote the incorporation found incompatible. *Syn1* is deemed as a neutral description of syncretism, while *syn2* denotes the end result of incompatible syncretism. Although they both may denote the same activity, the distinction should be maintained because not all syncretism ends up satisfactory.

There is another usage of syncretism that we should not ignore. "*Syncretism 3*" (*syn3*) refers to compatible syncretism. The difference between *syn3* and *syn2* splits hairs but this distinction is important and necessary. As with the two sides of a coin, they refer to the same activity or process but with different evaluated results. In fact, legitimate syncretism is evidential. A vivid example of this is the concept of "homoousion."

25. Kane, *Syncretism*, 48–89.
26. For a fuller discussion on the aspect of power in syncretism, see Kane, *Syncretism*.

We have listed five different approaches to delineate both the meaning and its application in the subsection "A Brief Review." Now we have reduced these five approaches to three, but is this reduction appropriate and acceptable? The etymological approach seeks to ascertain syncretism from a historical point of view. Its meaning is implied in *syn2* and *3*. Both the process and power play approaches address the dynamic aspects of syncretism, which seems not to be reflected in *syn1* and *2*. However, these two aspects are, in fact, presupposed throughout any discussion on compatibility. "Syncretism three-in-one" seems to be a simple and direct way to demarcate syncretism for a clear discussion.

Inculturation and Syncretism

Terminology Matters

Before discussing how inculturation relates to syncretism (*syn1, 2,* and *3*), we have to address the terminology of inculturation. Inculturation is a term used mainly by Catholic missionaries and theologians. Its primary meaning is similar to that of indigenization and contextualization but with a focus on incarnation. It is well known to researchers in this area that indigenization was the first terminology used to denote the process of self-identification and building a new nation in postcolonial era. As indigenization of personnel and governance happened, cultural and religious indigenization followed. Nicholls noticed that contextualization began to be used in 1972 and earned its support from many, especially evangelicals.[27] Contextualization involves indigenization and more, going beyond by including "the process of secularity, technology and the struggle for human justice which characterized the historical moment of nations in the Third World."[28] It is an attempt to "respond meaningfully to the gospel with the framework of one's own situation."[29] In short, the difference between indigenization and contextualization is that the latter seriously focuses on the contemporary factors in cultural change.[30]

---

27. Nicholls, *Contextualizaton*, 20.
28. Nicholls, *Contextualizaton*, 21.
29. Nicholls, *Contextualizaton*, 21.
30. Nicholls, *Contextualizaton*, 22.

Inculturation as a term first appeared in 1959[31] and later became an official term used by Catholics in the discussion of indigenization and contextualization. Most importantly, the coining of this term emphasizes the role of incarnation in words and deeds in the gospel and culture contact. V. C. Vanzin considered that Christianity must "incarnate" in its culture.[32] Pedro Arrupe further claimed,

> Inculturation is the incarnation of Christian life and of the Christian message in a particular cultural context, in such a way that this experience not only finds expression through elements proper to the culture in question (this alone would be no more than a superficial adaptation), but becomes a principle that animates, directs and unifies the culture, transforming and remaking it so as to bring about a "new creation."[33]

This definition, firstly, considers culture, including past and present, as an organic whole. Secondly, it treats the culture with respect and aims to identify the elements which are proper to the culture to engage in dialogue with Christianity. Finally, it seeks to create a "new creation" through transformation and remaking of the culture through the gospel. Inculturation seems to be more inclusive than contextualization and indigenization. Choosing it to denote the interaction between gospel and culture is more appropriate.

Syncretism: An Inevitable Phenomenon But Not Necessary Result in Inculturation

Syncretism (*syn1*, 2 and 3) relates closely with inculturation. Nicholls considers it inevitable in the process. He quotes the Willowbank Report saying that when the church seeks to express its life in local culture, it has to face the problem of cultural elements no matter how good or evil they are.[34] Bevans even claims that anyone who engages in contextual theology or inculturated theology, "engages in a process of syncretism."[35] Kamstra also recognized that with prophetic religions such as Christianity and Islam,

---

31. Dhavamony, *Christian Theology*, 88.
32. Dhavamony, *Christian Theology*, 90.
33. Dhavamony, *Christian Theology*, 91–92.
34. Nicholls, *Contextualizaton*, 29.
35. Bevans, "Fair or Foul?," 91.

their prophets have to employ the speech, concepts, and situation of the audience in communicating with the target culture, to make their message comprehensible. Syncretism is unavoidable and it is so human that "to be human is to be a syncretist."[36]

Schreiter in his study of local theology once proposed a mapping of construction of inculturated theology.[37] This mapping demonstrates that *syncretism 1* is inevitable.

Church Tradition   **Culture**

Church Tradition	Culture
The Opening of Church Tradition through Analysis (4)	The Opening of Culture through Analysis (2)
	Previous Local Theology (1)
Christian Tradition seen as a Series of Local Theology (5)	Emergence of Themes for Local Theology (3)
Encounter of Themes with Parallel Local Theologies (6)	
	The Impact of Church Tradition on Local Theologies (7)
The Impact of Local Theologies on Church Tradition (8)	
	The Impact of Local Theologies upon the Culture (9)

Syncretism happens in stage 2 and 3 when the local Christian community begins to engage in cultural analysis and identifies cultural themes for inculturated theology. Although we emphasize the inevitability of *syn1*, it does not imply that *syn2* (syncretism that is incompatible) will necessarily

36. As quoted by Pye, "Syncretism," 60.

37. Schreiter, *Local Theologies*, 25. The figure of the mapping proposed is reproduced here for demonstration purposes.

result. Schreiter's model highlights that there is step 6 to ascertain the compatibility through dialogue with the tradition of other inculturated theologies included in "church tradition."

As highlighted earlier in this paper, the process approach emphasizes that *syn1* is a hermeneutical process that involves reinterpretation, reconfiguration or reconception. The findings remain temporary until completing its dialogue with other inculturated theologies for credentials in orthodoxy. *Syn1* will then be classified as *syn2* or *3*. In this process of syncretism or incorporation, its end remains open. This is where the "unnecessary" aspect of the statement "syncretism is inevitable but not necessary" stands.

Foul or Fair Play

In order to become part of church tradition, inculturated theology must go through examinations fostered by other inculturated theologies and church tradition as a whole.[38] While Boff maintains a positive evaluation of syncretism considering it a "positive and normal process for Catholicism,"[39] he has not overlooked the importance to scrutinize the compatibility with inculturated theology. He also suggests that there are six kinds of syncretism: addition, accommodation, mixture, agreement, translation, and adaptation.[40] He claims that not all of these six types are compatible with the essential catholicity of the divine message.[41] For *syn1* to be accepted into church tradition, it must be a syncretism that "arises from the essential core of Christian faith that is embodied in the symbolic framework of another culture" and which is "converted in such a way that it ceases to be what it was, at its roots, and becomes an expression of the Christian faith."[42] Boff continues to stipulate criteria to ascertain *syn1*: Scripture, the tradition of the universal church that expresses the Christian experience, decisions of the episcopal synods that discern the "objectification" developed by the people of God, and the tradition of Jesus, prophets, and the liberating message of God in history, spiritual worship, and ethical commitment.[43] While Boff's suggestion indeed reflects the possible criteria and process of

38. Schreiter, *Local Theologies*, 34.
39. Boff, *Church*, 89.
40. Boff, *Church*, 90–91.
41. Boff, *Church*, 93.
42. Boff, *Church*, 101.
43. Boff, *Church*, 104–6.

examination, Stephen Bevans's imagery is more comprehensive in describing what the compatibility test is.

Bevans suggests utilizing the imagery of the "fair or foul play" of baseball to determine if a certain *syn1* is acceptable or compatible.[44] Bevans's idea is inspired by Justo González's understanding of the nature of doctrine which functions as the foul lines on a baseball field.[45] These foul lines can determine the compatibility of any inculturated theology. The merit of this imagery is that it sets the boundary but not the exact spot that the ball should target. Bevans continues to explain by quoting González, that "There is no rule that says that the ball must be hit to a particular area of the field. As long as they stay within the foul lines, players have a great deal of freedom."[46] It is also true for inculturation. The function of the criteria is boundary setting but not the area where the "ball" should land, as long as it is within the boundary. This gives younger churches freedom to develop their own theologies.

Church Tradition and Inculturated Theology

Christianity is a religion with a long history. From formation years onward, it experienced debates on orthodoxy in different phases, particularly through the first five hundred years. Although the basic doctrines seem to be settled and accepted by the wider Christian community, when Christianity entered the Third World, which was more pluralistic in culture and religions, it faced new challenges. These challenges included inculturated rites, practices, and theologies, which arose from their particular Christian experiences. Whether these particular Christian experiences are compatible with church tradition or other formerly accepted inculturation theologies remains in question. Schreiter's mapping suggests that any inculturated theology must engage in dialogue with "church tradition," which represents different compatible inculturated theologies, in order to be accepted as part of it. This dialogue (step six of the mapping), in fact, involves power plays in discourse and theological construction.

When we expect the newly developed theology to undergo scrutiny by church tradition, it seems that church tradition assumes a superior role in theological construction. If we agree that the "younger churches" are equal

---

44. Bevans, "Fair or Foul?" 88–103.
45. Bevans, "Fair or Foul?" 90.
46. Bevans, "Fair or Foul?" 90.

in their experience of the "Jesus event" and all theologies are inculturated, parties at both ends should be equal. What are the grounds for putting church tradition first? From the discussion on syncretism above, the determination of syncretism (*syn2* and *3*) always involves the issue of "with-in" and "with-out." It is simply the case that the "insider" and "outsider," as well as cleric and lay persons, understand synthesis or incorporation differently. What is the justifiable reason to give church tradition supremacy in the power play? Perhaps, the principle of "first among the equals" may help solve this problem.

Church tradition can be considered both the founding members and the constitution of an association. To register as a government-recognized association, we need founding members as "patrons" who bear responsibilities. In its development stage, founding members assume the role to determine new memberships. As the association grows, the governing body may elect new delegates other than founding members to continue this role and responsibilities. These newly elected delegates assume the responsibilities that the founding members assumed. This can be parallel to compatible local theologies in Schreiter's mapping. However, the constitution of the association can be deemed as the church tradition which upholds all those compatible local or inculturated theologies. Just as any new proposal of changes must undergo an examination with the constitution for compatibility to be accepted, "younger churches" have their rights and autonomies to propose new theologies. Whether to accept it, the right rests with the church tradition (in association terms, the founding members, their delegates, and the constitution).

This imagery justifies the priority of the "first" of the church tradition. However, it does not justify any power play beyond this. Plays of power seem unavoidable in many aspects of activities. The issue is not to eliminate power plays but to clearly define an examination on compatibility that is equal and fair.

Is Wang Zheng Syncretic?

We have so far addressed syncretism and inculturation from the side of theory. We now turn to an example of Chinese inculturated theology to attend this issue in a concrete way. To give a full account of Wang's thought is beyond the scope that this paper allows, so we will limit our discussion of Wang's thought relevant to the accusation of syncretism (*syn2*).[47]

Wang Zheng, a Controversial Catechist

Wang Zheng of late Ming is a controversial person. He is deemed the fourth principal Christian in Ming.[48] However, research on him, in comparison to the Three Pillars, is inadequate. This study will highlight who he was in the context of controversy, his inculturated theology, and the evaluation of his thought.

Wang Zheng (王徵) was born in 1571 to a peasant family in the Shaanxi province.[49] He was a literatus who earned his doctoral degree (*jinshi*, 進士) in 1622 and was assigned the post of Prefectural Judge in Guangping and Yangzhou respectively. He was also appointed as an army commander at the frontier of Northeastern China to guard against the Manchurian invasion. This duty ended after a coup among the soldiers and after he was given amnesty, he retired from all government duties. Although he was a literatus and heavily influenced by Confucianism, he was also very religious. He first believed in Buddhism and later converted to Daoism.[50] However, he found that Confucianism, Buddhism, and Daoism could not help Chinese people (including himself) be upright or moral, nor help the government tackle its chaotic fate. He converted to Christianity by the influence of *Qike* (《七克》, *The Seven Victories*) of Diego de Pantoja. His conversion can be deemed as moral/ethical in nature.[51] Among his extant writings, the trilogy adequately represents his Christian thought. In this trilogy, the first book (according to both the sequence of composition and thought development), *Xueyong Shujie* (〈學庸書解〉, "An Exposition on *Daxue* and *Zongyong*"), is an exposition to the Confucian classics: *Daxue* (《大學》) and *Zongjung* (《中庸》). It serves as the premise of Wang's inculturated thought. The second book, *Weitian Airun Jilun* (《畏

---

47. For a full account of Wang Zheng's thought and work, see the writer's unpublished PhD thesis. Wong, "Filial Piety."

48. Standaert, *Handbook*, 404–5.

49. Hummel, *Eminent Chinese*, 807–9. See also 宋伯胤編 (Song), 《明涇陽王徵先生年譜》, 3.

50. 王徵(Wang), 《畏天愛人極論》, n6868, 1b.

51. Standaert, *Handbook*, 410. For discussions on conversion, see Rambo, *Religious Conversions*.

天愛人極論》, *Ultimate Discussion of the Awe of Heaven and Care of Human, WTARHL hereafter*), the main body of Wang's thought, is a catechism in its nature. *Renhuiyue* (〈仁會約〉, *Constitution and Regulation of the Humanitarian Society*) is the constitution and regulation of a benevolent society that Wang Zheng founded and serves as a sequel to *WTARJL*.

Wang Zheng was undoubtedly a Christian. However, his thoughts and behavior were criticized by some as syncretic and unfaithful to Christianity. These criticisms yield a good case study for the topic of syncretism and inculturation.

Eric Zücher, a Dutch sinologist, criticized that he hardly discussed the doctrines of incarnation and atonement in *WTARJL*.[52] Jacques Gernet, a French sinologist, also commented that Wang Zheng was a syncretist who incorporated the Christian God as the master of the pavilion of local deities. He said:

> Some, indeed, thought they had found a way to reconcile everything: it was by granting to this Master of Heaven the foremost place, that of the Sovereign on High of the Chinese . . . meanwhile retaining beneath him the whole heteroclite pantheon of China: Buddha, Bodhisattva, the gods and immortals of the Taoists, all the figures of the tradition of the literate elite and countless other deities too, each one being somehow delegated with a part of the universal power of the Master of Heaven. That is what it proposed by one of the interlocutors in an imaginary dialogue written by the convert, Wang Zheng.[53]

Gernet's comments are mainly based on the incidents where Wang Zheng, in his service as Prefectural Judge, led the people in his jurisdictions to say petitions to *Haotian Shangdi* (昊天上帝, the Supreme God in Heaven),[54] and on another occasion when he mentioned *He Bo* (河伯, river god).[55] In fact, Wang Zheng, also built a shrine that housed local sages who had contributed to the region.[56] These incidents appear to support Gernet's comment that Wang was a polytheist.

Huang Yi-long, a Taiwanese historian, considered that Wang Zheng's behavior betrayed his faith; a two-headed snake who practiced dual

52. Zücher, "Social Action," 274.
53. Gernet, *China*, 76.
54. 王徵(Wang),〈兩理略.活閘救秧〉, 17.
55. 王徵(Wang),《兩理略.肥城治水》, 11.
56. 王徵(Wang),《兩理略.建閣崇賢》, 36–38.

religious commitment to Confucianism and Christianity.[57] He complained that Wang Zheng had once visited a fortune teller with a friend.[58] Wang Zheng also took a young girl of age fifteen as his concubine, which was clearly forbidden by the teaching of missionaries.[59] Huang also criticized that Wang Zheng committed suicide in 1644 to demonstrate his loyalty to the last emperor of the Ming dynasty.[60] Huang considered Wang unorthodox because his deeds seemed contrary to Christian behavior.

It is noteworthy that these critics of Wang Zheng are not professional theologians per se but sinologists and a historian. The theological grounds for their critiques should be carefully reviewed. We will address these criticisms in the following subsection.

Wang Zheng's Inculturated Thoughts and Behavior

Although Wang Zheng was more a catechist than a theologian, his Christian thought is a good example for the study of inculturated theology and syncretism. In this subsection, we will first address his thoughts on man, God, the God-man relation, and salvation. Then, we will attend to what has been labelled as Wang's syncretic behavior. Due to the scope of this paper, direct quotation will only be given when necessary. Otherwise, references will be given for further study.

Tianming and God's Commandments

The first part of Wang's Trilogy, *Xueyong Shujie*, is an exposition by Wang Zheng concerning the two Confucian classics: *Daxue* and *Zhongyong*. This exposition was written in 1624, which reflected Wang faithfully following the Confucian tradition in encouraging his audience to attend moral cultivation. On the one hand, he followed Gao Panlong's (高攀龍) understanding of *Daxue* and *Zongyong* by emphasizing personal cultivation of morality.

---

57. 黃一農(Huang), 〈儒家化的天主教徒〉, 144–46.

58. 黃一農(Huang), 〈明末中西文化衝突之析探〉, 231. See also 黃一農(Huang), 〈儒家化的天主教徒〉, 167.

59. 黃一農(Huang), 〈明末中西文化衝突之析探〉, 223. Wang, in fact, was excommunicated by the church and in his final years he wrote a confession to the church regarding this matter. See also 王徵(Wang), 〈崇一堂日記隨筆.附錄祈請解罪啟稿〉, 176–77.

60. 黃一農(Huang), 〈明末中西文化衝突之析探〉, 154.

On the other, he connected this personal cultivation with the Mandate of Heaven (*tianming*, 天命). According to the tradition of Confucianism, the *Dao* (*The Principle*, 道) confers to humans their human nature (*xing*, 性), which makes moral cultivation possible. *Dao* is the metaphysical ground of morality in human beings. To substantiate this claim, Wang quoted the opening clauses of the first chapter of *Zhongyong* saying, "What Heaven has conferred is called nature; accordance with this nature is called the path of duty; the cultivation of this path is called instruction."[61] In saying this, Wang skillfully united human nature, *xing*, with the Mandate of Heaven. If one seeks to understand the Mandate of Heaven, what one should do is search inwardly. Later in *WTARJL*, this Mandate of Heaven is synonymous with the objective commandments of the Christian God (*Tianzhu*, 天主).[62] Confucianism is considered a philosophy which puts much emphasis on the human capability of living morally through self-discipline and cultivation. However, Christianity is a religion that highlights man's inadequacy of self-aided salvation and emphasizes external redemption. The Mandate of Heaven or the will of God is crucial in this aspect. Through *Xueyong Shujie*, Wang cleverly identified the Mandate of Heaven and its relation to human nature through a breakthrough between Confucianism and Christianity. Apart from this, he also transformed the understanding of mankind from moral agent into rational soul in *WTARJL*.

The Great Parent and Man

The second book of the Trilogy is *WTARJL*, which is catechism in nature. *WTARJL* is based on the works of Jesuit missionaries such as Ricci's *Tianzhu Shiyi* (《天主實義》, *The True Meaning of the Lord of Heaven*)[63] and is formatted as dialogues between the catechist and interlocutor. In this book, Wang utilized the "father and son" relationship of *wulun* (五倫, the Five Relationships) in Confucianism as an analogy for God and man's relationship. He considered God was the Father of mankind and used different ways to address God as the Father.[64] The most vivid name of the Father

---

61. 王徵(Wang),〈學庸書解〉, 109.
62. 王徵(Wang),《畏天愛人極論》, 43b–44a.
63. Standaert, "Wang Zheng's," 167–68.
64. Names such as "Pater" (罷得肋), "the original father-mother" (本生父母), "the true original father-mother" (元初真父母), "the father of all" (大公之父), and "the supreme divine father of all" (上帝公父).

is *Dafumu* (大父母, The Great Parent).⁶⁵ This concept of *Dafumu*, is believed to be inspired by the concept of *qing* (乾) and *kun* (坤), which Song Confucian Zhang Zai considered to represent the creating power in this universe.⁶⁶ Its creation of mankind is deemed similar to that of a father and a mother. It is noteworthy that when Wang named God as the Great Parent, he was not saying that God was dual in number nor dual-gendered. The term "parent" refers to God's creation as an analogy to parental procreation in mankind. In fact, he followed the Christian teaching of God in such a manner that *Dafumu* had not attracted any substantial criticism. However, the role and personhood of God the Father is so prominent in his thought that he was criticized for neglecting the doctrine of the Son and his salvation. Before turning to the discussion on this criticism, we will continue to address what Wang taught about man.

Wang Zheng followed the Catholic teaching on the human soul. To Wang Zheng, the human soul is imperishable and the rationality that rests in the soul are the distinctive features of the human soul compared to the souls of animals and plants.⁶⁷ This differs from Chinese belief, where the human soul consists of two elements, *hun* (魂) and *po* (魄), which will separate from each other at death and perish afterwards. The rationality of mankind is crucial because it provides the grounds for mankind to understand the objective Mandate of Heaven. Unlike the inward-searching of the Mandate of Heaven by Confucians, Wang pointed towards a new direction—to understand the commandments of God rationally. This redirection also affected how Chinese people anticipated what salvation should look like.

It is true that Wang rarely mentioned Jesus and rarely addressed anything about Jesus's salvation. Instead, he seemed to put much emphasis on moral teaching. This is indeed what Zücher criticized him for. However, Zücher's criticism seems overexaggerated. While it was common for the Jesuit missionaries and Christian literati to mention the Son and in particular, the incarnation and Jesus's passion, these discussions are comparably rarer than teaching on God the Father. There were social and cultural factors that contributed to this. Late Ming was a patriarchal society where a father would enjoy a superior status. Confucian teaching on filial piety

---

65. The first person who coined this term was Yang Tingyun (楊廷筠) and this terminology was widely accepted by missionaries.
66. 張載(Zhang), 〈乾清篇(西銘)〉, 62–63.
67. 王徵(Wang), 《畏天愛人極論》, 20b–21a.

placed greater emphasis on how the son should treat the father. In this social and ideological ethos, God the Father enjoyed a more prominent status in Christian teaching. Gianni Griveller also points out that it was extremely difficult for Christians to preach a God who was humiliated to the extent that he died on the cross as a criminal in late Ming. In such a social and ideological context, Wang Zheng was seemingly bound by his environment.

WTARJL as a catechism and its content was basically bound by its nature. Catechisms, in late sixteenth-century Europe, usually included the teachings of the creed, the Our Father (that is the Lord's prayer), and the Decalogue.[68] However, we should not overlook the fact that Wang had mentioned the incarnation and mission of Jesus, not in *WTARJL*, but in *Renhuiyue*.[69] In other words, what was labelled as "neglection" is mainly due to the limitation of the nature and tradition of catechisms. It seems that Wang's "neglection" was neither exceptional nor un-Christian in this context. The criticism of ignoring salvation is also groundless. Wang in *WTARJL* portrayed mankind as a prodigal son, who rebelled against God and should return to him as a filial son by observing his commandment through fearing God and administering charity to others.[70] He also on two other occasions addressed salvation. Firstly, in his poem "Echoing the 'Return Home' of Tao Qian," he portrayed mankind as a prodigal son wandering for a long time, and that it was time to return home to reunite with God, the *Shangdi*.[71] The second incident is that Wang implicitly mentioned baptism on a gospel tract calling its reader to accept this as a prescription to cure a human's immoral nature and deeds.[72] It is undeniable that this "homecoming" way of redemption is far from acceptable by the standard of penal substitutional theory. However, there are different theories in Christian tradition, such as recapitulation, ransom, satisfactory, and recently articulated "nonviolence," and these theories do not emphasize bloodshedding or retribution, but nonviolent ways to reunite with God. Consequently the "homecoming" theory can be considered compatible with church tradition.

---

68. Bradley, *Roman Catechism*, 84.
69. 王徵(Wang), 〈仁會約〉, 147–49.
70. 王徵(Wang), 《畏天愛人極論》, 7a–7b.
71. 王徵(Wang), 〈和陶靖節先生歸去來辭〉355–56.
72. 王徵(Wang), 〈活人丹方〉, 356.

Charitable Work

The third book of the trilogy is *Renhuiyue*. *Renhui* (仁會, humanitarian society) was a charity similar to other benevolent societies in late Ming except that it had significant Christian elements throughout. The founding philosophy of *Renhui* was based on 《哀矜行詮》 (*Exploration of the Practice of Compassion*) by Giacomo Rho[73] and the core concept, *ren* (仁), of Confucianism. This charity was founded with the purpose of serving those who were in need. Its services were limited to feeding the hungry, attending to the sick and burying the dead.[74] *Renhuiyue* is indeed a sequel to *WTARJL*. Wang highlighted in *WTARJL* that man should observe the commandments of *Tianzhu* (畏天, in awe of God) and love others through services (愛人, loving others). Wang, personally and individually, put this into practice through his services in the government.[75] *Renhui* was his effort on a corporate level. Membership is restricted to Christians, and Buddhists in particular were forbidden to join. It is also noteworthy that Wang in this book highlighted the mission and work of Jesus, portraying him as a model of *ren*, loving *Tianzhu* and others.

Polytheistic and Unfaithful

Gernet accused Wang of practicing and teaching polytheism. Gernet's criticism was mainly based on incidents showing that Wang lead local people in his jurisdiction petition to local deities and built a shrine for local sages. To accurately interpret these incidents, one has to put them in their social and cultural context. According to Wang's records of his services in both Guangping and Yangzhou, we find that the incidents that Gernet cited are factual. However, we must view them in the context of Confucianism and a Chinese culture of governance.

The responsibilities of a prefectural judge included not only legal matters, but also local policing, and educational affairs. Leading sacrifices to Confucius and making petitions to local deities for flooding and droughts were part of a government official's responsibilities. Even for those who had retired in their hometowns, they were still reckoned as literati with

---

73. 王徵(Wang), 〈仁會約〉, 140.
74. 王徵(Wang), 〈仁會約〉, 142.
75. 王徵(Wang), 〈兩理略.兩理略自序〉, 1.

authority, with the expectation to assume the leading roles in all these ceremonies. It is important to take this into consideration before making a judgment.

On the one hand, Gernet's judgment is not conclusive since we know nothing about Wang's motivation and thinking behind these incidents. On the other hand, we are certain that in *WTARJL* Wang fiercely attacked Buddhism for idolatries. Although Wang's criticism on Daoism was less intense, he clearly criticized Daoism as false teaching. Unless we have undisputable evidence to consider him hypocritical and subscribing to dual religions in practice, we should look into other possible interpretations of these incidents.

We find three other prayer scripts in 〈兩理略〉 (*Brief Compilations of Documents and Annotations of Prefectural Judge Offices at Guangping and Yangzhou*) addressed to *Shangdi*, the term that stood for the Creator God among Christians in late Ming.[76] In the "Petition for Sunny Weather," Wang mentioned guardian angels. He said, "It is the Creator God who grants guardian angels of nine levels to protect the people of the county . . ."[77] In the shrine he built, Wang put a tablet of *Haotian Shangdi* above all other tablets. This arrangement can be understood as putting the Christian God first and above all sages. This interpretation can be substantiated by the name given to this memorial shrine. It is named as *Jintiange* (敬天閣, Heaven Reverencing Shrine). Although heaven reverencing had a long tradition in Confucianism, here Wang subtly connected Confucianism to the Christian God. It is worth noting that both the missionaries and local Christians believed that the Confucian *Tian* was indeed the Christian God, *Tianzhu*. Furthermore, this shrine was built for commemoration and modelling purposes but not idol worshipping.[78] This textual and ideological evidence outweigh Gernet's superficial observation. It is more convincing to conclude that Wang, in conducting his service as a leader in seemingly "pagan" ceremonies, utilized his privilege to plant Christian elements in these cultural events.

Huang Yi-long criticizes Wang as a "snake with two heads" because he went with his best friend to see a fortune teller. Huang considers that this either involves subscribing to dual religions, or that Wang's thought remained at a theoretical level without changing his behavior. This incident

---

76. 王徵(Wang), 〈兩理略.祈晴文〉, 60-61.

77. 王徵(Wang), 〈兩理略.祈晴文〉, 60. Wang, in fact, also mentioned guardian angels regarding creation and the fall of mankind in 《畏天愛人極論》, 6b-7a.

78. 李九功(Li), 《問答彙抄》, 542.

happened in 1628, at the time Wang was about to complete his composition of *WTARJL*. This best friend, Zhang Man (鄭鄤, 1594–1639), recorded this incident of visiting a fortune teller in his 《崒陽草堂文集》 (*The Collected Works of Zhang Man*).[79] According to Zhang's record, Wang and Zhang each brought a new white writing brush with them and asked the fortune teller what their friendship and mutual understanding would be like in their old age with grey hair (referencing the white brushes). The answer of the fortune teller seems to be irrelevant as he told them that someone in their families would pass away in the near future. It is also worth noting that Zhang only recorded his own response but not Wang's. How Wang responded is unclear. How to evaluate this incident is controversial. It seems to us that Huang's criticism is biased and hasty.

Huang's other criticism concerns Wang marrying a concubine, which was forbidden by the church. Marrying a concubine is factual and cannot be denied. However, how to interpret this incident is another matter. When Wang passed the national examination and became a *jinshi*, he was urged by his parents to marry a concubine for lineage continuation purposes. Wang's reply reflected his faithfulness to the teaching of the church. He considered that passing the examination was God's grace and so he should not do things that were unpleasing to God, and he turned down his parents' appeal.[80] However, it seems that Wang did not maintain his stance enough and he finally married a concubine, Ms. Shen (申氏). He was then excommunicated by the church. He tried to be reinstated but without success. It was not until his later years that he finally came to a consensus with his concubine that they would terminate their marital relationship but remain as family members. He then wrote a confession on this matter.[81] After his confession he was reinstated into the church. Was Wang unfaithful to church teaching? The answer is a clear "yes." Was he a two-headed snake? Huang's comment is overexaggerated and stained with dislike without putting the incident in its social and cultural context. *Xiao* (孝, filial piety) was exceptionally important and paramount in ancient China. Marrying a concubine was not only a common practice among husbands who did not have an heir to continue their lineage but was also deemed a praiseworthy act of filial piety from both the husband and the barren wife because of their

79. 鄭鄤(Zhang), 《崒陽草堂文集》, 85. See also 黃一農(Huang), 〈儒家化的天主教徒〉, 166–67.

80. 艾儒略(Aleni), 《口鐸日抄》, 106.

81. 王徵(Wang), 〈崇一堂日記隨筆.附錄祈請解罪啟稿〉, 176–77.

contribution to the lineage. Having said that, we should not neglect the suffering it brings to the parties involved. However, Huang was so overwhelmed by the suffering of Wang's concubine that he made such a criticism.[82] The reality is that such an arrangement indeed causes suffering to all involved: the wife, the husband, and the concubine. There is no exception in Wang's case. Should Huang be aware of this and less hostile to Christianity, his comment would be more sympathetic and fairer.

The last doubt about Wang's Christian behavior is also made by Huang. He criticizes Wang for committing suicide by starvation for the last Ming emperor. Wang's case is complex and requires careful examination. First, we find that Wang had already prepared to die because of his refusal of Li Zicheng's (李自成) summons to serve in Li's court. Evidently, that those who refused to comply would be sentenced to death.[83] Wang's refusal would have caused him death eventually.[84] This fact should not be overlooked because Wang's death should not be classified as egoistic but altruistic in Durkheim's categories. Second, the Catholic Church rejects any form of suicide except that with double effect. Martyrdom is considered a death with double effect.[85] In view of this, we find that Wang's self-starvation can be interpreted as an act to demonstrate his loyalty to the emperor (aiming at a higher end). Although death is inevitably a natural result of self-starvation, death is not Wang's primary aim but rather the bad effect that it brings. Third, death for the emperor of the previous dynasty can be classified as martyrdom which demonstrates one's loyalty. Martyrdom for the government, in particular to the emperor, has been praised highly in Chinese culture. Wang's choice was common among Confucian literati of his time. Christian literati in late Ming were first-generation Christians. They had to find a way of living acceptable to their local culture and newly converted religion. Wang's self-starvation to death was obviously one of the many dilemmas that Christian literati had to face, reflecting the struggle of insiders. Dying for the emperor may be an act of syncretism in the eyes of "outsiders." However, to "insiders," it is a way to show their loyalty to

82. Huang once on his personal webpage stated that he would make a film on Wang Zheng if he could. He planned to focus on the life and suffering of the concubine. It reflects clearly how he felt for her and his resentment to Wang. Regrettably this webpage does not exist anymore and verification is not feasible.

83. 何冠彪(He), 《生與死》, 39, 140.

84. It is important to note that Wang was spared this time. However, his refusal and readiness to die for the cause remain true.

85. For discussion of double effect, see Stempsey, "Laying Down," 219.

Tianzhu through their loyalty to the emperor. This incident of Wang clearly demonstrates the issue of power play between "insiders" and "outsiders" that we mentioned earlier.

Evaluation

We start this section with a question, "Is Wang Zheng Syncretic?" The answer to this question is yes and no. Through his life and his thought, we find that he is syncretic in the sense of *syn1* and *3*. Wang as a Confucian literatus, identified cultural themes such as filial piety, *wulung*, in particular the relationship between father and son, and man as a moral agent to engage with Christianity. As a Christian, Wang proposed the concepts of the great parent, the prodigal son, the rational man with an imperishable soul, and homecoming as themes to dialogue with Confucianism. Viewed from both ends, his inculturated thoughts should be classified "fair play" in the sense of a baseball game, as the ball is within the compatible and acceptable boundary. Is it a perfect pitch or bat? Not necessarily, but it is "fair." Dialogue can go on and new themes will emerge. However, most importantly, Wang's thought created new perspectives that may bring new understanding of God, man, and the God-man relationship to Chinese culture. These new understandings are compatible with Confucianism, the major thread of Chinese culture. The seed is planted but whether it will flourish or wither is out of Wang's control. By the same token, Wang's thought on "homecoming" brings a new perspective to the study of atonement theories of the church tradition. As a theory of atonement, "homecoming" has merits in that it avoids the criticism of a violent God demanding retribution. The God in this theory is portrayed as a Father who longs for the return of a prodigal son with his love, kindness, and patience. Homecoming leads to a reunion in relational harmony that both the Father and the prodigal son have desired for so long.

On the one hand, Wang's behavior is neither perfect nor spotless from a Christian perspective. However, the transgressions in behavior were not intense. On the other hand, it is also worth noting that from a Chinese perspective, his behavior is more than satisfactory. Wang being caught in a dilemma is understandable because he and other first-generation Christian literatus in late Ming did not have role models to look up to and follow. Struggling in dilemmas seems to be unavoidable.

Wang's experience and effort provide us with an appropriate case for the study of inculturation and syncretism as a first-generation Confucian Christian in both the late Ming and the Chinese church. Through him, we learn that an emerging church or Christian individual, through inculturation, is able to contribute to church tradition. His portrait of God as a loving great parent who loves all mankind, a Father who patiently waits for the return of his sons is not only compatible to the teaching of the church, but also brings in a gentle, loving fatherly figure which softens the image of an indifferent fearful judge. His portrait of man as a returning prodigal son who is good in (original) nature but led astray by Satan, together with the kind and loving great parent form a beautiful and harmonious picture of a great family. These contributions will enrich church tradition and the Christian experience of God. Wang's case also encourages Chinese churches around the world, as well as other emerging Third World churches that their inculturation efforts will also be able to contribute to the great story of Jesus.

Wang's case also encourages emerging churches to be proud of their cultures. Cultures should be examined by the tradition of the universal church that has been best expressed the Christian experience.[86] However, it does not imply that we have to forsake every element of human cultures. Upholding the truth that Jesus is the ultimate and complete revelation of God does not imply that the God does not reveal himself to all cultures through general revelation. It is undeniable that God's truth is revealed in the incarnated Word through Hebrew and Greek cultures. To become a Christian does not require anyone to become a Christian of a particular culture.[87] We should be proud of being Chinese Christians with cultural heritage and practices which are different from other ethnic Christians but compatible to church tradition, when church tradition is, in fact, developed through different inculturated theologies.

Conclusion

Syncretism seems to be a stigma that deters "younger churches" from engaging in the development of their own inculturated theology. This phenomenon is mainly triggered by the misconception of syncretism.

---

86. Boff, *Church*, 104.

87. The issue of "white gaze" in Kane's book helps us to recognize how dangerous and harmful this prejudice is.

Syncretism in the sense of *syn1* is inevitable when a church "seeks to express its life in local cultural form." However, becoming *syn3* is not a logical outcome. It can be a *syn2* that will enrich the Christian tradition and lead to a Christian transformation within the receiving culture. Wang Zheng's attempt seems to be one of them. This paper, hopefully, has achieved its goal: to help "younger churches" offload the stigma of syncretism. May younger churches like the Australian Chinese church be encouraged to launch attempts to boldly and fairly establish an inculturated theology.

Bibliography

艾儒略(Aleni, Giulio). 《口鐸日抄》. 於耶穌會羅馬檔案館明清天主教文獻. 鍾鳴旦、杜鼎克編. 第七冊.台北: 利氏學社, 2002.

Bevans, Stephen. "Fair or Foul? Contextual Theology, Syncretism and the Criteria for Orthodoxy." In *Theological and Philosophical Responses to Syncretism: Beyond the Mirage of Pure Religion*, edited by Patrik Fridlund and Mika Vähäkanga, 88–103. Boston: Brill, 2017.

Boff, Leonardo. *Church: Charism and Power*. Eugene, OR: Wipf and Stock, 2012.

Bradley, Robert I. *The Roman Catechism in the Catechetical Tradition of the Church: The Structure of the Roman Catechism as Illustrative of the "Classic Catechesis."* Lanham, New York: University Press of America, 1990.

Dhavamony, Mariasusai. *Christian Theology of Inculturation*. Roma: Editrice Pontificia Universita Gregoriana, 1997.

Gernet, Jacques. *China and the Christian Impact: A Conflict of Cultures*. Translated by Janet Lloyd. Cambridge: Cambridge University Press, 1985.

何冠彪(He, Guan-biao). 《生與死: 明季士大夫的抉擇》. 台北: 聯經出版事業公司, 1997.

黃一農(Huang, Yi-long). 〈明末中西文化衝突之析探: 以天主教徒王徵娶妾和殉國為例〉. 於《第一屆全國歷史學學術討論會論文集—世變, 群體與個人》. 211-34. 台北: 台灣大學歷史系, 1991.

———. 〈儒家化的天主教徒: 以王徵為例〉. 於《兩頭蛇: 明末清初的第一代天主教徒》. 131-74. 新竹市: 國立清華大學出版, 2005.

Hummel, Arthur W., ed. *Eminent Chinese of the Ch'ing Period (1644-1912)*. Reprint, 807-9. Taipei: Southern Material Centre, 1991.

Kane, Rose. *Syncretism and Christian Tradition: Race and Revelation in the Study of Religious Mixture*. New York: Oxford University Press, 2021.

Kraemer, Hendrik. *Religion and the Christian Faith*. London: Lutterworth, 1956.

Leopold, Anita Maria, and Jeppe Sinding Jensen, eds. "Introduction to Part II." In *Sycretism in Religions: A Reader*, 14–28. New York: Routledge, 2014.

李九功(Li, Jiu-gong). 《問答彙抄》.耶穌會羅馬檔案館明清天主教文獻. 235-604.鍾明旦、杜鼎克編. 第八冊. 台北: 利氏學社, 2002.

Nicholls, Bruce. *Contextualizaton: A Theology of Gospel and Culture*. Downers Grove, IL: InterVarsity, 1979.

Pye, Michael. "Syncretism and Ambiguity." In *Syncretism in Religions: A Reader*, edited by Maria Anita Leopold and Jeppe Sinding Jensen, 59–67. New York: Routledge, 2014.

Rambo, Lewis. *Understanding Religious Conversions*. New Haven: Yale University Press, 1993.
Schreiter, Robert J. *Constructing Local Theologies*. Maryknoll, NY: Orbis, 1985.
宋伯胤編(Song, Bo-yin).《明涇陽王徵先生年譜》.西安：陝西師範大學出版社，1990.
Standaert, Nicolas. *Handbook of Christianity in China Vol. 1: 636–1800*. Leiden: Brill, 2001.
———. "Wang Zheng's Ultimate Discussion of the Awe of Heaven and Care of Human Beings." *Orientalia Lovaniensia Periodica* 29 (1998) 163–88.
Stempsey, William E. "Laying Down One's Life for Oneself." *Christian Bioethics* 4, no. 2 (1998) 202–24.
Vroom, Hendrik M. "Syncretism and Dialogue: A Philosophical Analysis." In *Syncretism in Religions: A Reader*, edited by Maria Anita Leopold and Jeppe Sinding Jensen, 103–12. New York: Routledge, 2014.
王徵(Wang, Zheng).〈仁會約〉.於《王徵全集》.139–56.林樂昌編.西安：三秦出版社，2011.
———.《畏天愛人極論》. Bibliotheque Nationale de France, Fonds Chinois, n.6868.
———.兩理略.兩理略自序〉.於《王徵全集》.1–2.林樂昌編.西安：三秦出版社，2011.
———.〈兩理略.祈晴文〉.於《王徵全集》.60.林樂昌編. 西安：三秦出版社，2011.
———.〈兩理略.活閘救秧〉.於《王徵全集》.16–17.林樂昌編. 西安：三秦出版社，2011.
———.《兩理略.肥城治水》.於《王徵全集》.10–11.林樂昌編. 西安：三秦出版社，2011.
———.《兩理略.建閣崇賢》.於《王徵全集》. 36–38.林樂昌編. 西安：三秦出版社，2011.
———.〈和陶靖節先生歸去來辭〉.於《王徵全集》. 355–56.林樂昌編.西安：三秦出版社，2011.
———.〈崇一堂日記隨筆.附錄祈請解罪啟稿〉.於《王徵全集》.176–77. 林樂昌編.西安：三秦出版社，2011.
Wong, Kai Tai Tony. "Filial Piety and Christian Piety: Wang Zheng and His Attempt to Inculturate Christianity in Late Ming China." PhD diss., La Trobe University, 2010.
鄭鄤(Zhang, Man). 《峚陽草堂文集》. 北京：北京愛如生數字化技術研究中心，2009.
張載(Zheng, Zai).〈乾清篇(西銘)〉.《張載集》.北京：中華書局，1978.
Zücher, Eric. "Christian Social Action in Late Ming Times: Wang Zheng and His 'Humanitarian Society.'" In *Linked Faiths: Essays on Chinese Religions and Traditional Culture in Honour of Kristofer Schipper*, edited by Jan. A. M. de Meyer and Peter M. Englefriet, 269–86. Sinica Lediensia 46. Leiden: Brill, 1999.

9.

Politics: A Topic That Cannot Be Avoided in Diasporic Chinese Churches

Jason Lam

Abstract

THE MAIN BODY OF this essay is divided into two parts. The first part offers a more technical but grand perspective—the development of contemporary Chinese theology—for articulating that political situation is a necessary element for theological reflection. The second part discusses why politics in diasporic Chinese churches is still an unavoidable topic for theology and ministry from the author's experience. The essay as a whole does not try to draw a comprehensive solution or to suggest some pastoral blueprint for Chinese churches on the topic of politics; they are important but can only be made in a concrete situation with a living community. The aim of this essay is to try to pinpoint from history and contemporary phenomena that although many Chinese churches may try to avoid politics, their operations have manifested their theological thinking in relation to the topic. On this basis the author suggests that if avoiding politics is a passive approach which may bring about pastoral shortfalls, Chinese churches in diaspora may consider how to address the topic proactively with congregants—not trying to silence the disharmonic tones but to let everyone have the chance to express him or herself despite some thoughts which are immature. It is for the sake of letting everyone know that different opinions will always exist, but with the same faith one must strive to achieve unity. It could be a more positive way and in accord with pastoral needs.

1. Politics: An Element That Cannot Be Avoided in Chinese Theology

From the outset this paper must declare that it is not aimed at producing a conventional piece in political theology or public theology. The underlying question is simply: "So what would count as 'theological' in a Christian community?"[1] For many Chinese Christians, theology is something unfathomable and out of touch; it is only for experts and ministers. Thus, today there is still a view among some believers that theology is unnecessary because it is far away from ordinary congregants. Historically, *theologia* or knowledge of God can truly be rendered as a classical discipline steeped in rational thinking. Nevertheless, theology can never occur without a living faith community.[2] In this vein, contemporary Christians avoid theology on one hand, while on the other they try to reclaim it. This is not only a phenomenon in the Chinese churches but is quite common in global Christianity.

For the church, if theology must in some way be related to the congregants, then she must address the topics they are facing. This essay chooses a thorny topic for Chinese churches today: politics, in the context of diasporic areas—outside of mainland China, Taiwan, Hong Kong, and Macau. A Chinese theology at large should take the concerns of mainland China into consideration as it covers the largest geographical area with the biggest population; Taiwan and Hong Kong occupy another special position due to political and historical reasons. Even if we are addressing the situation of overseas Chinese churches, most of the congregants today are from mainland China, although the majority in the past were from Taiwan and Hong Kong. Seen in this way, there have already been changes on this platform over the years. The political and social situation in the last few decades brought about the changes, and many pastoral and theological issues are closely connected to these changes. Nevertheless, regardless of where one

---

1. This question is raised by Mary McClintock Fulkerson and led to a discussion on her "Ethnography," 115.

2. For the dual sides of theology, cf. Farley, *Theologia*; for a Chinese reflection, cf. Lam, "Typological Consideration," 93–109.

is situated, many Chinese Christians share the same experience: politics is a topic the church wants to avoid. There are many reasons contributing to this phenomenon, including an immature or wrong view on the church and state relationship,[3] cultural conservatism, an intent to avoid differentiation due to conflicting positions, and even to escape from political consequences.[4] Nonetheless, since the anti-extradition law movement emerged in June 2019, Hong Kong has become a focus for international news.[5] On top of that, Christianity is an outstanding element in some scenarios and thus Chinese churches can hardly avoid being included in the discussion. Theological reflections are produced, and responses are made from various stances. However, it is not easy to find a space for accumulating different reflections and producing further analysis. Yet it is a pastoral situation that the church finds herself sitting in.

Many churches have found themselves encountering a dilemma of handling this situation—of advancing or retreating from the topic of politics. Political theology, public theology, theological ethics, and so on, have become heated topics in academia and even marched in the public realm of the Chinese-speaking world. Nevertheless, most congregants find these discourses filled with out-of-place theological jargons, but they are the majority of the present faith community. Therefore, as a piece on contextual theology, this essay does not want to deal with the topic only from a theoretical dimension; this approach would only suffocate ordinary believers. However, a description on the context is still necessary. But the author believes that starting the discussion from personal experience and producing reflection upon it would be more appropriate for most congregants. It is also relevant for the topic of politics and it is one of the themes for the emerging approach of "lived theology."[6] The author must state from the beginning, however, that this essay does not try to draw a comprehensive solution or to suggest some pastoral blueprint for Chinese churches; they are important but can only be made in the concrete situation with a living community. The aim of this essay is rather narrow—trying to pinpoint from history and the contemporary phenomena that although many churches

---

3. 郭承天 (Guo), 《華人政治神學》, 112–65.

4. For the development of Christian mission in China, cf. Latourette, *History*; Bays, *New History*.

5. For a historical description of the event, cf. Purbrick, "Report," 465–87.

6. For the approach, cf. Marsh et al., *Lived Theology*; Maynard et al., *Pastoral Bearings*.

may try to avoid politics, the operation of the Chinese churches has manifested their theological thinking in relation to the topic. On this basis the author suggests that if avoiding politics is a passive approach which may bring about pastoral shortfall, Chinese churches in diaspora may consider how to address the topic proactively with the congregants—not trying to silence the disharmonic tones but letting everyone have the chance to express him or herself despite some immature thoughts. It is for the sake of letting everyone know that different opinions will always exist, but with the same faith one must strive to achieve unity. It could be a more positive way and in accord with pastoral needs, as Paul Ramsey wrote: "before there can be a Christian social ethic, understanding of the fundamental moral perspective of the Christian must be deepened and clarified."[7]

As this is an essay addressing the topic of politics, the author should first state his own situation and conditions. He was born and grew up in Hong Kong and received his foundational theological education there. In 2000, he went to the UK for advanced theological study and engaged in pastoral ministry for four years. Afterwards, he returned to Hong Kong for fourteen years, travelling frequently between mainland China, Taiwan, and Hong Kong to promote Sino-Christian theology.[8] In early 2019, the author moved to work at the Melbourne School of Theology until now—almost four years.[9] In the meantime, he is observing his motherland at a distance as an outlander. Very often, he finds himself interacting with the diasporic Chinese and local communities; he thus has different lenses to see and examine the development of the social and political situation of the Chinese communities and can understand to some extent the reasons that they want to avoid politics but in vain. Under these conditions, the author must admit that though working as a theologian for many years, he has no intent and is not able to discuss the topic as an expert. At some points, he can only offer his own thought as a narrative portraiture, such that reflection may be produced afterwards by himself and others. This echoes the approach of lived theology—allowing the voices of non-professionals to be

---

7. Ramsey, *Christian Ethics*, xxxiii.

8. For the information of the Institute of Sino-Christian Studies in which the author participated, cf. "Institute"; for an overview of Sino-Christian theology, cf. Lai and Lam, *Sino-Christian*.

9. For further information, see Melbourne School of Theology, "Upcoming Events"; for the history of the Chinese churches in Australia, cf. 賴德明 (Lai),《澳洲華人基督教會史初探》.

heard.[10] But the author is standing on the embarrassing position between the two sides. Therefore, this essay will be divided into two main sections: in the first part, it will offer a more technical but grand perspective—the development of contemporary Chinese theology—for articulating that political situation is a necessary element for theological reflection. In the second part, the author will discuss why politics in diasporic Chinese churches is still an unavoidable topic for theology and ministry from his personal experience.

2. The Development of Contemporary Chinese Theology and Its Relation to Politics

As mentioned above, mainland China as the largest geographical area with the biggest population in the Chinese-speaking world is a significant factor in theological reflection. In this part, we will thus first have a brief analysis of the development of Christianity and theology on this land in relation to the political situation. Afterwards we will proceed to articulate the issues encountered by the diasporic communities. The analysis below will be relatively grand and "technical" but will also provide the background that non-professionals could and should know.

2.1 Different Forms of Christianity and Theology in Mainland China[11]

In 1949, the Chinese Communist Party (CCP) took control of mainland China. It is no secret that the orthodox state teaching is atheism, which is in ideological conflict with Christianity and all forms of theistic faith. As a result, the Christian churches and in fact all institutional religions were suppressed and experienced a difficult time during the early reign of the regime, especially during the Cultural Revolution (1966–76). But since the end of the 1970s the policy of Reform and Opening Up has been implemented and, at least to some extent, religions have been tolerated over the

---

10. For the characteristics of this approach, cf. Holman, "Daring to Write," 80–101; Wigg-Stevenson, *Ethnographic Theology*. Chu and Perry has provided two portraitures with different political stances of the Hong Kong Christians; cf. Chu (朱安之) and Perry, "Gospel," 422–34.

11. This part is adapted and revised from Lam, "Theological Reflection," 300–306.

last forty years.¹² This is not to say that the conflict between communism and religion is settled. Rather, after the regime declared its primary aim to be developing the economy, the issue of ideological conflict has often been treated as a secondary matter. At times it may even go so far as to consider religion a means for social cohesion, as long as the religious communities in question are not seen to be making trouble for the government. Under this situation the development of Christianity and theology in mainland China is closely related to the political situation.

Undoubtedly, the sociopolitical situation is just one of the dimensions affecting the shape of Christianity in a given place and time. Nevertheless, no one can escape from this background and the Christians living in a given context must try to accommodate to it. What are the possibilities of Christianity and theology that have already been embodied in the People's Republic of China (PRC) for the last seventy years, especially after the Reform and Opening Up policy? From the view of historical development, there have been registered churches and unregistered/house churches since the reign of the CCP. Their political and thus theological orientations are different.¹³ Higher quality Christian studies began to emerge in the late 1980s and Sino-Christian theology has developed since then. The interesting point is that many participants are not churchgoers.¹⁴ In Alexander Chow's *Chinese Public Theology* they are described as three major types of Chinese public theology and are put in chronological order of development. It is noteworthy that he regarded urban intellectual Christianity as the latest type rather than on parallel with the registered churches, although it is a subset of the unregistered churches. Urban intellectual Christians are participants of unregistered churches, but their involvement in social issues provides clear features compared with the conservative stance of the rest.¹⁵

12. Madsen, "Religious Renaissance," 17–42; Yang, "Religious Revival," 8–25.

13. For the early history of this period, cf. 邢福增 (Ying), 《基督教在中國的失敗？》.

14. It thus aroused vigorous debate on whether the discourse produced should be considered as Christian theology. The most widely read one is undoubtedly the so-called "Cultural Christian" debate appearing in the Hong Kong Christian newspaper *Christian Times* 時代論壇, issue 419 (September 10, 1995) to issue 456 (May 26, 1996); all of these discussions have been collected in 漢語基督教文化研究所編, 《文化基督徒》, 96–196. For reviews and discussions, see Lee, "Cultural Christians," 53–62; Chan, "Conceptual Differences," 63–82; for a recent review from another perspective, see Lam, "Sino-Christian," 97–119.

15. Chow, *Chinese Public Theology*, 48–114. One of the representatives is undoubtedly the pastor of the Chengdu Early Rain Reformed Church (*Qiuyu zhi fu guizheng*

I believe that this perspective is viable as a result of the sociopolitical change of the last few decades in the PRC. Since a quasi-free market has been established and certain resources (economic and political) are shared by the people, a (quasi-) open and liberal society has been felt in the last few decades; hence more progressive types of public theology have emerged.[16] Many people are asking the question: What if China's economy stops growing or grows less rapidly? This is no longer a conditional clause but a matter of fact; the economic and political situation of the country has become less stable than before. Therefore, various phenomena have occurred more often, for example, provocative Christians are arrested, unregistered churches of large size are raided, the crosses and even buildings of some official churches are pulled down, and intellectuals find that the space for producing their voices in academia shrinks. This is also a reason why Chinese Christians have had an ambivalent view of China's economic impact and the related explanations for the last ten years or so. Theological responses are also encountering challenges and difficulties.

For making a further analysis of the above pluralistic situation of the PRC, I make use of Stephen B. Bevans and Roger P. Schroeder's renowned work *Constants in Context* for convenience. They articulated three types of theology of mission on the basis of several theological models before them:

A. Mission as saving souls and extending the church
B. Mission as discovery of the truth
C. Mission as commitment to liberation and transformation.[17]

Needless to say, in actual practice the three types are not mutually exclusive but complementary. The registered and most unregistered churches mainly focus on saving souls and church extension (type A) in order to avoid suppression from the state. Apart from the political situation there are other factors behind such as cultural conservatism and the background of the missions to China. But it is noteworthy that nowadays even the

---

jiaohui 秋雨之福教會), Wang Yi 王怡, who was recently sentenced to prison for nine years. Because of their social vision, many of them have claimed attachment to some form of Calvinist theology. For a recent survey of the whole trend, cf. Fällman, "Calvin," 153–68.

16. For a more detailed analysis, cf. 李向平 (Li), 《中國當代宗教的社會學詮釋》; for a related theological reflection, cf. 林子淳 (Lam), 〈操控還是信任？〉, 37–62.

17. Bevans and Schroeder, *Constants*, ch. 2; it is mainly built upon the models suggested by Sölle, *Thinking*, and González, *Christian Thought*.

unregistered churches find that at times they may have to keep silent and make compromises if the truth they learn from Christian tradition is in conflict with the interests of the state.[18] The non-ecclesial nature of Sino-Christian theology gives it a chance to voice out in the public realm of the PRC and has thus become a special force of Chinese Christianity for the last few decades.[19] It concerns discovering the truth from the Christian tradition (type B). Some participants may even have a heart to commit to social liberation and transformation (type C), as they write in the public realm about their findings.[20] Nevertheless, some concessions have to be made in expressions and even the choice of study topic, as the platform is state controlled. Given that it is not easy to identify a visible community, expansion (type A) can hardly be a primary concern. It seems that only urban intellectual Christians have tried to actualize all missional models, which is why they often court the risk of being raided by the regime. In a nutshell, most types of Christianity and the related theology in the PRC are seeking ways to survive under the rule of an authoritarian regime with an atheist ideology by some forms of self-limiting. Marie-Eve Reny described this phenomenon in her recent book as "containment" (*ezhixing* 遏制性)—the conditional and bounded toleration of a group outside state-sanctioned institutions:

> Toleration is *conditional* insofar as it involves a bargain. State security actors grant religious leaders some autonomy in exchange for complying with a set of conditions. Rules may be implicit or explicitly stated. The authorities expect religious leaders to keep a low profile and share information about their internal activities with public security bureaus. They further expect unregistered pastors to refrain from crossing red lines (*guo hongxian* 過紅線) deemed unacceptable by the regime . . .[21]

---

18. Chow in *Chinese Public Theology*, 92, drew our attention to an article in *China Daily*. See Wu and Cui, "House Churches." Another very distinguished work in this area is Reny, *Authoritarian Containment*. Therefore, Chow did not find a distinguished type of public theology produced by those churches that did not make provocative actions in his book.

19. 李向平 (Li), 〈漢語神學〉, 57–69.

20. For an earlier set of analysis, cf. the theme of 《道風》 on "Sino-Christian Theology and Public Space (漢語神學與公共空間)"; cf. also Xie, "Why Public?," 381–404; Lam, "Sino-Christian."

21. Reny, *Authoritarian Containment*, 6.

In other words, the party-state, or the local government officials can tolerate the existence of different kinds of Christianity, insofar as they do not threaten the perceived political security of the regime. Nevertheless, in the last few years, when the economic and political pressure on the state has increased, we have seen the augmentation of attacks on Christianity. Obviously, this kind of bargain in exchange for survival space is largely controlled by the hand of the regime. In view of this increasing harshness, some may ask whether engaging in this bargain is a wise tactic in the long run. Taking the question to another level, one may even ask if it is right to exchange (part of) the autonomy of the church for survival in the face of unjust persecution. Agreeing to enter this perverted game, as interpreted by Reny, is a risk-averse behavior that usually pays off. Nevertheless, this kind of informal agreement also isolates those communities that do not see it as appropriate and produce distrust between both sides. It may also strengthen the resilience of the authoritarian regime.[22] Whether it is worthy and ethical for Christians in mainland China to do so is truly a difficult question of faith in relation to politics.

2.2 Recent Development with the Interaction of Diasporic Communities

The above analysis is obviously penned by someone outside mainland China as discourses related to politics and Christianity are sensitive in this place. For many years scholars including the author of this essay have produced similar studies. China studies scholars in the broad sense, including theologians who study Chinese church-state relations in Hong Kong and elsewhere, understanding that their work may not be transmitted in the public platform of the PRC. But after crossing the border (for people in Hong Kong that is the Shenzhen River 深圳河) they can enjoy the freedom to express themselves.[23] Thus, all types of mission and theology as articulated by Bevans and Schroeder can be found in Hong Kong and diaspora in the past.[24] Nevertheless, as Christianity has never become a dominant religion in most Chinese societies, most Chinese churches have focused

---

22. Reny, *Authoritarian Containment*, 16.

23. The Shenzhen River is the natural dividing line between Hong Kong and Mainland China and several custom control channels are established along it.

24. For contemporary theological discourses outside Mainland China, cf. 何光滬、楊熙楠 (He & Yeung) 編,《漢語神學讀本 (下)》.

on saving souls and extending the church (type A). But as time goes on the academic strength and political concerns of Chinese Christianity have grown. Type B theology aiming at discovering truth has grown in some Chinese communities. However, academic theology in mainland China appears relatively not willing to go too far towards social liberation and transformation (type C) compared with other places; their responses can at most be in theoretical articulation rather than in concrete actions.

Since the end of 2007 when the Chinese government rejected the possibility of a general election for the chief executive of Hong Kong, the region has entered a politically unstable period. The Umbrella Movement occurring in 2014 may be seen as a historical watershed and in 2019 the world has witnessed tremendous social unrest.[25] As some Hong Kong Christians and churches had high profile participation in these events, theological discourses produced around this time had more concerns with liberation and transformation (type C). Moreover, they have appeared on international platforms and attracted a wide range of audience.[26] Seen against this, the academic theology which has been developing in mainland China and has also produced voices on public platforms, appears conservative. The difference is undoubtedly shaped by the sociopolitical situation and interactions between different perspectives of Chinese Christians in Taiwan, Hong Kong, and other diaspora are found. Nevertheless, their differences are mainly due to accidental historical development rather than theological construction with intent. When discussions have developed as time goes on, the gaps between the believers in different places would multiply. Apart from the difference of political orientation, cultural and educational background, social and economic conditions, and even denominational stances, clergies and church leaders may also have different views from the mass. The consequences would be felt on the theology produced and even pastoral concerns and strategies.

Hong Kong has been an important exchange station between East and West for a long time. It is not only said for business sectors but also academic realms. However, since the implementation of the Reform and Opening Up policy, some mainland higher institutes have begun to accumulate their own experience in exchange with the outside world. Even

---

25. For the changing church-state relationship, see Soper and Fetzer, "Church and State," 121–45.

26. For the participation of Hong Kong Christians in the movement, cf. Chan, "Protestant Community," 380–95; Ng and Fulda, "Religious Dimensions," 377–97; Tse and Tan, *Theological Reflections*; Kwok and Yip, *Hong Kong Protests*.

in Christian studies Hong Kong has lost the role as a mediator in some areas. If Hong Kong gradually loses its characters of a Special Administration Region and becoming just another ordinary city in the PRC due to the changing political atmosphere, then the development of theology would be greatly affected. Room for developing mission and theology concerning social liberation and transformation would shrink and may become hard to commit to in actions. Theological discourses may return to a more conservative side but that is difficult to get into the mainstream public platforms as in most Chinese societies. Since the National Security Law in Hong Kong was passed on June 30, 2020, the borderline at Shenzhen River seems to have disappeared from the angle of freedom of speech. The Chinese government has become more sensitive to Christianity at the same time. Scholars and institutes in Hong Kong are encountering similar difficulties as in the mainland. They include the shrinking of discussion space and some sensitive themes, and the consideration of the consequence of voicing out. The special features of a diasporic platform are disappearing in Hong Kong.

This new situation may appear quite normal to mainland scholars who have been living in similar conditions for decades. In the past Hong Kong has provided them a convenient local (but out of border) platform. They may use their own language to express their academic findings. For those who are fluent in other languages, foreign platforms may provide a similar function, including research resources and the possibility of expression. But they cannot enjoy the convenience of using their mother language and close cultural cognates abroad (there is also a political barrier in Taiwan), and the audience is different. For the last few decades many diasporic research institutes related to Chinese Christianity were established and have made contributions. As mentioned above, however, they are living in different cultural and political circles and the governments may not always have a good relationship with the CCP. Thus, it has made Hong Kong look so distinctive and allowed it to enjoy prosperous growth in the past.

As mainland scholars have acquired foreign languages and gained more experience from international academia, it seemed that diasporic institutes would flourish. However, the future has become more ambiguous since the COVID-19 pandemic burst out. Since international travel is hindered, the whole academia has been affected. It takes time to have the past situation restored and the presupposition is that one is willing to live with the virus. But again, it highlights the difference of the PRC (and Hong

Kong at present) and makes restoring normal academic exchange difficult in this region.[27] From the very beginning of the pandemic the whole world including the academia has been exploring alternative ways to alleviate the problem. Various ways of online exchange have been developed. The PRC is never behind in applied technology but all kinds of exchange including internet technology has always been a sensitive area in authoritarian societies. Anything related to Christianity risks treading on thin ice. People are still observing the impacts produced after the "New Measures on the Administration of Internet Religious Information Services" (which requires preregistration for posting any religious content) became effective on March 1, 2022. Most expect that the operations of churches, especially unregistered ones, will be severely impacted. Mainland academia is likely to experience some direct impacts too. Even for diasporic communities, they may find difficulties making academic exchanges, even for genuine scientific studies. One may expect that the pandemic will finish one day and the diplomatic relations between countries often change. Nevertheless, in the near future, Christianity and related studies will certainly be affected in the PRC.

3. Role and Situation of Diasporic Platforms

Since the 1950s, not only Christian theology but other disciplines have made use of diasporic Chinese platforms for outlets due to the unstable political situation in mainland China. But the effectiveness depends largely on the quality, population of users, and the liquidity of the platform. Hong Kong as a diasporic platform, as mentioned above, may lose its special features in the past. Can other places provide complementary functions or even become a substitution? It largely depends on the sociopolitical development of the PRC and Hong Kong. This is a topic for Chinese Christianity and studies of China in the broad sense. Paradoxically, this kind of study, though taking China as its subject, may not be able to speak out on her own land or may encounter difficulty when it wants to publish. It thus manifests the importance of the diasporic platforms for the Chinese-speaking world. As the content of the studies includes political, economic, and social analysis, if it is also related to Christianity, then a public theology may be produced in the process and attract scholars from other disciplines.

27. In early 2023 Mainland China opened the border again and this may lead to a new situation. But this essay cannot make any analysis at the time of completion.

It would become a genuine kind of public theology done with interdisciplinary studies in an open space. This is a topic less noticed by Chinese churches in the past.

3.1 Description from the Experience of a Diasporic Theologian

In the past, Sino-Christian theology developed in the PRC has always claimed to be a kind of public theology, since it takes the human and social sciences in mainland China as its basis and uses public discourse to speak out and attract non-Christians. It has truly been a spectacular phenomenon in the history of Chinese Christianity. Nevertheless, public theology in the general sense is a discourse which speaks out on contextual issues; it may produce a prophetic voice, which is sensitive under the current political atmosphere in the PRC. Thus, some have already written that Mainland academic theology at this stage should take the role of a servant rather than a prophet, serving the prevailing (government) viewpoint rather than critiquing it.[28] This could be seen as a phenomenon of "containment," as Reny coined it. Even if scholars have emerged in mainland China insisting on doing Christian theology, their studies must comply to the norms of the quasi-liberal platform. That means they can only publish with an "objective/neutral" interdisciplinary style. For those who are trained in dogmatics and biblical studies, this may not be the ideal approach. If they want to produce their works in conventional theological styles, they may only do so on the non-open ecclesial platform in mainland China or those in diaspora.

Surely there are many open platforms in Europe, America, and other places. But as mentioned above, the scholars cannot use their native language and that is not ideal especially if it aims to produce a local theology. In addition to the issue of language, for confessing scholars it may not be easy to separate the two roles of priest and prophet. Therefore, critical discourse taking Chinese Christianity as the subject has often appeared in the areas of history, sociology, and political science outside the PRC. It is worthwhile to ask if after a rational analysis can one produce constructive theology? It would be difficult in mainland academia when conventional theological discourse can hardly appear on the public platform. In Hong Kong an increasing pressure has been felt. If the discourse were written in Chinese, in the future it may only try to find its outlet in diaspora (but there are other difficulties in these places as explicated below). Some people

---

28. 卓新平 (Zhuo), 〈中國教會與中國社會〉, 249.

have long been trying to work out in this way. But the problem is that how effective can an effort be made outside of the original context. Even if some valuable results were produced, could they be transmitted back to the original place or at least make an exchange without being regarded as political infiltration? From this angle we may clearly perceive the crucial function of Hong Kong for so many years. But in the future, we may only hope that the diasporic platforms may provide some complementary functions.

The situation of mainland China and Hong Kong today was foreseen by one of the Sino-Christian theology initiators, Liu Xiaofeng 劉小楓. Apart from his early theological outline, people have mostly noticed his introduction of the political theologies of Carl Schmitt and Leo Strauss in the last two decades. Nevertheless, in his early work on Sino-Christian theology the concept of "esoteric writing (隱微寫作)"—a writing style for those in danger of persecution, was already articulated.[29] At that time, scholars in Hong Kong and even mainland China were living in a relatively open situation, however, the concept has escaped attention but may be helpful today. If scholars on the largest Chinese platforms have the difficulty of voicing out, then those in diasporas, especially confessing Christians, seem to have the duty to help them speak. Nevertheless, although theology cannot distance itself from the social, economic, and political situation, it must first construct itself as a theology rather than being another discipline or an instrument of other subjects. It has been the issue encountered by Sino-Christian theology, and Christians in diaspora may learn from this lesson.[30]

Various theologies in diaspora and exile from Hong Kong people scattered in different places have already arisen in these years.[31] But they are still in a stage of infancy and must be allowed time to develop. Regardless of the concepts used—diaspora, exile, remnant, or others from the Hebrew Bible—they emphasize that the subjects involved are separated from the original place but have a sentiment of longing to return or to make a contribution back home. Thus, they echo with the exilic experience of Israel but differ from the ordinary experience of migration. In Taiwan and other diasporic Chinese communities, many do not have the same nostalgia as

---

29. 劉小楓 (Liu), 《漢語神學與歷史哲學》, 69–72, referring to Strauss, *Persecution*. Some differences can be detected if we compare the Mainland and Hong Kong version of Liu's works. It can be taken as an example of esoteric writing.

30. Lam, "Sino-Christian."

31. E.g., 何兆斌 (Ho), 〈「餘民神學」芻議〉; 胡志偉 (Wu), 〈「流放神學」的初探〉; 陳韋安 (Chan), 〈從聖殿神學到流放神學〉.

the newcomers from Hong Kong. Local theologies in places like Taiwan are already well developed, and the people can analyze the political situation of Hong Kong and Mainland from a more distant perspective. The Christian population is small in most Chinese societies; and in diaspora, it is usually a minority. Now there is a relatively large number of Hong Kong people moving to these places, bipolar influences are felt.

As the Chinese population on these platforms is not large, producing and transmitting constructive theology is not easy. Now there are newcomers with mission and vision, it seems that the influence would be positive. However, as they are nostalgic and have close links to the homeland, the sentiment may not be easily shared and echoed by those already settled and may even stir up conflict if they embrace different political and theological positions. Thus, in recent years the taboo of discussing politics in diasporic churches is not less than those in Hong Kong. Some churches even try to avoid it in order not to produce differentiation within a small community. Nevertheless, in this crisis people may still try to produce some positive development. A genuine type of public theology can only be constructed if appropriate sociopolitical analysis can work out. If Chinese Christians want to develop theology on these platforms, it would be a necessary issue to overcome. Since the 2000s, many issues related to Mainland, Taiwan, and Hong Kong have become the international focus. Diaspora are the places Chinese scholars can meet other people in different circles easily and directly. How to deal with these issues is a difficult but crucial topic for Chinese theologians in the future. But undoubtedly it would be a thorny pastoral issue at the same time for most diasporic churches.

3.2 The Need for Hearing the Voice of the Congregants

Finally, our focus has come to the diasporic platform. As a key topic of this essay, it seems that we should have produced a description of this platform earlier. However, "diaspora" can hardly be analyzed independently without first dealing with the "homeland." In addition, the contextuality of "diaspora" is a complicated issue. Last June, the author participated in a conference on "Chinese Theology" held by Yale Divinity School with "Academic and Diasporic Theologies" as the focus. A young participant shared a topic on "Chinese American theology" and gave much food for thought to diasporic Chinese Christians. From his own experience it was pointed out that "Chinese American" is a concept not easy to deal with. Apart from living in the

USA, what are the characteristics they share? Not that they are of the same ethnic group? Nonetheless, "Chinese" is a pluralistic grouping; most of them may come from mainland China, Taiwan, and Hong Kong, but not a few are descendants of Chinese communities in countries such as Thailand, Vietnam, Singapore, and Malaysia. Thus, they have different living contexts and cultures. Some may have arrived in the USA recently, but others are local Chinese descendants. Their acquaintance with the Chinese language and participation in ethnic Chinese churches may differ greatly. Therefore, it is not easy to articulate the common features of a "Chinese American." Even if one wants to take examples for reference, C. S. Song 宋泉盛 may incline to name himself as a Taiwanese while Kwok Pui-lan 郭佩蘭 would identify herself as a Hongkongese. This has already shifted the focus from the cultural aspect to the thorny question of political orientation.

The same situation of "Chinese Australian" is also true for me as I have only been in Australia for four years; our plurality is not less than those living in the USA. The census of Australia in 2021 shows that more than half of the residents have one of the parents as immigrant. About 5.5 percent are Chinese descendants from the abovementioned countries.[32] Apart from showing an interesting figure this also raises a challenge to the local Chinese churches: What is "Chinese Australian theology"? What kind of cultural background should it take into consideration? Besides the issues of language and culture, it also concerns the problem of political orientation, which is the topic many Chinese churches want to avoid, so as to minimize the chance of differentiation.

Even from the everyday experience of overseas Chinese, we know that we cannot identify ourselves as typical "Chinese." The place of origin, the length of stay overseas, and even the language and habits used differs from one to another as mentioned above. The political issues emerged in the Chinese-speaking world from the last decade have provided churches an additional obstacle for uniting believers together with the "Chinese" banner. Be this as it may, partly because of the social unrest, there have been increasing newcomers in the Chinese churches which has brought about chances and challenges. As mentioned in the beginning of this essay, we cannot provide a comprehensive analysis or pastoral strategy in the face of this situation. Nevertheless, we would point out why politics has to be

---

32. Australian census data can be retrieved from the official website. See Australian Bureau of Statistics, "Population."

taken into theological and pastoral consideration in spite of the difficulties it brought about.

As an immigrant from Hong Kong, I will use some examples that happened there for illustration. The churches in Hong Kong should have borne the brunt if politics is seen as the element of bringing in differentiation. It has in fact produced many splits. Nonetheless, some significant points can be collected as time goes on. The Umbrella Movement occurring in 2014 can be seen as the blasting point and the anti-extradition law movement brought the social unrest to a climax. Be this as it may, the Hong Kong Theological Education Association (HKTEA), which is comprised of fourteen major seminaries, issued a statement in 2014 to request the government and police to recognize the rights of protesters, to condemn all violent behaviors, and to ask different parties to communicate with patience.[33] In 2019, apart from the general request just mentioned, the HKTEA even asked the government to postpone the amendment to the extradition ordinances because of the intensity of social unrest.[34] Although there was some thought that these statements were conservative and ambiguous, it should be counted as a breakthrough in Hong Kong Christianity. Although there have been the two camps (progressive and conservative) of churches emerging over the years, both sides issued statements requesting to postpone the amendment of the extradition law.[35] Seen in this way, even when the controversial political event was in progress, if churches were willing to communicate with reason and patience, consensus can still be made to a certain extent if they really take care of the society at large.

Chinese churches overseas may have more concern about the differences among the congregants than between congregations and denominations. It is true that the personal political inclination cannot be altered within a short time and is related to everyone's background, media, and denominational stance, for example. Moreover, political orientation should not be taken as a prime objective of pastoral care. However, it may affect the ministry. In recent years, some new churches have emerged in Hong Kong, and they have highlighted political orientation for ascertaining their internal coherence. It seems to be a pastoral strategy; but it is difficult if not impossible to take this approach from a theological point of view, as a church accepts its congregants based on a political rather than faith position. St.

33. 〈神學教育協會聲明〉.
34. 田淑珍 (Tian), 〈神學教育協會十四院校聯署譴責暴力, 深望暫緩修例〉.
35. Cf. Albert Lee's analysis in "Dialogue," 151–52.

Paul might have emphasized his Jewish national identity, but when talking about the ministry of the gospel he would say that in Christ one should not differentiate between Jews and gentiles. No partiality can be given to his own kin. There is a closer blood tie between different kinds of "Chinese" than between Jews and gentiles. It is thus difficult to find a reason for division due to political orientation in the church. It is not to say that church ministries cannot be divided into different groupings, especially from the perspectives of language and age groups. It is particularly helpful for overseas churches. Nonetheless, as all congregants are under Jesus Christ, the ministry of the gospel should not be differentiated. Within a short period, we may accept the partition between congregants with opposing political orientations to avoid severe conflict. But in the long run it would become a kind of apartheid. Moreover, Chinese churches in diaspora are living in a highly pluralistic cultural context and may have multiple language and cultural groups. We know that ministries for different groups have emerged due to convenience and pastoral needs. And many churches are struggling to achieve unity between different groups when pastoral strategy is being discussed. It is not a new issue as seen from the early church: Jews and gentiles were living in tension. Christianity has been encountering various issues of differentiation; politics is just one of those but intensified in recent years for the Chinese churches. If Christians who embrace the same faith are not willing to communicate and reconcile, it is not quite possible for those who do not commit to the same faith. But it is interesting that the Chinese churches have never abandoned evangelism and type A theology has always been the mainstream. If congregants stop communicating due to different political inclinations, it is not a good witness inside and outside of the church apart from a lack of theological reason.

Due to the issue of witnessing, many overseas Chinese churches have thus chosen to keep silent on politics for the sake of avoiding conflicts. Nevertheless, as mentioned above, many newcomers have arrived precisely due to the social unrest. Therefore, this approach may produce pastoral difficulty when encountering their needs. With believers in Hong Kong as our example again, some research points out that beside the drops in the confidence level in the government and constitutional system, social unrest and many concrete scenarios have brought about depression, post-traumatic stress, and different sorts of psychological issues for them.[36] In

---

36. Ni et al., "Depression," 273–84.

a broad sense, it is a phenomenon of human security being threatened.[37] We can imagine that this will spread out to overseas Chinese churches as many people from Hong Kong move to a diaspora. Although the issues originate from political events, if the Chinese churches want to offer adequate pastoral care, it is not reasonable to stop them from sharing their stress and traumatic experience. One of the reasons for these newcomers to leave their motherland is that it is a place where they cannot speak out. If after leaving and arriving in diasporic churches they find that it is still a place where their voices are blocked, it would increase their feeling of powerlessness. They may even find that the churches in the diaspora are not the resting place for them. This is certainly a pastoral issue to take note.

Seen in this way, the question is how to let congregants of one faith with different (political) opinions share themselves openly and be accepted without being attacked. It is not to say that the church has to affirm believers' political stances and ideas unreservedly. Some political approaches conflict with the Christian faith and the church should point it out, for example, Nazis in WWII and the apartheid in South Africa. It would become the pastoral and teaching concern of the church.[38] But even if there were not social unrest in the Chinese-speaking world, different issues have emerged in the last few decades and brought about different opinions (e.g., divorce and same-sex marriage). How we can make the church a place all can share with faithful principles has always been an issue. Historically, it is true that in the interaction with the world, especially with political powers, the church has not usually been in control. Nevertheless, it does not mean that Christians have no choice but to conform to all of the world's demands. Otherwise, the church would become merely one more human grouping in this world. Arne Rasmusson reminded us that the politics of the church are different from the politics of the world. We should not merely endorse some existing political agenda; otherwise, the church would become just another agent for a political circle or ideology. In other words, we should be aware that the church is not a political party and has no intention of offering an agenda for solving the political matrix at hand. We are not a political alternative but an alternative to politics.[39] Thus we should bring

---

37. Luk, "Human Security," 1–10.

38. It is really not an easy topic for the church; for a simple rendering with a concern on spirituality, see 龔立人 (Kung), 〈情緒政治/靈性教會．靈性政治/情緒教會〉, 136–70.

39. Rasmusson, *Church as Polis*, 208–19, 331–34.

in our "imagination" through a critical theological reflection, such that we would not be satisfied merely with what we are at present but challenging ourselves to become the people we should be as God wills for us.

It is a fact that though we know the question and the thoughts, it does not mean that we can handle them easily. For example, the difference of denominational theology is a problem the ecumenical church has not been able to solve for five hundred years. It is related to the heart of the Christian faith, but one can understand that it would not be sorted out within a short time. Nevertheless, churches around the world have never avoided the idea that unity should be a direction all must strive for. Christianity has been struggling with similar issues over the years in different places. Perhaps we may change our perspective. The immediate question is not how to sort that out from a rational calculation, but "Who is my neighbor and who is the subject of my mission?" From time to time, it is found that we are not the one to set the question but one must be sensitive to the chances and challenges God is giving to his people. Therefore, the "Chinese churches" should not only pray to increase the number of congregants but ask the will of God in this time. This is the question for every generation for the sake of his kingdom.

Bibliography

Australian Bureau of Statistics, "Population." https://www.abs.gov.au/statistics/people/population.

Bays, Daniel H. *A New History of Christianity in China*. Chichester & Malden, MA: Wiley Blackwell, 2012.

Bevans, Steven B., and Roger Schroeder. *Constants in Context: A Theology of Mission for Today*. Maryknoll: Orbis, 2004.

Chan, Shun-hing. "Conceptual Differences between Hong Kong and Chinese Theologians: A Study of the 'Cultural Christians' Controversy." In *Sino-Christian Theology*, edited by Pan-chiu Lai and Jason Lam, 63–82. Frankfurt: Peter Lang, 2010.

———. "The Protestant Community and the Umbrella Movement in Hong Kong." *Inter-Asia Cultural Studies* 16 (2015) 380–95.

陳韋安 (Chan, John Wai-on).〈從聖殿神學到流放神學〉.《時代論壇》February 4, 2022.

Chow, Alexander. *Chinese Public Theology: Generational Shifts and Confucian Imagination in Chinese Christianity*. Oxford: Oxford University Press, 2018.

Chu, Ann Gillian, and John Perry. "'If the Gospel We Preach Disregards Human Rights, I Would Rather Not Preach This Gospel': Towards a Lived Theology of Hong Kong Churches." *Theology Today* 79, no. 4 (2023) 422–34.

Fällman, Fredrik. "Calvin, Culture and Christ?: Developments of Faith Among Chinese Intellectuals." In *Christianity in Contemporary China: Socio-Cultural Perspectives*, edited by Francis Khek Gee Lim, 153–68. New York: Routledge, 2012.

Farley, Edward. *Theologia: The Fragmentation and Unity of Theological Education*. Philadelphia: Fortress, 1983.

Fulkerson, Mary McClintock. "Ethnography in Theology: A Work in Process." In *Lived Theology: New Perspectives on Method, Style, and Pedagogy*, edited by Charles Marsh et al., 115–33. Oxford: Oxford University Press, 2017.

González, Justo L. *Christian Thought Revisited*. Maryknoll: Orbis, 1999.

郭承天 (Guo, Cheng-tian).《華人政治神學: 恢復與調適》.新北：韋伯，2021.

何光滬 (He, Guanghu) and 楊熙楠 (Daniel H. N. Yeung) 編.《漢語神學讀本 (下)》.香港：道風，2009.

何兆斌 (Ho, Siu-pun).〈「餘民神學」芻議〉.《時代論壇》June 8, 2018.

Holman, Susan R. "Daring to Write Theology without Footnotes." In *Lived Theology: New Perspectives on Method, Style, and Pedagogy*, edited by Charles Marsh et al., 80–81. Oxford: Oxford University Press, 2017.

"Institute of Sino-Christian Studies." www.iscs.org.hk.

漢語基督教文化研究所 (Institute of Sino-Christian Studies) 編.《文化基督徒: 現象與論爭》.香港：漢語基督教文化研究所，1997.

龔立人 (Kung, Lap-yan).〈情緒政治/靈性教會．靈性政治/情緒教會〉.《天國與人間》.陳韋安 (John Chan) 編，136–70.香港：明風，2016.

Kwok, Pui-lan, and Francis Ching-Wah Yip, eds. *The Hong Kong Protests and Political Theology*. Lanham: Rowman & Littlefield, 2021.

Lai, Pan-chiu and Jason Lam, eds. *Sino-Christian Theology: A Theological qua Cultural Movement in Contemporary China*. Frankfurt: Peter Lang, 2010.

賴德明 (Lai, Tony).《澳洲華人基督教會史初探》.墨爾本：墨爾本福音堂，2022.

Lam, Jason. "A Typological Consideration of Sino-Theology." *Quest* 4, no. 11 (2005) 93–109.

林子淳 (Lam, Jason).〈操控還是信任？中國教會登記問題引發的社會學與神學反思〉.《當代中國研究期刊》9, no. 2 (2022) 37–62.

———. "Is Sino-Christian Theology Truly 'Theology'? Problematizing Sino-Christian Theology as a Public Theology." *International Journal of Public Theology* 14 (2020) 97–119.

———. "Why Does Theology Still Matter for Chinese Christianity? A Theological Reflection on Contemporary Christian Mission in China." In *Proclaiming the Gospel, Engaging the World*, edited by Michael Bräutigam et al., 300–306. Eugene: Wipf & Stock, 2021.

Latourette, Kenneth Scott. *A History of Christian Mission in China*. New York: MacMillan, 1929.

Lee, Albert. "Is Dialogue in the Church Still Possible after the Hong Kong Protests?" In *The Hong Kong Protests and Political Theology*, edited by Pui-lan Kwok and Francis Ching-Wah Yip, 151–52. Lanham: Rowman & Littlefield, 2021.

Lee, Peter K. H. "The 'Cultural Christians' Phenomenon in China: A Hong Kong Discussion." In *Sino-Christian Theology: A Theological qua Cultural Movement in Contemporary China*, edited by Pan-chiu Lai and Jason Lam, 53–62. Frankfurt: Peter Lang, 2010.

李向平 (Li, Xiangping).《中國當代宗教的社會學詮釋》.上海：上海人民出版社，2006.

———.〈漢語神學:「無形的教會」與「公共的信仰」〉.《道風》32 (2010) 57–69.
劉小楓 (Liu, Xiaofeng).《漢語神學與歷史哲學》.香港: 道風,2000.
Luk, Bryan Tzu Wei. "Human Security and Threats Associated with the Impacts of 2019 Hong Kong Social Unrest." *International Journal of Peace and Development Studies* 12, no. 1 (2021) 1–10.
Madsen, Richard. "Religious Renaissance in China Today." *Journal of Current Chinese Affairs* 2/2011, 17–42.
Marsh, Charles, et al., eds. *Lived Theology: New Perspectives on Method, Style, and Pedagogy*. Oxford: Oxford University Press, 2017.
Maynard, Jane F., et al., eds. *Pastoral Bearings: Lived Religion and Pastoral Theology*. Plymouth: Lexington, 2010.
Melbourne School of Theology. "Upcoming Events." cf. www.mst.edu.au.
Ng, Nancy, and Andreas Fulda. "The Religious Dimensions of Hong Kong's Umbrella Movement." *Journal of Church and State* 60 (2017) 377–97.
Ni, Michael Y., et al. "Depression and Post-Traumatic Stress during Major Social Unrest in Hong Kong: A 10-year Prospective Cohort Study." *The Lancet* 395 (2020) 273–84.
Purbrick, Martin. "A Report of the 2019 Hong Kong Protests." *Asian Affairs* 50, no. 4 (2019) 465–87.
Ramsey, Paul. *Basic Christian Ethics*. Louisville, KY: Westminster John Knox, 1993.
Strauss, Leo. *Persecution and the Art of Writing*. Chicago: University of Chicago, 1988.
Rasmusson, Arne. *The Church as Polis: From Political Theology to Theological Politics as Exemplified by Jürgen Moltmann and Stanley Hauerwas*. Notre Dame: University of Notre Dame, 1995.
Reny, Marie-Eve. *Authoritarian Containment: Public Security Bureaus and Protestant House Churches in Urban China*. New York: Oxford University Press, 2018.
Sölle, Dorothee. *Thinking about God*. London: SCM, 1990.
Soper, J. Christopher, and Joel S. Fetzer. "Church and State in Post-Handover Hong Kong." *Taiwan Journal of Democracy* 16, no. 2 (2020) 121–45.
田淑珍 (Tian, Shuzhen).〈神學教育協會十四院校聯署譴責暴力, 深望暫緩修例〉.《時代論壇》June 14, 2019.
Tse, Justin K. H., and Jonathan Y. Tan, eds. *Theological Reflections on the Hong Kong Umbrella Movement*. New York: Macmillan, 2016.
Wigg-Stevenson, Natalie. *Ethnographic Theology: An Inquiry into the Production of Theological Knowledge*. New York: Palgrave Macmillan, 2014.
胡志偉 (Wu, Chi-wai).〈「流放神學」的初探〉.《時代論壇》September 4, 2020.
Wu, Yiyao, and Cui, Xiaohuo. "House Churches Thrive in Beijing." *China Daily*, March 17, 2010. http://www.chinadaily.com.cn/cndy/2010-03/17/content_9600333.htm.
Xie, Zhibin. "Why Public and Theological? The Problem of Public Theology in the Chinese Context." *International Journal of Public Theology* 11 (2017) 381–404.
Yang, Fenggang. "Religious Revival and Religious Deficit in China Today." *Chinese Law and Religion Monitor* 8, no. 1 (2012) 8–25.
邢福增 (Ying, Fuk-tsang).《基督教在中國的失敗?》.香港: 道風,2012.
卓新平 (Zhuo, Xinping).〈中國教會與中國社會〉.《基督宗教與當代社會》.卓新平、薩耶爾編.北京: 宗教文化出版社,2003.
〈神學教育協會聲明: 強烈譴責任何暴力行為〉,《時代論壇》October 5, 2014.

Subject Index

Acts, book of
    cultural conflict in, 91–107
    table fellowship in, 100–101
    Acts 6:1–7, 91, 93–107
Aleni, Giulio (艾儒略), 171n80
Anglocentric theology, 47, 48, 50, 52–53, 59–61, 64, 66
Aquinas, Thomas, 110
Arrupe, Pedro, 158
Asian American theology, 47, 48, 54–57, 67
Asian American Quadrilateral (AAQ), 57–61
    Lee, Daniel D., 47, 57, 65
    Lee, Sang Hyun, 47, 57, 61, 65
    Ong, Andrew, 47, 57, 64
    theology of liminality, 47, 61–64
Auddy, Ranjan Kumar, xviii
Augustine, 141
Australian Bureau of Statistics (ABS), 18, 36, 37, 72n2
Australian Chinese Christians
    contextual theology for, 47–70
    history of, 1–27
    identity of, 48–49, 50–54
    necromancy and, 71–90
Australian University of Theology, v, vii, 22, 51

"Banana Christianity," 50
Barth, Karl, 61, 109, 133
Bevans, Stephen, 158, 161
Boff, Leonardo, 160
Bosch, David J., xviii
Brueggemann, Walter, xvi

Calvin, John, 109n2, 110n11, 111–13, 115–16, 117–18, 120
canonical-linguistic approach, 123, 141, 145
Cheong Cheok Hong (張卓雄), 3, 9–10, 16–17
Chia, Philip P. (謝品然), v, xv
Chinese Christian Church (CCC) at Milsons Point, 18–20, 38
Chinese churches in Australia
    conflict in, 91–92, 103–6
    contextualization in, 28–46
    expansion of, 17–23
    history of, 1–27
    politics in, 177–80
Chinese immigrants, 2, 4, 18, 28–29, 31, 35–39, 41–43
Chinese Methodist Church in Australia (CMCA), 20–22

SUBJECT INDEX

Chinese Presbyterian Church, Sydney, 13–16, 19, 38
Chinese Theological College Australia (CTCA, 澳洲華人教牧神學院), xi, 22, 24
Coe, Shoki (黃彰輝), xv, xix, xxi
Confucianism, 58–59, 125n4, 128, 131, 138, 143, 163–74
contextualization
    Chinese churches, 28–46
    definitions of, xv–xix, 157–58
    for Chinese Australian evangelicals, 47–70
    process of, 28–46, 154
    Shoki Coe on, xv, xxi
cultural conflict, 91–107
cultural studies, approaches of, 128–32, 137–140

Dafumu (大父母, The Great Parent), 149, 167
diaspora, Chinese, xxi, 65–66, 91, 123, 177
divination. *See* necromancy

evangelism, 32, 48, 67

fuji (扶箕), 75–77
fundamentalism. *See* restorationism

Gernet, Jacques, 149, 164, 169–70
gold rush, 2, 4–10, 13, 58
González, Justo, 161

He, Guanghu (何光滬), 132–33, 138n106, 144
Hellenists vs. Hebrews, 93–94, 98–103, 105–6
hermeneutics, 126–28, 133–37, 141–42
Hesselgrave, David J., xvii
Hiebert, Paul, 29, 49, 53, 61n53
homogeneous unit (HU) principle, 32–35
Hong, Andrew, 54–55
Huang Yi-long (黃一農), 149, 164–65, 170–72

inculturation
    and syncretism, 157–62
    definition of, xix, 157–58
    Wang Zheng and, 149–76
indigenization
    approaches to, 124–45
    definition of, xviii, xix, 124–25
    of theology (本土神學), 124, 132–33, 135–37, 141–45

Jesuit missionaries, 166, 167
John Young Wai (周榮威), 9, 13–15, 16, 17

Keller, Timothy, xvii
kingly office of Christ, 108, 110, 112, 116–19
Kraemer, Hendrik, 151, 153–55
Kuyper, Abraham, 64

Lam, Jason (林子淳), ix, xxi, 143, 177, 180
Law, Rev. Denis, xx, 2, 24
leadership succession, 92, 101–3, 105–6
Lee, Daniel D., 47, 57, 61, 65
Lee, Sang Hyun, 47, 57, 61–63, 65
Leung, Ming (梁明生), ix, xx, 91
liminality, theology of, 47, 57, 61–64
Lindbeck, George, 135, 139, 142
Liu, Xiaofeng (劉小楓), 126–28, 133–34, 136–37
Lui, Ka Shing Samuel (呂家聲), ix, xx, 28
Lung, Grace (歐陽惠), x, xx, 47, 56

Mak Sai Ying (麦世英), 2
McGavran, Donald, 32–35
migration, 2–4, 13, 15, 17–18, 28–29, 31–32, 35–39, 43, 49, 58, 65
ministry, church, 108–22
    and *munus triplex Christi*, 108–22
mission, xv–xxi, 1–27, 28–46
    in Australia, 1–10
Moy Ling, James, 11–13
multiculturalism, 30–31, 35, 37, 40–41, 43, 44, 59–60

SUBJECT INDEX

munus triplex Christi (threefold office of Christ), 108–22

necromancy
    in 1 Samuel 28, 71–90
    in ancient Hebrew context, 78–82
    in Chinese culture, 74–77
neo-Calvinism, 47, 57, 64–66
Nicholls, Bruce, 150, 157, 158

Ong, Andrew, 47, 57, 64–66

politics, in Chinese churches, xxi, 177–80
power dynamics, 151, 155–56, 161–62
Presbyterian Church. *See* Chinese Presbyterian Church, Sydney
priestly office of Christ, 108–10, 112, 114–16
prophetic office of Christ, 109, 110, 112, 119–20

racialization, 57, 60–61
Rah, Soong-Chan, 52–53
restorationism, 126–27

1 Samuel 28, 71–90
Saul, King, 71, 73, 77–78, 82, 85–87
Schreiter, Robert, 155, 159, 161
self-theologizing, 49, 56, 66–67
Silent Exodus, 53, 54
Sinicization
    approaches to, 124–45
    definition of, xix, 124–25
Sino-Christian theology, ix, 126–28, 132–33, 136, 142, 143, 180
syncretism
    and inculturation, 157–62

definitions of, 149–57
Wang Zheng and, 149, 162–74

table fellowship, 100–101, 104
theology
    Anglocentric, 47–48, 50, 52–53, 59–61, 64–66
    Asian American, 47–48, 54–57, 67
    Chinese Australian, 47–70
    contextual, xv–xxi, 28–46, 47–70
    Indigenous (本土神學), 124, 132–33, 135–38, 141–45
    of liminality, 47, 61–64
    political, 177–180
    Sino-Christian, ix, 126–28, 132–33, 136, 142, 143, 180
Tien, Hung-En (Tallis) (田宏恩), x, xx, 123
Tseng, Tim, 49
Tsoi, Grace Kwan Sik (李君皙), v, x, xv, xx, 71

Wang, Wally (王光正), x, xx, 108
Wang Zheng (王徵), xxi, 149–50, 162–74
    and Confucianism, 163–74
    and inculturation, 149–76
    as catechist, 163–64
    criticisms of, 164–65, 169–73
Wesleyan Chinese Mission Church, 10–13
White Australia Policy, 4, 15, 17, 23
Wong, Kai T. (黃啟泰), xi, xxi, 149
Wu, Jackson, xvii

Zhaohun (招魂), 74–76
Zhou, Yun (周韻), xi, xix, 1
Zücher, Eric, 149, 164, 167

Scripture Index

OLD TESTAMENT

Genesis
10 — 64
28:10–17 — 78

Exodus
18:13–27 — 103

Leviticus
8:8 — 78
16:6 — 115
19:31 — 78, 81
20:6 — 81

Numbers
11:1–30 — 103

Deuteronomy
1:9–18 — 103
13:1–2 — 119
17:14–20 — 117
18:9–14 — 81
18:10–11 — 78, 87n62
18:15–19 — 119
18:21–22 — 86

1 Samuel
2:6 — 85
15 — 85, 86
15:23 — 87
15:23 — 87
15:30–31 — 85
28 — v, xx, 71, 73, 76, 77, 78, 81, 82, 88
28:18 — 87
31 — 86

1 Kings
3:5–15 — 78

1 Chronicles
12:32 — 39

Psalms
68:5, cf. 146:9 — 98

Proverbs
15:25 — 98

SCRIPTURE INDEX

Isaiah
8:19	78

Jeremiah
49:11	98

Hosea
1–3	120

NEW TESTAMENT

Matthew
5:17–18	134
28:19–20	40

Mark
9:35	118
10:45	118

Luke
2:36–38	98
5:27–39	101
5:30	100, 100n34
7:11–17	98
7:36	100
7:36–50	101
9:1–2	102
10:38–42	96
15:2	100, 100n34
16:21	100
18:1–8	98
19:23	100
21:1–4	98
22:14–30	101
22:21	100
22:30	100

Luke-Acts
	95n14, 96, 100

John
1:14	129
13:5	118
15:26–27	112n17

Acts
1:8	100
1:13	94n12
1:21–26	97
2	94, 95
2:8	130
2:14	94n12
2:40–42	98
2:42	102
4	97
4:34–35	95
5	97
6	35, 95, 98, 100n32, 101, 103, 104
6:1	96
6:1–6	34, 100
6:1–7	91, 93–95, 97, 100
6:7	95
6:11–14	94n10
8	102
10	94, 102n42
12	94n10, 102n42
15	102n42
16:34	100
20:21	140

Romans
9:4–5	134

1 Corinthians
9:22	32, 130
14:21	140
15:24	118
15:28	118

2 Corinthians
11:22	94

Galatians
3:28	28, 34
4:4	134

Ephesians

2:13	140
4:3	32

Philippians

3:5	94

Hebrews

1:1–3	120
2:17	129
7:27	115

1 Peter

5:2	32

Revelation

21	64

www.ingramcontent.com/pod-product-compliance
Lightning Source LLC
Chambersburg PA
CBHW070253230426
43664CB00014B/2518